VESNA PAVLOVIĆ

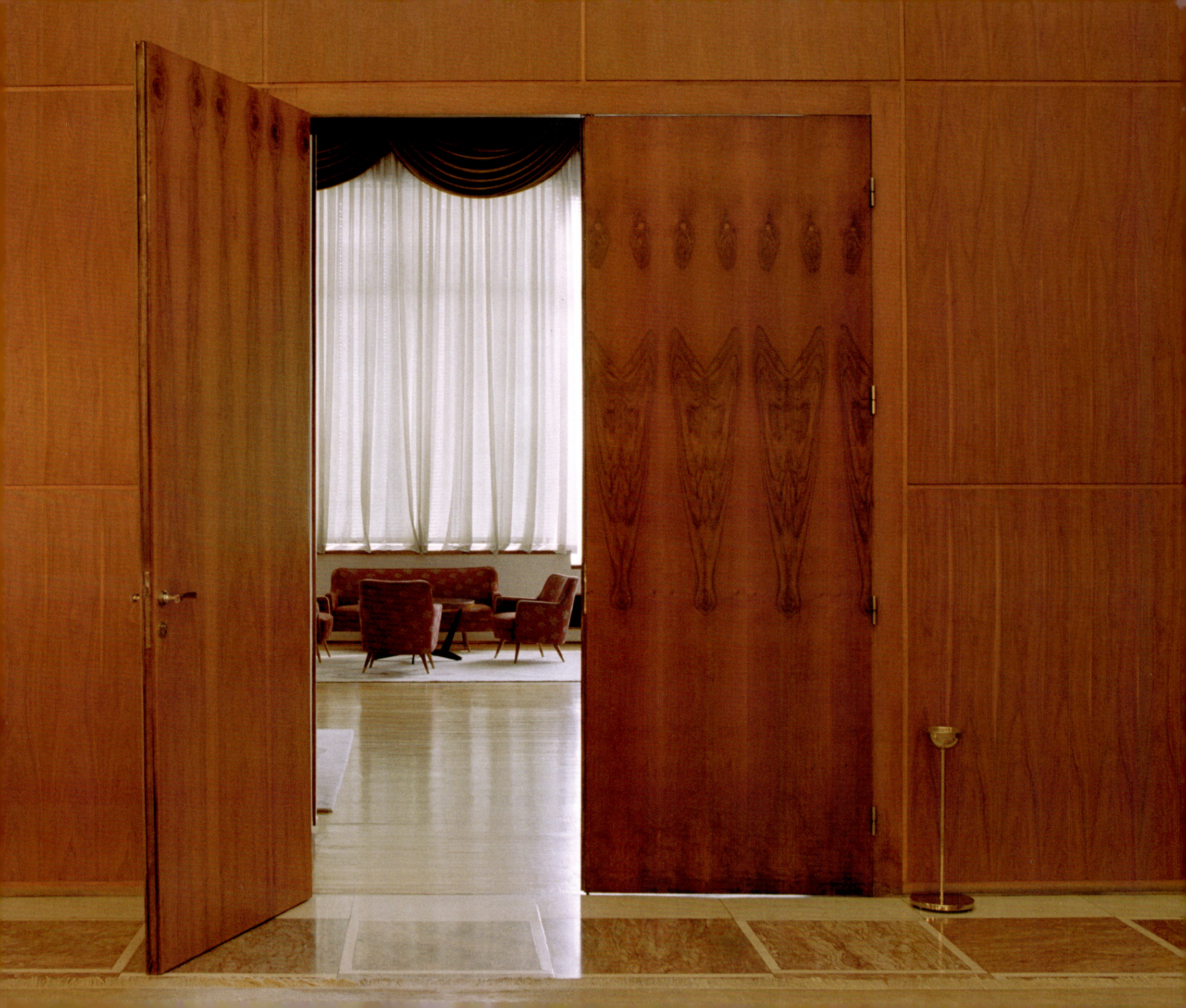

VESNA PAVLOVIĆ
STAGECRAFT

VESNA PAVLOVIĆ

Essays by Jelena Vesić, Branislav Dimitrijević,
Jordan Amirkhani, and John J. Curley

VANDERBILT UNIVERSITY PRESS
Nashville, Tennessee

LIBRARY OF CONGRESS CATALOGING-IN-PUBLICATION DATA

Names: Dimitrijević, Branislav. Vesna Pavlović. | Vesić, Jelena, 1974–
  Stagecrafting. | Pavlović, Vesna, 1987– Photographs. Selections.
Title: Vesna Pavlović : stagecraft / [photography by] Vesna Pavlović.
Other titles: Stagecraft
Description: Nashville : Vanderbilt University Press, [2021] | Includes
  images recorded by Pavlović between 1999 and 2019 in Yugoslavia. |
  Includes bibliographical references.
Identifiers: LCCN 2020044653 (print) | LCCN 2020044654 (ebook) | ISBN
  9780826501837 (hardcover) | ISBN 9780826501844 (epub) | ISBN
  9780826501851 (pdf)
Subjects: LCSH: Documentary photography—Yugoslavia. | Architectural
  photography—Yugoslavia. | Photography—Political aspects—Yugoslavia. |
  Photographers—Yugoslavia—Biography. | Pavlović, Vesna, 1987–
Classification: LCC TR820.5 .V47 2021 (print) | LCC TR820.5 (ebook) | DDC
  770.39/87—dc23

LC record available at https://lccn.loc.gov/2020044653
LC ebook record available at https://lccn.loc.gov/2020044654

COVER IMAGE: *!No pasaran!* and *Kolona*, Đorđe Andrejević Kun. Inside the
Federal Executive Council Building, Belgrade, Serbia. From Collection/
Kolekcija series (2003–2005)

CONTENTS

In 2018 I returned to Belgrade as Fulbright Research Fellow. Working with photography students and colleagues at the University of Belgrade allowed me to have a fresh look on the post-WWII era of former Yugoslavia. While in Belgrade I was exploring my personal archive and wondered about the meaning of the images of past and present. I am indebted to my friend and collaborator art historian Jelena Vesić, who helped me in this process of imagining an exciting new reading of my photographs. This became *Stagecraft*, an intimate exploration of my documentary aesthetic of highly charged ceremonial spaces of Yugoslav socialism.

Stagecraft begins with *Herzlich willkommen im Hotel Hyatt Belgrad, April 1999*. Taken while on journalistic assignment for *Die Zeit* magazine during the times of war, this image, capturing a representative of the foreign media in a space that offers a false sense of safety, marked a conceptual shift in my photography. The photographs in the book, from vacant hotel spaces to two art collections of the cold war opposites, and the visual translation of the historical archives of the Museum of Yugoslavia, all convey a reflection on the very idea of the image and how it relates to memory and ideology. The photographic grain reminds us of an *analogue moment* in time, a brief pause, a site of memory.

This book largely benefited from my time as a Fulbright Research Scholar in Belgrade, and from the generous funds of the Vanderbilt University Chancellor Fellowship and the College of Arts & Science Dean's Office. The Museum of Yugoslavia and the Department for Historiography of Radio Television of Serbia continued to provide the logistical and collegial support during the production of the book. Vanderbilt University Press allowed me the time and space needed for such an encompassing endeavor. Hadley and Luke stayed home in Nashville during my year in Belgrade, which was a tremendous gift. I remain in gratitude to the essay contributors Jelena Vesić, Jordan Amirkhani, Branislav Dimitrijević, and John. J. Curley, who took an extraordinary consideration and critical reflection of my work.

Thank you.

Vesna Pavlović | Nashville, 2020

Introduction

JELENA VESIĆ

Stagecraft by Vesna Pavlović is what we can call a *cinematic book*—a publication consisting of a visual sequence of four photographic series (Hotels, Collection/Kolekcija, Fabrics of Socialism, and Sites of Memory), and four thematic essays. The images recorded by the artist between 1999 and 2019 and the corresponding critical reflections result in this exciting edition to be published by Vanderbilt Press in 2021.

The American, Serbian, and Yugoslav social and aesthetic contexts are crucial for the personal and artistic development of Pavlović. She received her BFA in cinematography from the University of Belgrade, Serbia—in the city where she was raised—continuing her photographic journeys at Columbia University, New York. Moving to the US, Vesna Pavlović lived in Atlanta, New York, Washington, DC, Seattle, and Nashville, where she currently teaches photography at Vanderbilt University.

With her series Hotels, Pavlović was one of the first artists who raised the question of the aesthetic-political form of Yugoslav socialist modernism. In the extended aftermath of the Cold War, the period during which the most of her pictures were created, she polemicized (in visual language) with the stereotypical views on socialism as dehumanizing ideological force. Rethinking the architectural symbols of the distinctively Yugoslav *third path of socialism*—the politics of non-alignment and self-management that opposed the binary power of the two political blocs—Vesna Pavlović approached the image of socialism in a different way.

The visual sequence of *Stagecraft* unfolds as a cluster of photographic reflections, opening to its readers and viewers the road toward the "better past," or provoking differentiated critical thoughts on history and its "staging in pictures." The uncanny spaces of Hotels offer a deadpan gaze to the "ceremonial interiors" of the Palace of Federation of Yugoslavia and Chase Manhattan bank in New York, telling stories of and about the twentieth century through a particular aesthetics inspired by Cold War ideologies. These images are witness to the crisis of modernity and socialism in our contemporary encounter with the endless process of transition to global capitalism.

The multitude of vacant interiors designed in the fashion of monumental modernist chic of 1950s and 1960s are silently staring at the viewers of Pavlović's series Collection/Kolekcija. These "empty/deserted stages," once hosting important political performances, today appear as mausoleums or "theme rooms" celebrating the modernist idea of total design (*gesamtkunstwerk*). They stand for Pavlović's interests in the relations between the domains of documentary photography and staged situations, examining how documentary photography is always already staged by the very language of photography. Her affinity and curiosity for a certain unsettling quality of the image that is at the same time cold and vacant in terms of event offers a radical detachment from the logic of the so-called decisive moment, an expressive gesture of documentary photography that Henri Cartier-Bresson famously outlined in his same-titled book from 1952. What Vesna Pavlović looks for in a documentary image is what I can recognize as *non-decisive moments of contemplation*; she is *stagecrafting* documentary photography, creating the "event of an image."

In her Fabrics of Socialism series, the artist explores the archive of Museum of Yugoslavia in Belgrade, revisiting the black and white photos of ceremonial visits of the president Josip Broz Tito to the countries of the Non-Aligned Movement that offer profound monumental representations of postwar ideologies of friendship and global peace. We follow Tito's travels to Brasilia, then to Rome, and his visits to a number of African countries. However, Vesna Pavlović remains faithful to her research of the photographic matter, and of the very way the images are staged and presented to their viewers, offering profound insight into the ideological apparatuses and visual philosophy of the analogue photographic image.

This publication includes four essays dedicated to reading the image from various perspectives and positions that among themselves enter a certain relation of dialogical thinking. Written by international curators, art critics, and theorists—Branislav Dimitrijević, Jordan Armikhani, John J. Curley, and Jelena Vesić—the essays analyze the photographic image in the knot of its imaginary, symbolic, and real potentials. Their analysis includes understanding of the location or the site of exposure; examining the geopolitical background, the historical and social meaning; and reflecting theoretically and critically on the aesthetic and material existence of images. The photographs by Vesna Pavlović are taken as both an example and a case study, bringing together theoretical theses and visual material in the form of a *cinematic bind*.

As the editor of the publication I would like to thank Vanderbilt University Press for their professionalism and precision in the production of this book. I would especially like to express my gratitude to the writers with whom Vesna and I tightly collaborated, sharing concepts, experiences and interpretations, exchanging ideas and books. Without their patience, openness, and friendly acceptance of all the propositions and criticism occurring in the editing process this book would not have been possible. Last but not least I am thankful to my long-term friend and collaborator Vesna Pavlović who took me on yet another photographic journey; in her signature manner, once again she was at the same time as reliable as an anchor and as adventurous as a sail on a pushing wind. Thank you!

Jelena Vesić

Vesna Pavlović
The Photographic Staging
of the Nonperformative

BRANISLAV DIMITRIJEVIĆ

* Darka Radosavljević and Dejan Sretenović, eds., *Reality Check* (Belgrade: Centre for Contemporary Art, 1999).

† Branislava Anđelković, Branislav Dimitrijević, and Dejan Sretenović, *On Normality: Art in Serbia, 1989–2001* (Belgrade: Museum of Contemporary Art Belgrade, 2005.)

‡ Shkelzen Maliqi, "O normalnosti (On normality)," *Vreme*, nos. 521, 522 and 523 (December 2000–January 2001).

p. 51

A series of photographs from 1999 entitled Herzlich willkommen im Hotel Hyatt Belgrad, April 1999, marked a turning point in the artistic output of Vesna Pavlović. In her capacity as a photojournalist, Pavlović was expected to document the spectacle surrounding the NATO bombing campaign of Serbia: explosions, demolished buildings, dramatic situations on the streets, people reacting on the ground, anger, and protests. Pavlović was local, but while working with foreign journalists she spent some time in the hotels where they stayed, particularly the Hyatt Regency—the most luxurious hotel in Belgrade at the time.

In one photograph from the Hyatt series, we encounter a scene of utter tranquility at the hotel swimming pool. Against the backdrop of polished grey and white tiles reflecting on the surface of the water, we see a man dressed in a white bathrobe, his head wrapped in a blue towel, reclining leisurely on a deckchair and dialing his mobile phone. The title of the series and the quoted date of its production (April 1999) point explicitly to the period of the bombing, but the juxtaposition of that date and this "peaceful" scene provoke a question about what could in fact be treated as an accurate representation of the war.

The photo initially appeared in a collection of postcards with greetings from the bombed city, designed by artists invited by the Centre for Contemporary Art.[*] It was later republished as the cover of the catalogue for *On Normality*, an exhibition of Serbian art of the 1990s.[†] It became an emblematic illustration of the desire for normality, for the ability to secure a retreat from antagonistic tensions, an oblivious, self-assured withdrawal from social participation and political struggle. The title of the exhibition was taken from a text by the Albanian theorist Shkelzen Maliqi, who coined the term "religion of normality" and described it as being "rather on the side of surrender and of acknowledgment of the primacy of evil, even perhaps of making an implicit excuse for it, a defense of human dignity which is not to be found in hiding and escaping but in active resistance."[‡] Whether the bather in Pavlović's photograph was a foreign journalist or some local businessman who could afford to relax in a luxurious hotel, this work presented one of the most characteristic symptoms of the human condition in our present times.

The Belgrade Hyatt can be listed in a line of emblematic hotels providing the illusion of safety and normality in the midst of a war mayhem—like the Holiday Inn in Sarajevo during the siege, or the Hôtel des Mille Collines in Kigali during the Rwandan genocide,

* Marc Augé, *Non-Places: Introduction to an Anthropology of Supermodernity* (London: Verso, 1995), 86.

† For a discussion of the shift from the planned economy to the market economy in Yugoslavia in the 1960s, and the cultural symptomatology of this shift, see Branislav Dimitrijević, *Potrošeni socijalizam / Consumed Socialism* (Belgrade: Fabrika knjiga, 2016).

or the famous Hotel Continental in Saigon, or the Commodore in Beirut. These hotels represent a paradoxical setting that structurally incorporates yet phenomenologically excludes the event of war. They are conventionally understood as spatial exemptions, as neutral places, as extra-territories. They operate in the midst of a dramatic situation—and yet they are still just "regular" hotels. They play the role of what Marc Augé calls a "non-place": a zone in which "the individual feels himself to be a spectator without paying much attention to the spectacle." [*]

In Vesna Pavlović's photographs, the nondramatic scenes from the hotel and the indistinct atmosphere of its interior approach the performativity of an event from a different angle. For a photographer whose work was primarily dedicated to documenting persons and actions related to the marginalized yet uncompromising activities of civil society in the Serbian 1990s—the anti-war movement and the independent artistic scene during the regime of Slobodan Milošević—the change portrayed in a sequence of Pavlović's photographs of hotel interiors (1999–2002) is symptomatic of a historical break in Serbia and the Balkans at the turn of the millennium. That break signified a turning away from the period of war and insecurity following the disintegration of Yugoslavia, and toward the period of an alleged social and political "normalization."

The NATO bombing in fact belongs to both periods: it was an act of war, but an act that was internationally represented as a humanitarian military project meant to bring normalization. Pavlović's photographs are therefore both about the normalization of war and about the fantasy of normalization—the fantasy that was quintessential for the paradigmatic socio-political shifts in Europe after 1989 when the Yugoslav wars symptomized a radical version of the so-called "transition" from the socialist to the capitalist realm.

The Belgrade Hyatt opened in 1990, the year one could mark as the last in the history of the Socialist Federal Republic of Yugoslavia. The hotel itself was a signifier of the transitional processes that had in fact already begun in Yugoslavia in the mid-1960s, when major political reforms introduced elements of the free-market economy in the midst of the socialist methods of production, material conditions, and ideological framework. [†] Following the Hyatt series, Pavlović brought her camera inside other hotels built in the same period in Yugoslavia. The series that developed consisted of vacant hotel interiors; it unraveled their emptiness and obsolescence in the transitional process that left them neglected and abandoned. Pavlović did not select better known hotels like those

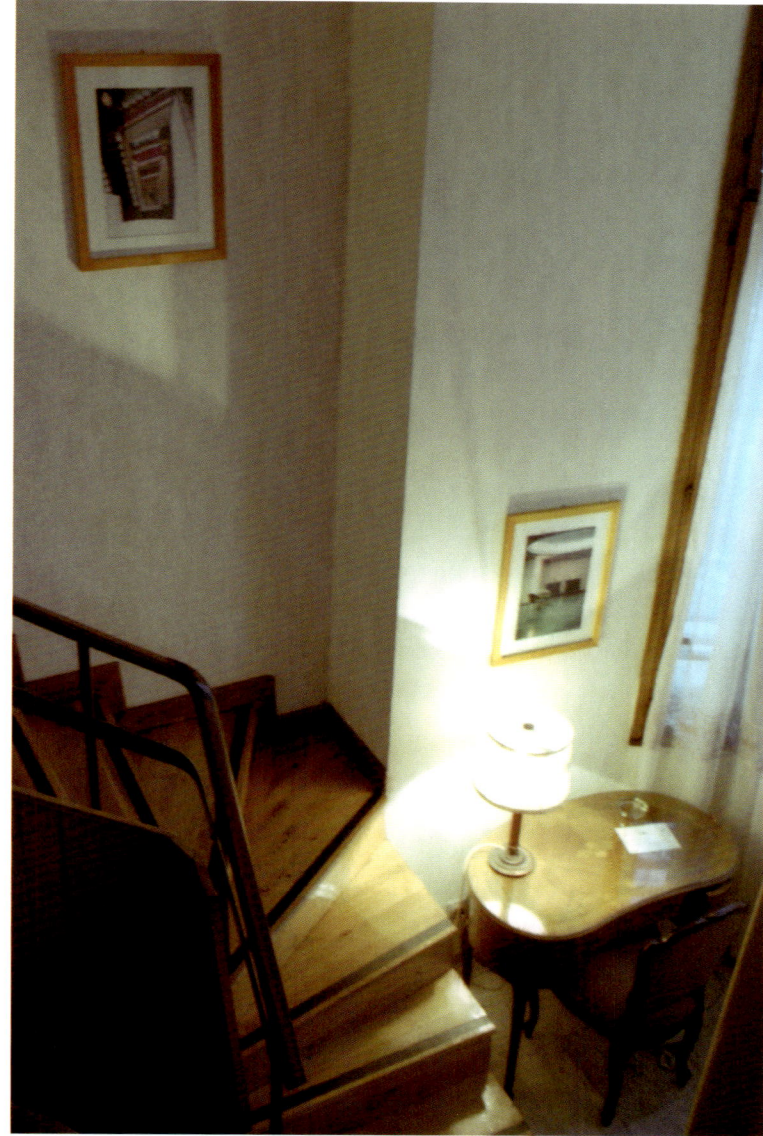

Figure 1. *Moskva in Moskva* (*Moscow in Moscow*, 2001), from the Hotels series, Belgrade 2011. Courtesy of the artist

* See Maroje Mrduljaš, "Toward an Affordable Arcadia: The Evolution of Hotel Typologies in Yugoslavia, 1960–1974", in Martino Stierli and Vladimir Kulić, eds., *Toward a Concrete Utopia: Architecture in Yugoslavia, 1948–1980* (New York: Museum of Modern Art, 2018), 78–83.

Branislav Dimitrijević

on the Adriatic coast,* but rather those operating in dormant small cities outside the influence of tourists. These deadpan images, taken always from eye level, gaze straight at a setting as though opening up a silent dialogue with the encountered objects themselves. In these photographs, we are already witnessing objects relating and communicating with each other, formulating a world of their own without needing people to inhabit them.

One project particularly stands out as the moment when Pavlović's "medium" became site-specific. Her photographs of the interior of the Moskva Hotel in Belgrade (an early twentieth century art-nouveau building in the city center) were exhibited in the lobbies, corridors, and rooms of the same hotel. The exhibition, *Moskva u Moskvi* (*Moscow in Moscow*, 2001, Figure 1), interfered with the way the signified and the signifier are simultaneously matched and separated. The placement of the photographs in the actual environment they record created a sense of alienation through tautology—this was not a space waiting for some performative event to happen, it was something of a non-event, an interchange between images and the space that went beyond and outside any further human intervention.

This "mechanicality" of the photographic gaze signaled a major shift in understanding the photographic attitude of Vesna Pavlović's work. In the 1990s, her approach to photography was subjective, involved, and empathic. She documented the events and their protagonists and engaged in political and artistic movements; her angles were wide, her contrasts were bold, and her viewpoints were dynamic. After the Herzlich willkommen series, the shift was conceptual and contextual. This shift to what is usually defined as "deadpan" photography has opened another photographic position in her work, which moved her away from the subjective and emotional, but engaged her in relations more speculative, detached, or even post-human in their theoretical foundations.

The series that followed, Collection/Kolekcija, was partly produced outside of Serbia/Yugoslavia. It was a combination, a merger, of two sites that hosted major art collections: Chase Manhattan Bank in New York and the Palace of Federation in Belgrade. Both buildings function as symbols of the political systems they extol. On one hand was David Rockefeller (a paragon of post-war American capitalism and cultural investment) building the Chase collection to enhance the working performance of the bank employees and to beautify modern corporate office spaces with works by the most significant artists of the time. On the other hand there was the Communist Party of Yugoslavia, furnishing

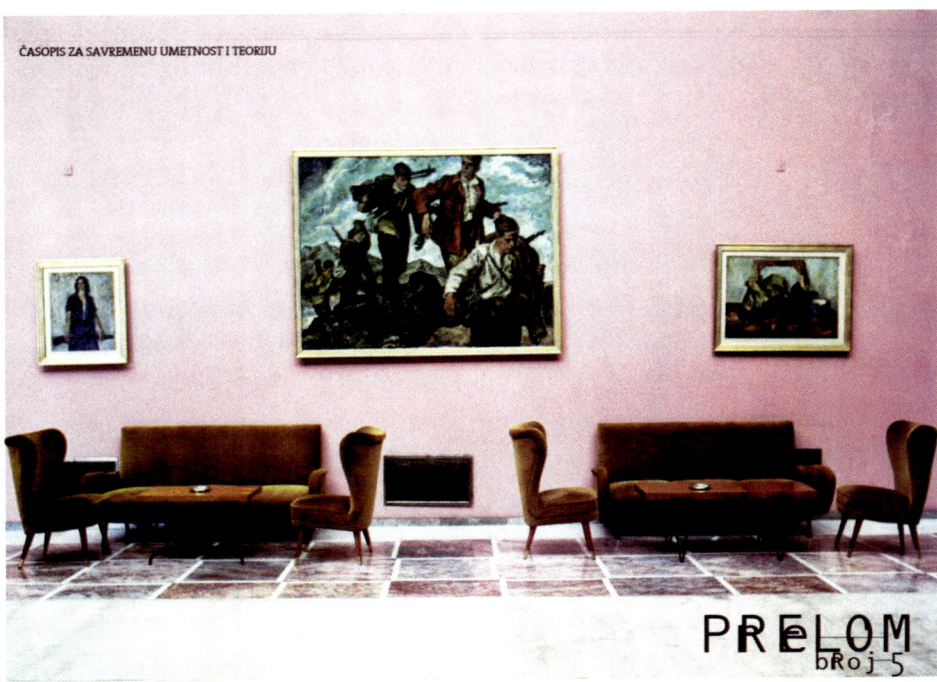

ČASOPIS ZA SAVREMENU UMETNOST I TEORIJU

PRELOM
bRoj 5

Figure 2. *Prelom*, no. 5 (Spring/ Summer 2003), magazine for contemporary art and critical theory

a huge building for the Yugoslav government with works of art referring to the anti-fascist struggle during World War II, but also with works of art representing the notion of "autonomous" artistic freedom as purveyed by official Yugoslav cultural policy. Both interiors in Pavlović's photographs are empty, deserted. We recognize them as similar not only in their original ambition, but also similar in the atmosphere they generate. They look like vacant stage sets for some play that was once performed there, or sites of modern archaeology that take us back to a time when progressive modernism was to become a language that transcended ideological boundaries. These photographs are striking visual essays about the vague distinction not just between architecture and politics but also between observation and imagination.

One photo from this series was published on the front page of *Prelom*, a journal for contemporary art and critical theory, in 2003 (Figure 2). This publication was the first after the disintegration of Yugoslavia to theoretically address the "Partizans politics" (i.e., the political and cultural practices of the communist revolution and national liberation after World War II). The photo of a pink wall inside the Palace of Federation holding three paintings—the largest one depicting a group of partisan soldiers advancing through rough mountainous terrain (Đorđe Andrejević Kun, *Kolona*, 1946)—and two sets of armchairs, couches, and tables with ashtrays on them, provides an ambiguous visual representation of a ceremonial socialist space stretched between the memory of the heroic, past-perfect times and the dried-out present-perfect. Again, the photograph is about the impossibility of inhabiting this space by contemporary means and with actual bodies. The artistic strategy here goes against the mode in which contemporary artists tend to deal with the Yugoslav socialist heritage (whatever we imply by this vague term), which has been to engage with it in a performative action, as a mode of re-performing the leftovers of history.

Pavlović's photographs are about physical sites where time becomes layered and compacted. We engage with the moment a photograph was taken, though the actual moment a photograph was taken is not always contemporaneous with the event that imbues the image with meaning. What her photographs affirm is that photography is not simply about the recording of an event, about an image of the event, but rather it is an event of the image.

"Yugoslavia" has come to invoke images, buildings, gestures, ideas, and propositions that are locked inside an entirely different social, economic, and cultural contemporaneity. Artists and

* See, for example, Owen Hatherley, "Concrete Clickbait: Next Time You Share a Spomenik Photo, Think about What It Means," Calvert Journal, November 2016, www.calvertjournal.com/articles/show/7269/spomenik-yugoslav-monument-owen-hatherley.

Branislav Dimitrijević

scholars have made an attempt to understand why and how the socialist system collapsed, and how to preserve its legacy against a hostile ideological standpoint that regards this period as a grandiose delusion, a failed political experiment, or even a totalitarian prison. Contemporary artists have countered this dominant view by researching complex and layered aspects of Yugoslav socialism and proposing different readings of—and, more importantly, different modes of engagement with—this ambiguous past. This research was necessitated by the catastrophic post-Yugoslav condition that adopted a revisionist "totalitarian paradigm" in interpreting the recent past. This in itself has been meant to conceal the contemporary catastrophe—not only the wars of succession in the 1990s, but also the current economic stagnation, the abolition of the basic rights that were established in socialism (free health system, free education, social security, etc.), and general social and economic inequality.

However, this interest in Yugoslavia has become almost a formulaic artistic cliché. Photographers have recorded a massive number of images that are today circulated on the internet, images presenting sites and objects belonging to Yugoslav socialist heritage. The Palace of Federation became a very popular photographic site, along with other buildings and particularly the monuments (*spomeniks*) that, because of their unusual brutalist forms and unexpected sizes, have become clickbait.*

In the same period (the first twenty years of this century) Vesna Pavlović turned away from her deadpan approach toward a more inquisitive technique in which photography was no longer primarily a means of observing but also a means of inquiry. Her work turned to photographic archives and their immense agglomerations of stocked images. She got interested both in individual photographic archives as well as in public and institutional archives, like a photographic archive of the Museum of Yugoslavia in Belgrade. From this point on she was no longer a photographer producing photographs, but an explorer of her chosen medium and its material aspects of production, reproduction, and projection.

At an exhibition at the Gallery of the Museum of Contemporary Art in Belgrade in 2013 (Figure 3), Pavlović confronted archival images from various sources. On one hand were the images appropriated from anonymous personal archives, the type of photographs that could be summed up under the term "tourist photography," and on the other hand were photographs taken from the archive of the Museum of Yugoslavia that document the travels of president Josip Broz Tito during the period in which Yugoslavia played

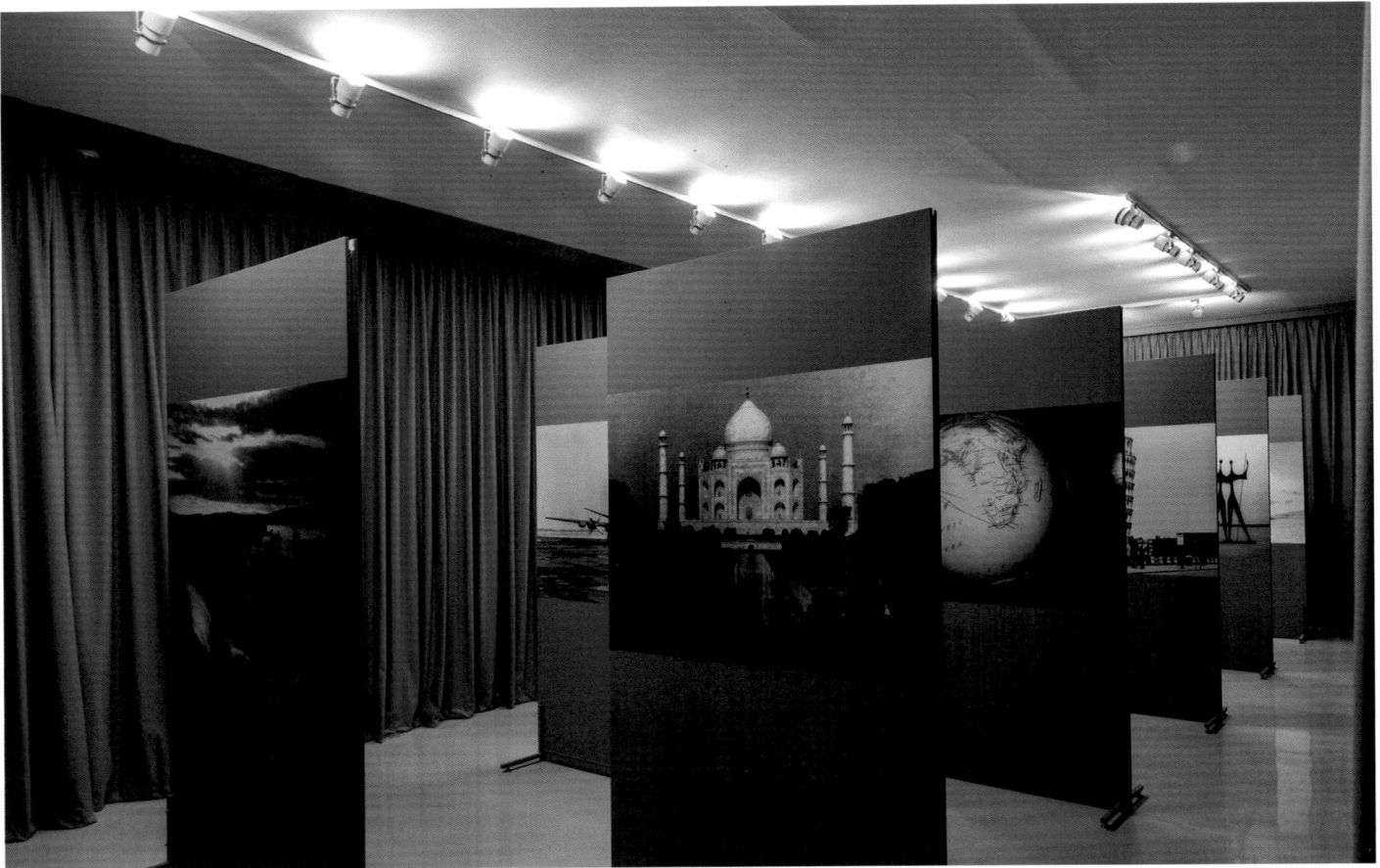

an essential role in the formation and the development of the Non-Aligned Movement. Both selections chronicle experiences and engagements with the sites, but they explore the *photographic* not only in its documentary function—as fabricated images of something—but also in its physical presentness through the mnemographic layering that is augmented each time an image is displayed in a shared physical space. This exhibition was about a research method wherein the artist discovers both semantic and syntactic properties of the tourist photography genre and its pragmatic and paradigmatic social role halfway between the private and the public. This investigation into the two types of archives, and the physical mode of co-presenting them, was aimed primarily at discerning the relations created between material space as we perceive it and imaginary space as a photographic representation—the way that these two (spaces) are brought together in the Lefebvrian concept of experienced space, the space as an experience.

For Vesna Pavlović, photography is not just a medium of representing an experience, but a material item involved in the

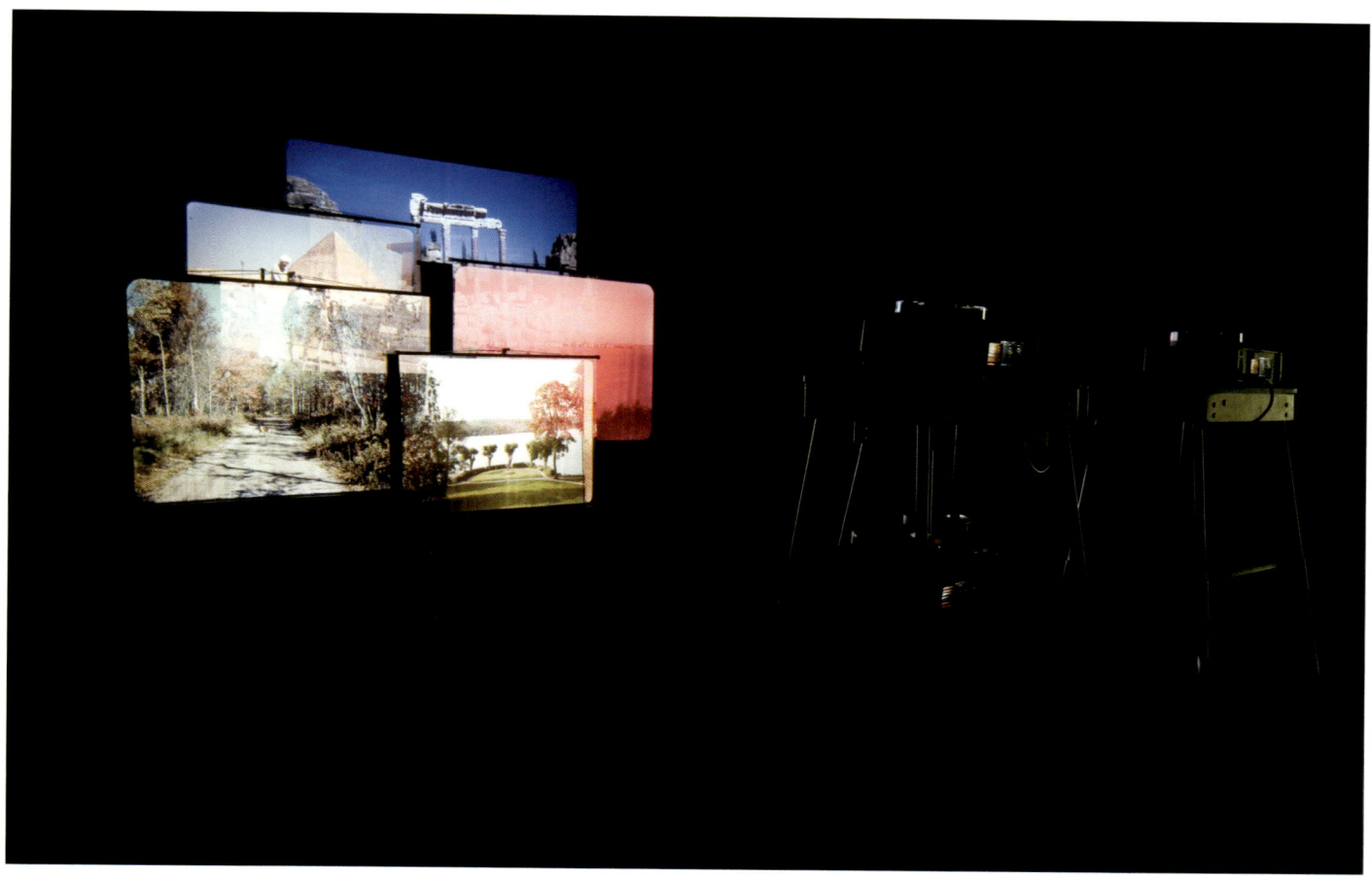

Figure 4. Vesna Pavlović, *Search for Landscapes* (2011), from the 12th Istanbul Biennial. Image courtesy IKSV / Photograph by Nathalie Barki

recollection of that experience—no matter whether it is the photographic slides' tangibility (represented at once as transparent images and as nontransparent physical objects) or the superimposition of slide projections that were once a part of the family experience of watching together. In her works, a photograph—along with everything materially connected to the photograph itself as well as to the conditions of the photographic display—is reproduced in new spatial situations (installations) where *the photographic* remembers its pre-digital history. This reflects on the translation and reproduction of different photographic archives, but also on the way archives emerge not as something found but rather as something constructed, something fictional containing both physical and imaginary experience. What is at stake is a construction of ways to establish the relations between, on the one hand, that which appears manifestly on a photographic image, and, on the other, the technical configurations of the making, reproduction, and projection of the photographic image.

Branislav Dimitrijević

* Jose van Dijk, *Mediated Memories in the Digital Age* (Stanford: Stanford University Press, 2007), 114.

† Victor Burgin, "Photography, Fantasy, Function," in *Thinking Photography* (London: Macmillan Press, 1982).

The exhibition *Reflections on Images* was based on the exploration of photo-archives but also on the modes of their re-materialization and their re-staging. Large prints of images from President Tito's journeys were pasted on thick free-standing panels used regularly during that period for gallery displays, and surrounded with similar "period pieces" with heavy, grey curtains enclosing the space. On the other side, diapositives from private archives were projected on overlapping screens, creating a three-dimensional layering of images that intersect and partially blend with one another. This installation, titled *Search for Landscapes*, commissioned for the twelfth Istanbul Biennial in 2011 (Figure 4), responds to a critical historical situation in which amateur tourist photography reached its climactic moment of hyper-production and intensive exchange due to social networking, wherein people "take less interest in sharing photographs as *objects* then as sharing them as *experiences*." * Pavlović explores pre-digital times, when the shared experience of a photograph was firmly grounded in photographic objecthood, in the materiality of photo albums, carrousels with framed slides, screens on tripods, and in general conditioned by the bulky technology of image making and image reproduction.

This new orientation continues with Pavlović's next and ongoing project, Lost Art, in which she delves into photographic archives not only with the intention of discovering lost imagery but also of recording the archives as repositories of obsolescent equipment and the conditions necessary to preserving the physical properties of photography. The photographic equipment and accessories themselves become objects of photographic reproduction.

Although primarily associated with the cinematographic, the notion of *suture* has been identified with the photographic as well following an influential proposition of the theorist Victor Burgin.† *Suture* is a psychoanalytic term that is also related to the theory of ideology. It suggests a viewer's self-recognition and subjectivization in the discursive field of photography, an interpellation of the viewer within the power of the photographic frame. In her latest cycle, Sites of Memory, Pavlović continues her exploration of the photographic archives related to the socialist Yugoslavia by trying to materialize the notion of suture in the process of the pre-fabrication of photographic material.

While in the Fabrics of Socialism cycle the re-materialization of the archival image occurred virtually on the folded textile used as a projection screen, here the archival photographs are printed

p. 163

on fabrics and then details of the image are cut off and replaced by extra-photographic patches that are manually sewn in. The photograph of this altered image is then digitally scanned and printed as a final print, thus opening an endless *mise-en-abyme* of the mnemographic process situated in this photographic stagecraft.

BIBLIOGRAPHY

Anđelković, Branislava, Branislav Dimitrijević, and Dejan Sretenović. *On Normality: Art in Serbia, 1989–2000*. Belgrade: Museum of Contemporary Art Belgrade, 2005.

Augé, Marc. *Non-Places: Introduction to an Anthropology of Supermodernity*. London: Verso, 1995.

Burgin, Victor. "Photography, Fantasy, Function." In *Thinking Photography*. Edited by Victor Burgin. London: Macmillan Press, 1982.

Dimitrijević, Branislav. *Potrošeni socijalizam / Consumed Socialism*. Belgrade: Fabrika knjiga, 2016.

Hatherley, Owen. "Concrete Clickbait: Next Time You Share a Spomenik Photo, Think about What It Means." *Calvert Journal*, November 2016. www.calvertjournal.com/articles/show/7269/spomenik-yugoslav-monument-owen-hatherley.

Maliqi, Shkelzen. "O normalnosti (On normality)." *Vreme*, nos. 521, 522 and 523, December 2000–January 2001.

Mrduljaš, Maroje. "Toward an Affordable Arcadia: The Evolution of Hotel Typologies in Yugoslavia, 1960–1974." In *Toward a Concrete Utopia: Architecture in Yugoslavia, 1948–1980*. Edited by Martino Stierli and Vladimir Kulić. New York: Museum of Modern Art, 2018.

Prelom, no. 5 (Spring-Summer 2003).

Radosavljević, Darka, and Sretenović, Dejan, eds. *Reality Check*. Belgrade: Centre for Contemporary Art, 1999.

Van Dijk, Jose. *Mediated Memories in the Digital Age*. Stanford: Stanford University Press, 2007.

Branislav Dimitrijević

Stagecrafting
Everything Here Is Both Lost and Gained in Translation

JELENA VESIĆ

* In the context of contemporary art and theory, Vesna Pavlović was one of the first artists who raised the question of Yugoslav socialist modernism in her series Hotels, while David Maljković independently and in a different medium of video-installation combined with drawings, maquettes, and collages dealt with the similar issues in his *Scene for New Heritage* (2004). The journal *Prelom* and its circle of editors and closest collaborators were the first to write about the topic in the larger framework of thinking of the twentieth century, Yugoslavia, and partisan politics. *Prelom* no. 5 (2003) published Vesna Pavlović's photo from the series Collection/Kolekcija on the front cover of the journal. *Prelom* no. 10 published a frame from Maljković's *Scene for New Heritage* (video II) on the front and back covers of the issue.

The topic of Yugoslav socialist modernism gained relevance over the previous few decades, but is only recently *museologize*d within the institutional context (the most well-known example would be MOMA's 2018 show *Toward a Concrete Utopia, Architecture in Yugoslavia, 1948–1980*).

What the *Stagecraft* book communicates to its readers and viewers can perhaps be summed up into the two claims on photography, both of which observe a certain entanglement between the medium of photography and the domain of "exhibiting," or what is sometimes called "the cultures of display." Being as broad as any material observation can be, and as specific as any artistic act requires, the two claims can also become the two theses.

1 .

The first claim says: each photograph in itself, in its very apparatus of representation, *is already a kind of exhibition*. As photography contains the capacity to reproduce and to be reproduced at the same time—what Walter Benjamin called *exhibition value*—this quality gives a specific meaning to reproduction as category; it shows that reproduction is always a certain act of translation. In her photo series Hotels and Collection/Kolekcija, Vesna Pavlović exercises the ability of photography to capture and transmit this "exhibition value" of its objects and scenes—to reproduce the aura in a contemporary sense. The aura, another term established by Benjamin, can be described as something that adds meaning and value to the object presented, as something that cannot be (easily, if at all) reproduced; it renders itself to the observer as a patina of the story, as a certain distance in time able to produce the *gloss of authenticity*. Can photography reproduce, stage, or craft the aura? What does the stagecrafting reconstruct, what does it place on stage as an event? How does it translate in space and time, through geographies and histories?

In Pavlović's photos the authenticity is not to be recognized in the facts recorded, but in her photographic thinking and translation of the *original scene*. The authenticity cannot be simply stated or declared. It operates—or not—depending on the very act of translation into the contemporary context. And Pavlović, with her photo series Hotels (2001) was among the first artistic and intellectual voices who posed the question of the heritage of Yugoslav socialist modernism and its political-aesthetical meaning[*]— in a time when such questioning was neither popular nor obvious. As an artist and photographer, she positions her questioning in the ambiguity of photographic visual representation mediated by many "curtains" (or shall we say *apparatuses*?) that reveal, project, hide, exhibit, and cover.

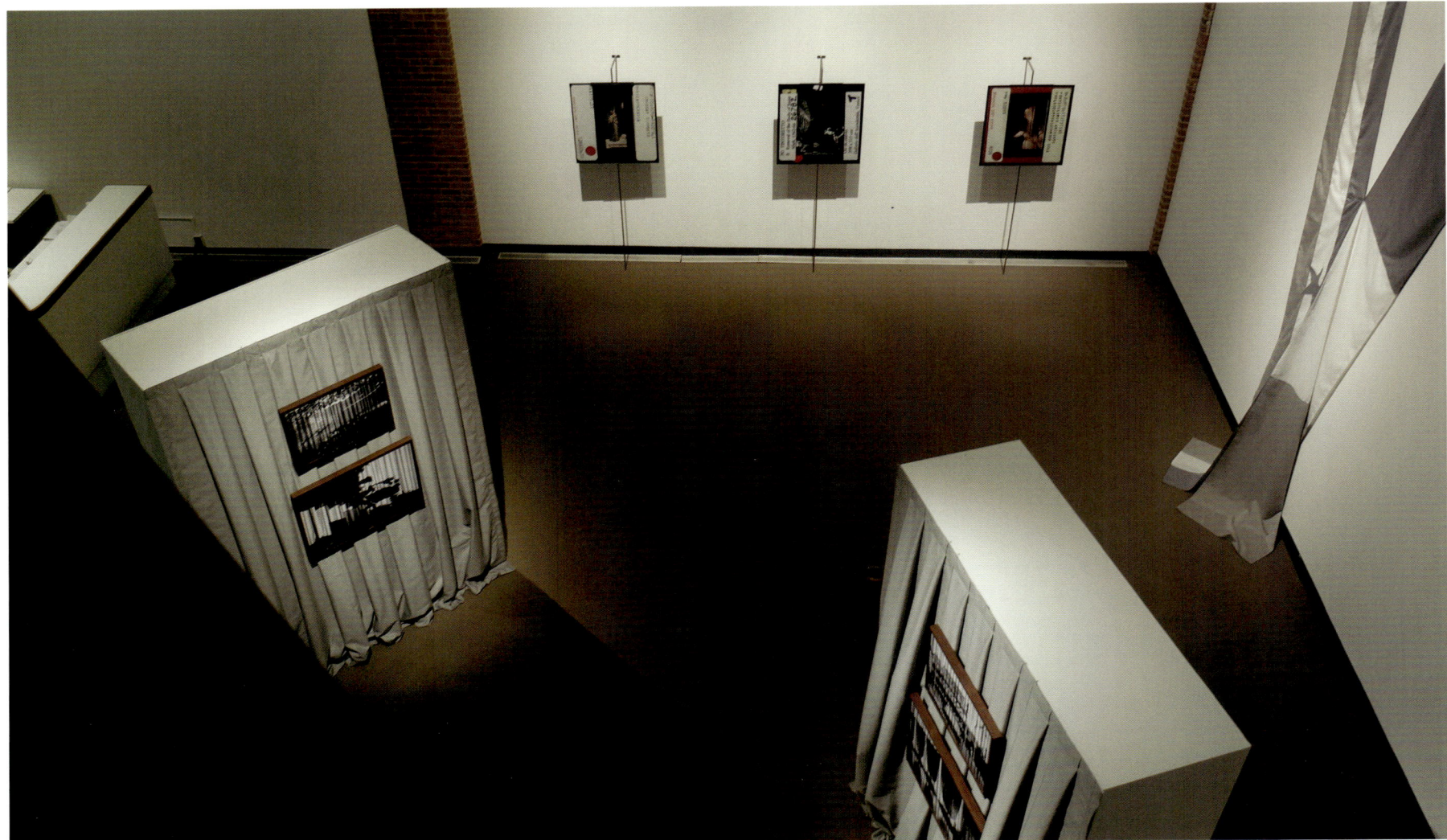

Figure 5. Vesna Pavlović, Lost Art (2017), installation view with *Elements of Choreography*, Hanes Art Gallery, Wake Forest University, 2017. Image courtesy of the gallery

* The *linguistics of exhibitionary* assume that the language of exhibition and its structure—including the study of grammar, syntax, and phonetics—can be studied scientifically and researched artistically.

2 .

The second claim of the *Stagecraft* project would be that photography, with its spatial-temporal characteristics, plays an active role in the linguistics of the exhibitionary and acts in the register of the exhibition.* The examples of such photographic thinking are the series by Pavlović that experiment with the forms of *spatialization of the photographic matter*, such as Search for Landscapes (2011), Reflection on Images (2013), Lost Art (2017) or Sites of Memory (2018, Figure 5). In these four series Pavlović moves from the classic photographic format to exhibition experiments and photographic installations. It is the period during which she starts spatializing both the production of display and the viewing experience itself.

* Recent works by Vesna Pavlović can be read as visual research of the archival practice. They are dealing with the way that photography communicates with the spatial (dis)positioning, determined by the Lefebvrean idea of "production of space."

† The provocative theme of the *Manifesta Journal*, no. 7—"The Grammar of the Exhibition"— opened up the issue of the language of exhibition-making and curatorial practice, and therefore, in art historical overview, of their place in artistic and intellectual discussions on authorship which were in classical tradition marked by the signature *ars liberalis*.

As with the first claim or thesis, she examines the theory of the pictorial (the idea of representation), probing the capacity of photography to display its objects and subjects and be part of the display itself. Historiographically speaking, in Pavlović's photographic oeuvre these two theses are at the same time divided and sewn together: thesis one from 1999 to 2009, thesis two from 2009 to present times.*

3 .

If we observe these two photographic theses in Pavlović's work, especially her experiments with the language of exhibition, it is of no surprise to find them situated in the larger debate about the exhibition as medium or the politics of display. Pavlović's entrance to the artistic scene overlaps almost perfectly with the development of what is today recognized as *the curatorial paradigm*, still a growing presence of the reflection of the very field of exhibition-making. Exhibitions became the main portal for observing and thinking art practice, offering a way of overcoming the modernist canon epitomized in the singularity of relation of artist-artwork and putting the accent on *art as collective experience*.

The ongoing debate on the concept of display as a form of curatorial arrangement of objects in space informs Vesna Pavlović's second photographic phase where she experiments with spatialized photographic forms and presents images that are both documentary and already stagecrafted for us. Such parallel thinking of the exhibition as a form and photographic matter as a medium makes Vesna Pavlović a contemporary artist. She is an artist who is acting *con tempora* (in her time, or with her time)—an artist who is aware of and in communication with the larger institutional and epistemic questions. Here Pavlović plays with the "grammar of the exhibition" and the very concept of the curatorial authorship over exhibition.

But, does the grammar of exhibition exist at all?

The *Manifesta Journal* (2009), which perhaps synthetizes this debate in the most useful way, presents the two opposing theses.† One denies the very existence of *the grammar of the exhibition* and its theoretical foundation, while another affirms the term and, what may be of interest for this book, explains the *exhibiting* precisely in the terms of stagecraft (as a *mise-en-scène*).

For Peter Osborne, exhibition-making is nothing more than a bureaucratic spice in the institutional apparatus of exhibition: "Curating has *no language*, and therefore has *no grammar*. . . . It cannot be distinguished from what it presents. Curating is also not

* Peter Osborne, "9 Points by Peter Osborne," in "The Grammar of the Exhibition," eds. Viktor Misiano and Nathalie Zonnenberg, special issue, *Manifesta Journal*, no. 7 (2009/2010): 23.

† Mieke Bal, "Exhibition as a Syntax of the Face," in "The Grammar of the Exhibition," eds. Viktor Misiano and Nathalie Zonnenberg, special issue, *Manifesta Journal*, no. 7 (2009/2010): 12–22.

‡ Brian O'Doherty, *Inside the White Cube: The Ideology of the Gallery Space* (San Francisco: Lapis Press, 1986; originally published in *Artforum*, 1976).

a genre—a genre of what? Of institutional management of art?" he wrote in his "9 Points."* An opposing thesis, coming from Mike Bal, placed the *exhibiting* in dialogue with the theatrical, stating quite unambiguously that to exhibit means "to place on stage," and that the very form of display is directly relational with the concept of *mise-en-scène*. In opposition to Osborne, Bal thinks that a curatorial language of exhibiting can be thought of on the level of syntax, that is, on the level of the relations between its elements: "*Mise-en-scène* is a syntax in three dimensions."†

Discussing the ideology of gallery space, the white cube, Brian O'Doherty wrote about how spaces such are galleries truly operate as a stage, even as a "proper" theatrical stage, in the sense of "separating the viewers from art."‡ In such an environment the "exhibition piece" unfolds as *tableau vivant*, a living picture of different spatial situations—the architecture, the disposition of artworks, the bodies of the viewers and the pattern of gaze scenes. Bal calls them "the actors" in whose mutual interaction the exhibition piece comes into being. The exhibition space and time for her are fictional; the same is true for Vesna Pavlović, who literary constructs a "prosthesis in time" for the objects of her photography, her photographic themes and scenes.

a .

The meaning of Vesna Pavlović's photographs is also derived from the specific circumstances of production of the photographic image within which the artist develops her autonomous artistic practice. The series Hotels (2001) is the first example of her artistic photography that came into being through what I would like to call the *(non)decisive moment*. In the 1990s and early 2000s Pavlović acted as photojournalist, working for various international press services, magazines, and publications, and producing commissioned images from the sites of war and transition. At the same time she uses (or even hacks) the existing infrastructure of the information industry for the sake of her autonomous artistic research. It is precisely the context in which she meets Yugoslav socialist modernism and its "cultures of display"—on the margins of production of the images of war, in transitory spaces and symbolic non-places.

Pavlović started photographing Hotels as temporary settings that she was staying in overnight as a photojournalist and that were almost never part of the itinerary of the official storytelling and image-making. She started recording these spaces as a personal

* I.e. Jan Van Eyck's coded signature on the image of *Arnolfini wedding*, in the form of the inscription of his witnessing on the wall above the mirror: "Johannes de eyck fuit hic 1434" ("*Jan van Eyck was here 1434*"). The inscription looks as if it was painted in large letters on the wall, as was done with proverbs and other phrases during this era.

† *The Decisive Moment*, a famous book by Henri Cartier-Bresson (New York City: Simon & Schuster, 1952) is used here as exemplary theoretical concept of the modern photojournalism.

p. 105

Jelena Vesić

note—artists sometimes do inscribe themselves as witnesses and protagonists of historical events, leaving the coded message "I have been here."* Hotels emerges as backdrop of a theatre where the traditional imagery of the war unfolding outside are suspended and absent from the view. If a decisive moment (from Cartier-Bresson's iconic book *The Decisive Moment*, 1952)† presupposes uncertainty, an unfinished action, and an unrepeatable moment that provides for one-chance shot, if it assumes that the body of the photographer is captured by the matrix of action (a photojournalist, falling on his back, pressing the shutter of the camera after running across the street—and boom!—*the decisive photo*), then the images of the Hotels series occur in the opposite way, precisely through non-action, as the non-decisive moments of contemplation.

The apparently still and silent images of Hotels do make the observer wonder about their inception; in order to do so, viewers can only empathize and imagine the photographer having a similar sentiment, being a subject of the same effect and affect induced by the images displayed to her eye. Together they stand still in front of the motionless scene that is silently gazing back. But if Pavlović appears as the meditative observer whose internal affairs cannot be easily told just by observing from outside, so are the spaces themselves; neither could be fully aware that this is a precise moment in which all this architecture has already lost its social function and will change its form dramatically or disappear very soon in what will become an endless transitional fix. Her inscription of "I have been here" takes place in the first years after the wars of the 1990s, when the hotels had already become monuments to socially distributed welfare, to the once-enthusiastic modernization of the country, evoking previous forms of mobility and business glamour, preceding the era of globalization. In her attempt to capture this representative image of the distinctive Yugoslav socialist state, of so-called "socialism with a human face," Pavlović was captured by the scenes in return (Figure 6).

At first glance, the images look detached from any activity. Hotels are scenes of absence: absence as the alienating presence of something that cannot be easily defined; absence as the artistic strategy of insinuating, of dislocating, of de-situating. The empty corridors and lounge spaces, the deserted dining rooms and conference halls are the pipes of memory or narrative and semantic portals that are pulling the viewers inside: they inhale us, suck us in, they push and drag us into the story.

Pavlović's observational photographic schism within the mainstream narrative on the totality of bloody Balkan wars, is a kind

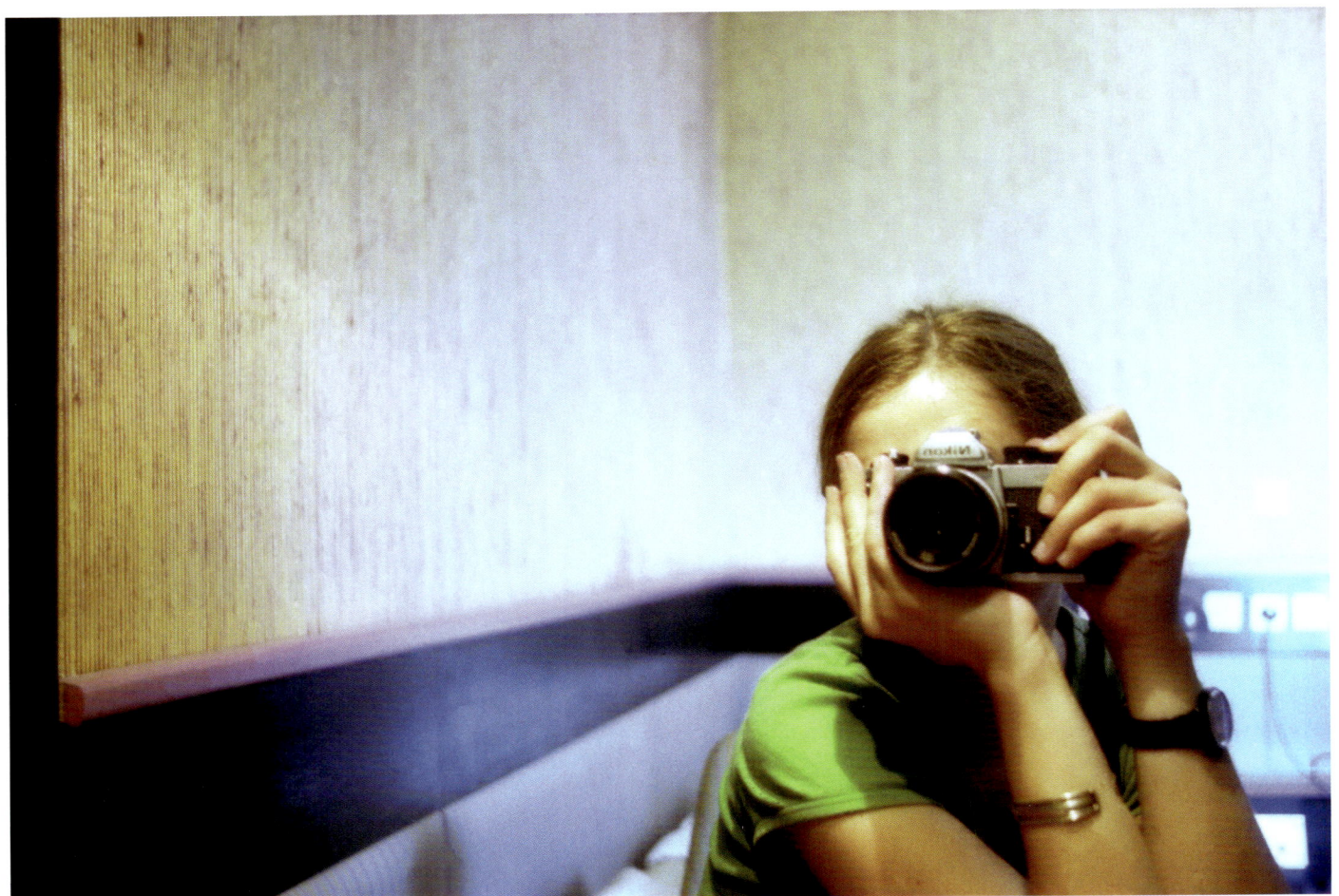

Figure 6. Vesna Pavlović, self-portrait in Hotel Lim, Priboj, 2002.

of a double exposure to the scene recorded, an overlap of real and mental images, of absence and presence, of the fact and the ghost: on the one hand *people act*, on another, the *architecture remembers*. This is the story of building and unbuilding of Yugoslavia. The calm scenes of Yugoslav socialist modernism and the turbulent scenes of war are bound together as parts of the same story. The twentieth century is put on display in reverse: from the series of freeze-frames from the 1990s and the end of Yugoslavia, back to its golden era of the 1960s and 1970s.

b.

What does Pavlović capture with her camera? What captures her?

In her early works the exhibition value of the image appears as a photographic capacity to display things *to us*, to outline a certain spatial-temporal composition. She records the already "curated" spaces with a certain disposition of art objects, furniture, and plants—in most cases the designed interiors of the 1950s, '60s, and '70s. Such interiors, observed in the register of contemporary exhibition practice, resemble the museological form of "period rooms," while in popular discourse they can be seen as "theme rooms" of representative spaces of the modern *époque* of the twentieth century. The "actors" in Pavlović's photographic plays are the corridors, the halls, the walls, the meeting rooms, the offices, and the views through the grandiose windows and atriums. The architecture is communicated in its *pure form*: emptied of life and the everyday; clean and frozen in time and space. But each frozen image, etymologically speaking, assumes a certain event, both before and after; it says "*I stand for the larger scenario.*"

The photographic series Collection/Kolekcija (2003–2005) engages with the modernist idea of the space as the total artwork—*gesmatkunstwerk*; it examines the way representative modernist spaces were formally and functionally constructed as displays for their visitors, observers, and users. The ambient and ideological representation of the capitalist West and of American context is shown in the series of the interiors of offices and lounges of the Chase Manhattan Bank building, while the halls and lounges of the Palace of Federation present the highly representative space of socialist Yugoslavia and of the Non-Aligned Movement. The viewers are, aware or not, caught in a Cold War aesthetic disposition; they are placed between the East and the West, between the spaces representative of the market economy and Capitalism and the spaces representative of the strong state apparatus and Socialism. However, the images from the series are neither unifying nor confronting the two aesthetics which could be all too easily mistaken for one and the same. The universal signifiers of modernism, functionalism, and abstraction seem to be able to join the two opposing ideologies in the same style. Only the details of occasional revolutionary iconography and the realist style of paintings in the Palace of Federation reveal the difference between these two ideological forms. Socialist modernism in the Collection/Kolekcija series is *a concrete utopia* of the twentieth century and its ideologies of better future. It is concrete in both senses: as universal signifier of modernization and social building, and as a specific Yugoslav political attempt to make socialism of self-management and non-alignment into an actual existing utopia.

Pavlović, in her photo series Collection/Kolekcija, presents two moments of exposure of the exhibition value of photography. One

pp. 123 & 121

Jelena Vesić

* If we observe the "exhibited" design of the space, the images, art objects, the furniture, the plants, the composition appears to us as a collage, the arrangement of things. It catches the spectator's eye as a scene that is already displayed. In the moment of photographing, or rather of exhibiting the photograph, these objects are appearing with the auratic patina and as a reflexive image of the original scene.

† About the concept of primary and secondary information, see Alexander Alberro, *Conceptual Art and the Politics of Publicity* (Cambridge: MIT Press, 1999); and John Slyce, "The Playmaker: Seth Siegelaub interviewed by John Slyce," *Art Monthly* 327, June 2009, artmonthly.co.uk/magazine/site/article/seth-siegelaub-interviewed-by-john-slyce-june-2009.

‡ Pierre Nora, *Realms of Memory: The Construction of the French Past*, ed. Lawrence D. Kritzman, trans. Arthur Goldhammer (New York: Columbia University Press, 1996).

is the exposure of the "original scene" when captured by the eye of the photographer or by the photographic apparatus.[*] Another is the photographic reproduction (translation, transmission) of the "original scene" that is now exposed for the second time, re-exposed through the exhibition. Representative space is always displayed to the multitude of gazes—imaginary, symbolic, or real. Such spaces are already *on stage*, yet Pavlović's stagecrafting provides them with a new exhibiting platform.

If we consider this Pavlović's play with the exhibition value of photography in the larger historical and theoretical framework of exhibiting, it recalls the logic of conceptual art curator Seth Sigelaub who, through his experiments with exhibiting, made a distinction between the two stages of exhibited objects. He speaks about primary and the secondary information;[†] *primary information* assumes live experience of observing art, while the *secondary information* presents the document, both staged and crafted, that witnesses about this once-live experience. (We already mentioned Pavlović's witnessing—*I have been here*). Primary and secondary information are the two moments where the production of the exhibition value occurs. It is not incidental that Vesna Pavlović titles the series Collection/Kolekcija, and it is not only because her photographic takes often include artworks or because the spaces she photographs are built as *total artworks*, but because of her "museologizing gesture" of theme-rooming, of presenting the image as the collection of our memories of the twentieth century—what French historian Pierre Nora calls *sites of memory* (*les lieux de mémoire*[‡]).

As the user of museum and exhibition knowledge, Vesna Pavlović escapes both the museological pitfalls of contemporary representation of the memory of socialism, and the twentieth century fetishism of totalitarian evil and nostalgia for socialism as "better past." (She escapes the entire palette of nostalgic, ahistorical approaches, the entire order of the stereotypical: images from the Cold War era as the times of naivety where the name of the enemy was clear, the golden times of espionage and simplified ideological clashes.)

C.

The second part of the thematic cut-out of Pavlović's photographic oeuvre presented in this book, her second thesis, develops in the interplay between the photographic matter and the idea of

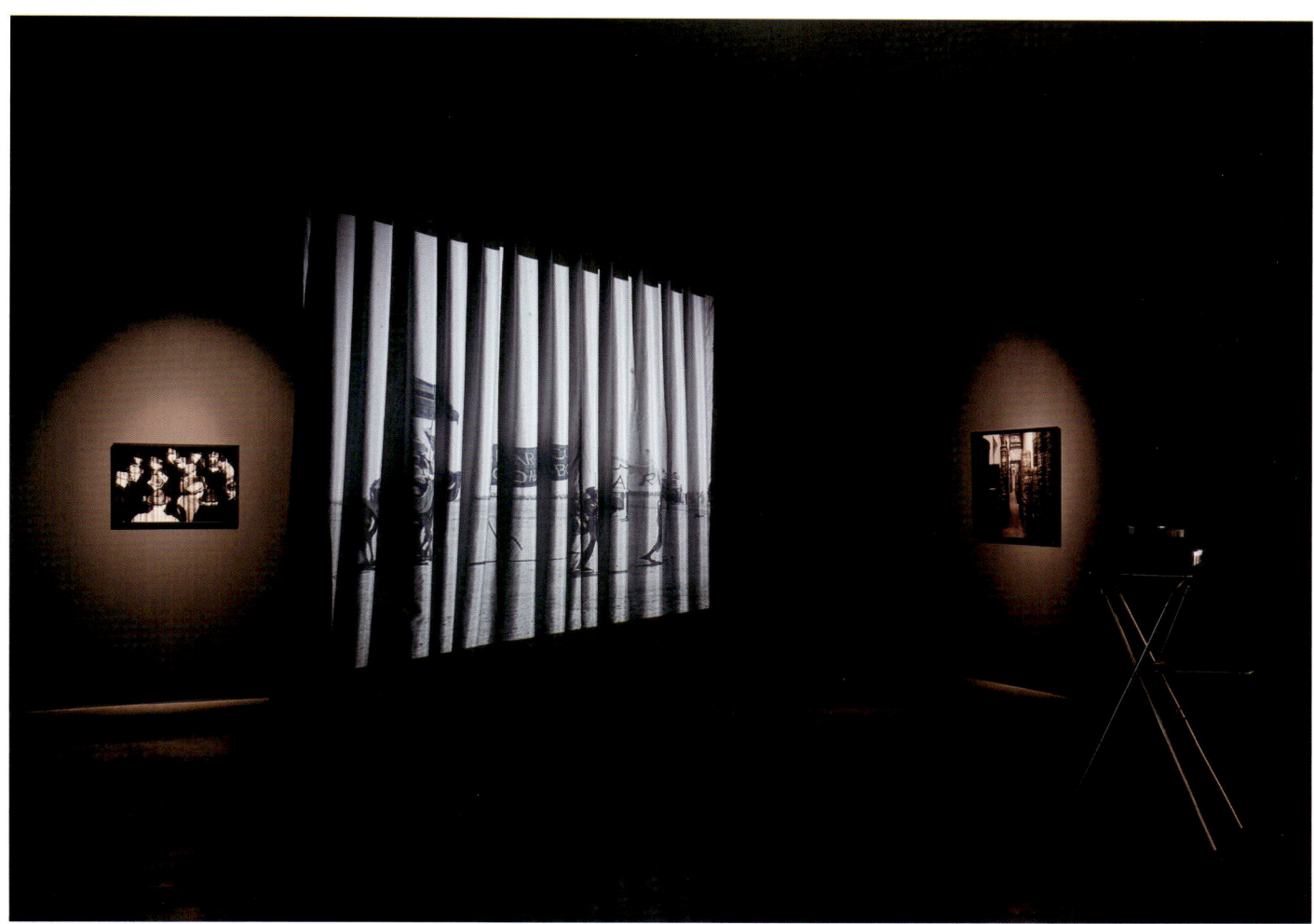

Figure 7. Vesna Pavlović, Fototeka (2013–2016), installation view at MAC International 2018, MAC Belfast. Image courtesy MAC Belfast / Photo by Simon Mills

Jelena Vesić

display-as-theater. In what can be called her American phase, Vesna Pavlović revisits the photographic field through the lens of the history of display of the twentieth century and beyond. Here the artist explores various forms of staging the image in the exhibition space; that is, she experiments with the forms of photographic spatialization. In parallel, she starts exploring the limits of a photographic image before it dissolves in space.

The archives of various different shapes and forms (including but far from limited to institutional archives) became one of the main resources of Pavlović's contemporary photographic practice marked by nondecisiveness, as exemplified by her exhibitions *Lost Art*, *Search for Landscapes*, and *Reflection on Images* (Figure 7). In these shows Pavlović explores the visual signification and the aesthetics of curtain, especially the way it was used in the exhibition compositions in different moments throughout the twentieth century. She focuses on the aesthetics of the pleated light gray curtains,

* Simon Sheikh, "Constitutive Effects: The Techniques of the Curator," in Paul O'Neill, ed., *Curating Subjects* (London: Open Editions, 2007).

† For more detailed reflection on the meaning of the screen and the curtain in Pavlović's exhibitions see Morna O'Neill, ed., *Vesna Pavlović's Lost Art: Photography, Display, and the Archive* (Winston-Salem: Hanes Art Gallery, 2018).

‡ It also corresponds with the title of the project *Decollecting*, in which Pavlović participated with her series Collection /Kolekcija. Curated by Annette Schemmel, the exhibition was displayed at FRAC Nord Pas De Calais, Dunquerque; Idem+Arts, Maubeuge; and De Garage Mechelen, Belgium. For more, see Annette Schemmel, ed., *Decollecting* (Dunkirk: Edition FRAC Nord- Pas de Calais, 2008).

a distinctive curatorial technique (to borrow a term from the theorist Simon Sheikh[*]) used for the background of artworks for the exhibitions of the late 1940s and 1950s. In the midst of her play with exhibiting, Pavlović inserts several visually memorable moments from the history of display, including different requisites, props, and backdrops, as a form of staging. In her three recent solo exhibitions, Pavlović "collages" the historical meanings of the *curtain* and the *screen*,[†] challenging the traditional affirmation of image-as-truth, of photography-as-truth, of any-record-as-truth. She presents the situations in which the observers encounter the spatial impossibility of photography to capture what could be assumed as *reality*.

Vesna Pavlović enters yet another stage of the use of the photographic—the stage of decomposition, and we can even say of *de-collection* (to directly confront the second thesis to the first, above, non-coincidently entitled Collection).[‡] Such de-collection of the visual, of rejecting any firm and stable visual take, a certain de-collage-ness of photography, emanates the distrust in visual-as-category that the artist, as many other of her contemporaries, put in the center of interest of today. Pavlović unbuilds the image, successfully transforming all the firmness of the photographic capture into a meltdown.

And precisely for that reason she uses the very exhibition as an installation form instead of exhibiting photographs in the gallery space, as was characteristic for her first phase. There is no container or border of the image; the image now "carries itself"; it melts into the space, it forms the space. Pavlović's use of curtains and screens in exhibiting her photographic matter is also a play on the historical use of media to distribute the image or to produce a display. She analyzes various technologies, from the analogue slide projection to a more contemporary digital postproduction of image. She doesn't deny nor celebrate this settled truth that all images are, indeed, constructed. Instead, she explores the instability of the image and ways to proceed with the awareness that the very field of the visual and the image itself is not a reliable source of truth.

Alberro, Alexander. *Conceptual Art and the Politics of Publicity*. Cambridge: MIT Press, 1999.

Bal, Mieke. "Exhibition as a Syntax of the Face." In "The Grammar of the Exhibition," edited by Viktor Misiano and Nathalie Zonnenberg. Special issue. *Manifesta Journal*, no. 7 (2009/2010): 12–22.

Cartier-Bresson, Henri. *The Decisive Moment*. New York City: Simon & Schuster, 1952

Lefebvre, Henri. *The Production of Space*. Translated by Donald Nicholson-Smith. Oxford: Basil Blackwell, 1991. Originally published as *La production de l'espace*. Paris: Anthropos, 1974.

Nora, Pierre. *Realms of Memory: The Construction of the French Past*. Edited by Lawrence D. Kritzman. Translated by Arthur Goldhammer. New York: Columbia University Press, 1996.

O'Doherty, Brian. *Inside the White Cube: The Ideology of the Gallery Space*. Santa Monica and San Francisco: Lapis Press, 1986. Originally published in *Artforum*, 1976.

O'Neill, Morna, ed. *Vesna Pavlović's Lost Art: Photography, Display, and the Archive*. Winston-Salem: Hanes Art Gallery, 2018.

O'Neill, Paul, ed. *Curating Subjects*. London: Open Editions and Amsterdam: De Appel, 2007.

Osborne, Peter. "9 Points by Peter Osborne." In "The Grammar of the Exhibition," edited by Viktor Misiano and Nathalie Zonnenberg. Special issue. *Manifesta Journal*, no. 7 (2009/2010): 23.

Schemmel, Annette, ed. *Decollecting*. Dunkirk: Edition FRAC Nord- Pas de Calais, 2008.

Sheikh, Simon. "Constitutive Effects: The Techniques of the Curator." In *Curating Subjects*. Edited by Paul O'Neill. London: Open Editions and Amsterdam: De Appel, 2007.

Slyce, John. "The Playmaker: Seth Siegelaub interviewed by John Slyce." *Art Monthly* 327, June 2009. artmonthly.co.uk/magazine/site/article/seth-siegelaub-interviewed-by-john-slyce-june-2009.

Jelena Vesić

Transnational Time
Unsettling Borders and Media in Vesna Pavlović's Oeuvre

JORDAN AMIRKHANI

* See Raqs Media Collective's performative text "An Ephemeris, Corrected for the Longitudes of Tomorrow: Speculations on the Orbit and Motion of Objects and Processes in Contemporary Art Today and Tomorrow" in Jill H. Casid and Aruna d'Souza, eds., *Art History in the Wake of the Global Turn* (New Haven: Yale University Press, 2014).

See Homi Bhabha's "After Words: Hybridity" in *Artforum* 35, no. 9 (May 1997), 11–13.

† See Claudette Lauzon's *The Unmaking of Home in Contemporary Art* (Toronto: University of Toronto, 2017).

‡ Lauzon, *The Unmaking of Home in Contemporary Art*.

INTRODUCTION

What is global is the distribution of chances that different places will speak to different people at different times. Nothing comes from just once place; nothing comes from just one time.
RAQS MEDIA COLLECTIVE[*]

For many, "home" is an easily named and singular origin, a particular space with a definable beginning where one's history and sense of self commences. My hometown, my community, my nation—each iteration provides a settlement from where one can be, belong, and become. However, for those who live and work across multiple "homes" and between different geographies, any notion of pure origins is difficult if not impossible to pin down. The work of artists who operate across borders and boundaries is rarely a direct reflection or extension of a singular national background and is instead an entanglement of the many cultural references that have accumulated along the way. As Homi Bhabha states, an artist who lives and works across and between borders will see their work make visible "the rough edges, the complex negotiations of aesthetic values that find themselves not only 'outside' the artwork . . . but 'inside' the work itself, both formally and affectively. These cultural contradictions, disjunctive historical spaces, identifications created on the crossroads—these are the issues that the arts of cultural hybridization seek to embody and enact."[†] As transnational and diasporic discourse has made evident, to address artists and their work as sites of national, cultural, and aesthetic "crossroads" is to recognize that "home" is a scattered and multiple location, and that any meaningful contextualization of art shaped by transnational conditions must find form for that flux.[‡]

The un-settlement of "home" and "origins" find productive form in the oeuvre of Vesna Pavlović, whose work since her arrival in the United States in the early 2000's unpacks the complicated terrain of making work as a Serbian/Yugoslav/and/or/-/American artist. While it is true that much of the context and poignancy of Pavlović's work is indebted to specific Serbian art historical and political legacies, this text turns its eye toward the artist's investments in and resonances with a more fluid and expansive field of contemporary photographic languages. Rather than sideline or ignore the heterogeneity of Pavlović's praxis in favor of a narrower nation- and identity-based interpretive framework, this intervention draws upon the accumulative archive of transnational references

* For more on Yugoslav modernism and its engagement with federalist republican political ideology, see Vladimir Kulić's essay "Building Brotherhood and Unity: Architecture and Federalism in Socialist Yugoslavia," in Martino Stierli and Vladimir Kulić, eds., *Toward a Concrete Utopia: Architecture in Yugoslavia, 1948–1980* (New York: Museum of Modern Art, 2018), 27–39.

that have shaped Pavlović's itinerant and deeply personal practice. Pavlović's destabilizing of photographic conditions and institutional apparatuses bears a quiet but potent resistance to the critical assumption that art made by those from "decidedly elsewhere" cannot "entirely belong" to the narratives granted unquestioningly to those whose "home" or origin is singular and definitive. What might it mean to think through these questions of here, elsewhere, and in-between through Pavlović's unique handling of the photographic medium, its institutional structures, and her own personal archive of identities and experiences? Contemporary art of the twenty-first century as a discourse is at its most powerful when its assumptions and concerns center the effects of a more global and de-centered geographical disposition, but as scholars of "the global turn" in art history have made evident, the specter of the "West" and its canon of aesthetic maneuvers can never be fully severed from the artists and works that live outside its reach. As a photographer operating in the late aftermath of the Cold War, and especially in her practice from the mid-1990's forward, Pavlović's education, influences, and career maps across and between an ecology of cultural spheres, turning her practice into a politics of location where each modality is neither stable nor totally fluent.

SOCIAL SPACE

Pavlović's politics of location as a position of "between-ness" is manifested in a variety of ways across her photo-based oeuvre, from subject matter to art historical context, medium to materiality, and can be subtly teased out of Pavlović's early photographic series Hotels—color photographs taken between 2000 and 2002 of 1960s modernist interiors designated as the official aesthetic of the "golden era" of Yugoslav socialism. Playing with the icon of a "hotel," Pavlović's series points to the temporal instability of the site itself. Hotels are locations that offer itinerants a home for a brief period, often acting as porous barriers between their ever-changing population of guests and the constellation of never-ending activities, transactions, and traffic that exists outside its walls. Providing an entrance and exit to travelers whose location is neither here nor there and whose relationship to their location is inherently contingent, Pavlović's Hotels series documents the physical demeanor of these spaces as a way of foregrounding the ongoing presence of the historical past at work within these sites due to their iconic status as icons of Yugoslav socialist modernism.* Quiet, intimate,

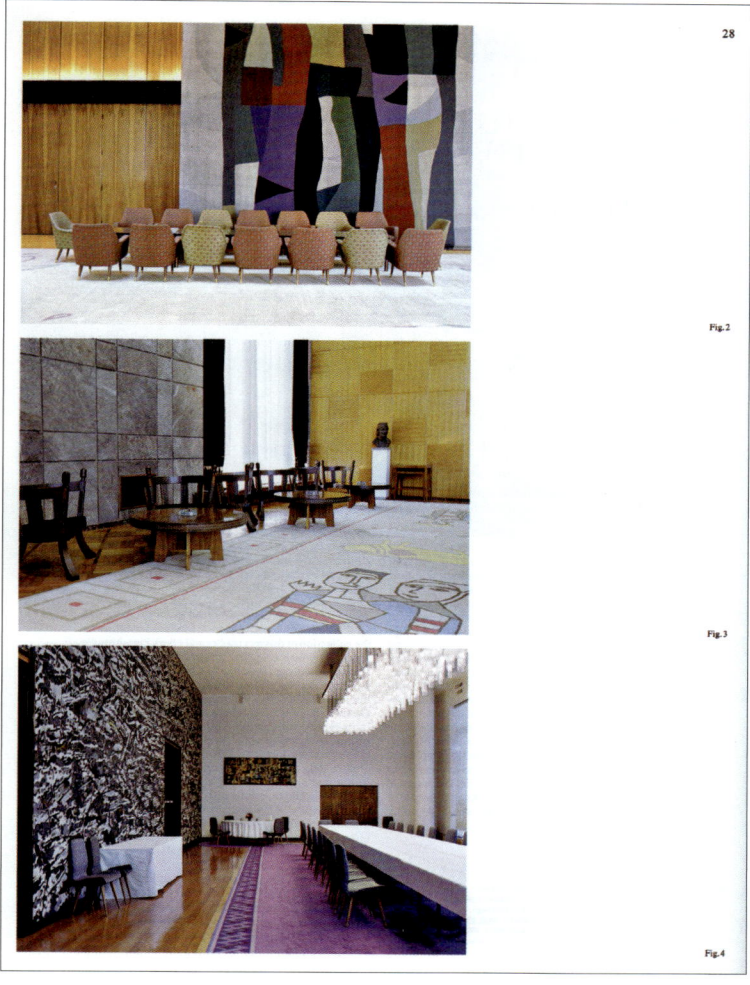

Fig.2

Fig.3

Fig.4

Figure 8. From Martino Stierli and Vladimir Kulić, *Toward a Concrete Utopia: Architecture in Yugoslavia, 1948–1980* (New York: Museum of Modern Art, 2018).

* Kulić, "Building Brotherhood and Unity," 27.

and seemingly abandoned, these hotels remained untouched while administrative buildings, including the former headquarters for the socialist party, lie in bombed ruin all around them. Pavlović's cold, deadpan style and uncanny photographic precision confront the tense anachronism of her "home nation" as both frozen and imploding in time, abandoned by history and still licking its wounds. Chunky, monochromatic lounge chairs and multi-person loveseats bask in the dim glow of aging yellowed light fixtures while a few folded napkins lying haphazardly on mid-century modern coffee tables point to the bodies that once frequented these rooms, the pageantry that these spaces once supported, and the collective body-politic that is no longer. In this series, the politics of location is foregrounded by a postwar ideal of the synthesis of aesthetics, space, and function conceived to celebrate a socialist federation, which, as architectural historian Vladimir Kulić has so powerfully expressed, continues to resonate as "an apt metaphor for the Yugoslav socialist state: a modern container for the collection of traditional ethnicities, brought together by their common struggle for liberation from fascism, class oppression, and underdevelopment" (Figure 8).* Thus, these spaces are neither neutral nor impotent in their abandonment, but reify the palpable sense of historical "between-ness" that remains so present in the current architectural, aesthetic, and public landscape of the country.

The aestheticization of politics is thus overt in Pavlović's images. Slick in their omniscient perspectives and pristine symmetries, details of surfaces and textures are rendered in exquisite clarity, while holes, broken shades, busted lightbulbs, and meticulous arrangements of furniture not only point to a bygone era but act as visual metaphors for the nation's struggle to marry Western capitalism with socialist ideologies and to complete its transition from Yugoslavia to Serbia. This transformation by the 1990s, under the leadership of Slobodan Milošević, allowed the leader to repackage Yugoslavia's legacy to serve his party's anti-Western, populist goals and marked an increasing right-wing nationalism that continues to spread across the world. By harnessing the photograph as a tool for technical documentation and its legacy as the avant-garde's tautological model of industrial progress, innovation, and at times, official propaganda, Pavlović's photographed spaces of leisure and sociality confront her country's political history from the sidelines. Spaces where parties, meetings, gossip sessions were held offer opportunities to visually "enter" the mysterious backstage arenas of power that so marked the age of Tito

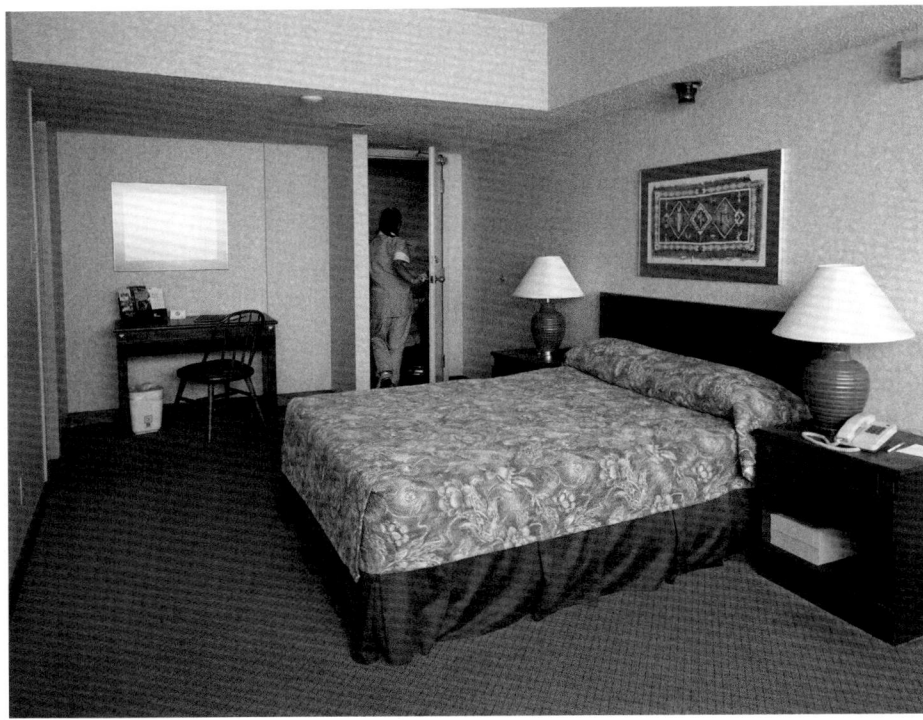

Figure 9. Jeff Wall, *Housekeeping* (1996), silver gelatin print, 192.0 × 258 cm. Courtesy of the artist

* See Michael Fried's text "Jeff Wall, Wittgenstein, and the Everyday" in *Critical Inquiry* 33, no. 3 (Spring 2007), 495–526.

and thus acknowledge the consequences of his administrative era. While many photographers from elsewhere have focused their energies on the massive "concrete utopian" monuments of the Tito era and shaped a photographic style that highlights the country's massive public monuments, virtuosic architectural feats, and colossal public spaces of modernism's last stance, Pavlović turns her attentions to the nooks, corridors, and intimate arenas where politics was constructed and performed on a smaller, less public, but no less potent scale. As Yugoslavia came and went, these photographs make clear that Yugoslavia's historical past haunts the interstices between public and private space.

However, to see Hotels as only participating in the narratives of Yugoslav political contexts does not acknowledge the series' resonance with a variety of external photographic conversations and debates, specifically, the direct and socially engaged lexicon of Anglo-American art and photography of the 1980s and early 1990s produced by artists such as Jeff Wall, Stephen Shore, Nan Goldin, and Tacita Dean. As art historian Michael Fried reminds us, Wall's art-history-minded, light-box photographs demand to be seen as a tableau, their painterly monumentality on the wall declaring themselves both "artifactual" as well as images of "beholding."* And yet Wall's photographs are not completely autonomous art objects either; the artist's subject matter points to political contexts and concerns outside the image despite Wall's overt concern with the medium-specific and formalist gestures of this photographic era. Wall's seemingly spontaneous documentarian aesthetic captures the politically fraught spaces, communities, and social fabric of America in an era of civil rights tensions and advanced high capitalism and point to Wall's consideration of form as much more than function. In this way, Wall and Pavlović share territory as photographers. While Wall has tried to distance himself from the messy world of politics in his statements and work, his persistent desire to circumnavigate or ignore the political resonances of the figures and locations in his photographs makes evident a keen awareness of the power of a clean formal polish to reveal and render strange the subjects and social narratives re-presented in his images. For example, Wall's image of a meticulously cleaned and orderly unoccupied hotel room belies its perfection in the title *Housekeeping* (1996, Figure 9), and instead presents a scathing photographic treatise on the invisible labor and politicized inequities of domestic work in spaces of leisure and tourism. Captured in an epic, "cinematographically" beautiful manner, Wall's photographs resonate with Pavlović's

* On the legacy of Stephen Shore's work see Ben Crair's essay "I Found Myself Seeing Pictures All the Time," *New Republic*, October 22, 2013, newrepublic.com/article/115243/stephen-shore-photography-american-surfaces-uncommon-places.

Jordan Amirkhani

own harnessing of a pristine and crisp visual aesthetic to critique these seemingly benign spaces of relaxation and entertainment. The work of both photographers belies powerful understandings of photography's aesthetic capacities—that an image can never be autonomous when the camera is pointed at subjects and spaces lodged deep within the collective unconscious of a community.

In addition, Pavlović's manipulation of rich color and textures in her photographs has an additional formal resonance with the colorful compositions of photographer Stephen Shore. Despite Shore's misleading assertion that his photographs depict "mere surfaces . . . and surfaces only," Shore's thoughtful elevation of personal objects and private spaces makes for sensitive encounters with the politics of the everyday and the impossibility of a neutral image.* Captured in these "perfect moments," Shore's tight compositions in his American Surfaces (1972–1973) series of motels, highways, and retail windows are indeed celebrations of the vernacular, democratic operations of the photographer and his choices. Like Pavlović, Shore's photographs are also images where bodies and politics reverberate outside the frame, absent from the depicted action but brought to bear on the image in the median between photograph and viewer. American Surfaces and Hotels point to the ways in which photographs for these two photographers enable a solidification of space and time where rooms and hotels are merely that, and of course, so much more.

Pavlović's centering of the social and communal spaces of a particular era and/or a particular cultural moment resonate with the photographic oeuvre of Nan Goldin as well, whose cinematic insider views of spaces and communities struggling to survive and celebrate in 1980's America have become iconic. While bodies are not physically present in the Hotels series, as stated earlier, their absence reverberates in the ideological conditions of the spaces, which were designated for the staging of the Yugoslav "body politic" and the political and social relations that shaped the workings of Yugoslav federalism and the ideologies of brotherhood and unity upon which the state depended during the Cold War. Physicality is thus represented not through the appearance of figures, but through the props, trappings, and stagings that bodies wander and live amongst. The interdependence between the body and its environment is articulated defiantly in Goldin's infamous photographic series The Ballad of Sexual Dependency (1986), a cohort of photographs that points to subjectivity as much more than a set of individual physical attributes, but as the relational, spatial,

* See Nan Goldin's quote from a 1996 interview on "The Ballad of Sexual Dependency" reprinted in Hilton Als' online essay "Nan Goldin's Life in Progress" for the *New Yorker*, June 27, 2016, www.newyorker.com/magazine/2016/07/04/nan-goldins-the-ballad-of-sexual-dependency.

† In 2004, Pavlović's Hotels series was included in the exhibition *Rearview Mirror* at Kettle's Yard in Cambridge, United Kingdom. Curated by Elizabeth Fisher, this exhibition presented the work of artists engaged with issues of historical memory and the relationship between past and present and included work by Tacita Dean, Joachim Koester, Siemon Allen, Omer Fast, and Vesna Pavlović, among many others. John J. Curley addresses Pavlović's work in relationship to Tacita Dean in his essay "Curtain Call: History Taking a Bow" written for Morna O'Neill, ed., *Vesna Pavlović's Lost Art: Photography, Display, and the Archive* (Hanes Art Gallery, Wake Forest University, 2018).

‡ Quoted in Tacita Dean: *Analogue*, exhibition catalogue (Basel: Steidl/Schaulager, 2006) 8–9.

and communal emanations that leave their traces on/in spaces, others, and time. Goldin's desire to "create a history by recording a history" through her photographic series reminds that making a photograph is indeed making a history for oneself and others.[*] Pavlović's series of hotels thus do much more than merely document abandoned historical spaces, but stage the constellation of events and memories that rendered these spaces disavowed by the dynamic forces of history. Just as Goldin grants us access to spaces and selves under threat in Ronald Regan's America, so too does Pavlović mine the spaces of a postwar transformation of the post-Yugoslav project still writhing under the dreams, appropriations, and misleadings of a restrictive national mythology.

Pavlović's engagement with the flexibility and fictionalization inherent in the medium of photography resonates deeply with a cohort of artists working internationally over the past thirty years on issues of historical preservation and memory, and shares this generation's critique of the photography as an agent of truth and direct, unassailable clarity. Keen to unearth the itinerant nature of historical and photographic materials so often collected in and framed by Enlightenment-laden value houses like museums, libraries, and national collections, Pavlović is also deeply sensitive to the obsolescence of photographic technologies and processes of time-based images that over the course of time are rendered unusable, inefficient, and even absurd. Pavlović's praxis stimulates tremendous resonance with artists such as the British filmmaker and photographer Tacita Dean, whose commitment to a set of artistic practices dependent upon time-based imagery and the destabilization of the veracity of images riffs with Pavlović's own fascination with historical memory, medium-specific obsolescence, and the relationship to historical time and cultural shifts.[†] Dean's *Kodak* (2006, Figure 10) is a strong example of this: shot using color stock and five rolls of obsolete black-and-white 16mm film, this forty-four-minute film was shot in the original Kodak factory in Chalon-sur-Saône, France. For Dean, this film is not only a meditation on the beauty and capacity of Kodak analogue film, but a reflection on the current state of photography itself: "the point is that it's a medium that is just about to be exhausted."[‡] Not only have digital processes replaced (and in some way annihilated) traditional methods of the medium, the loss of these methods points to forms of historical shift; from the twentieth to twenty-first century image regimes, the modern to the postmodern, the destruction of the analogue's image efficacy and potency in a

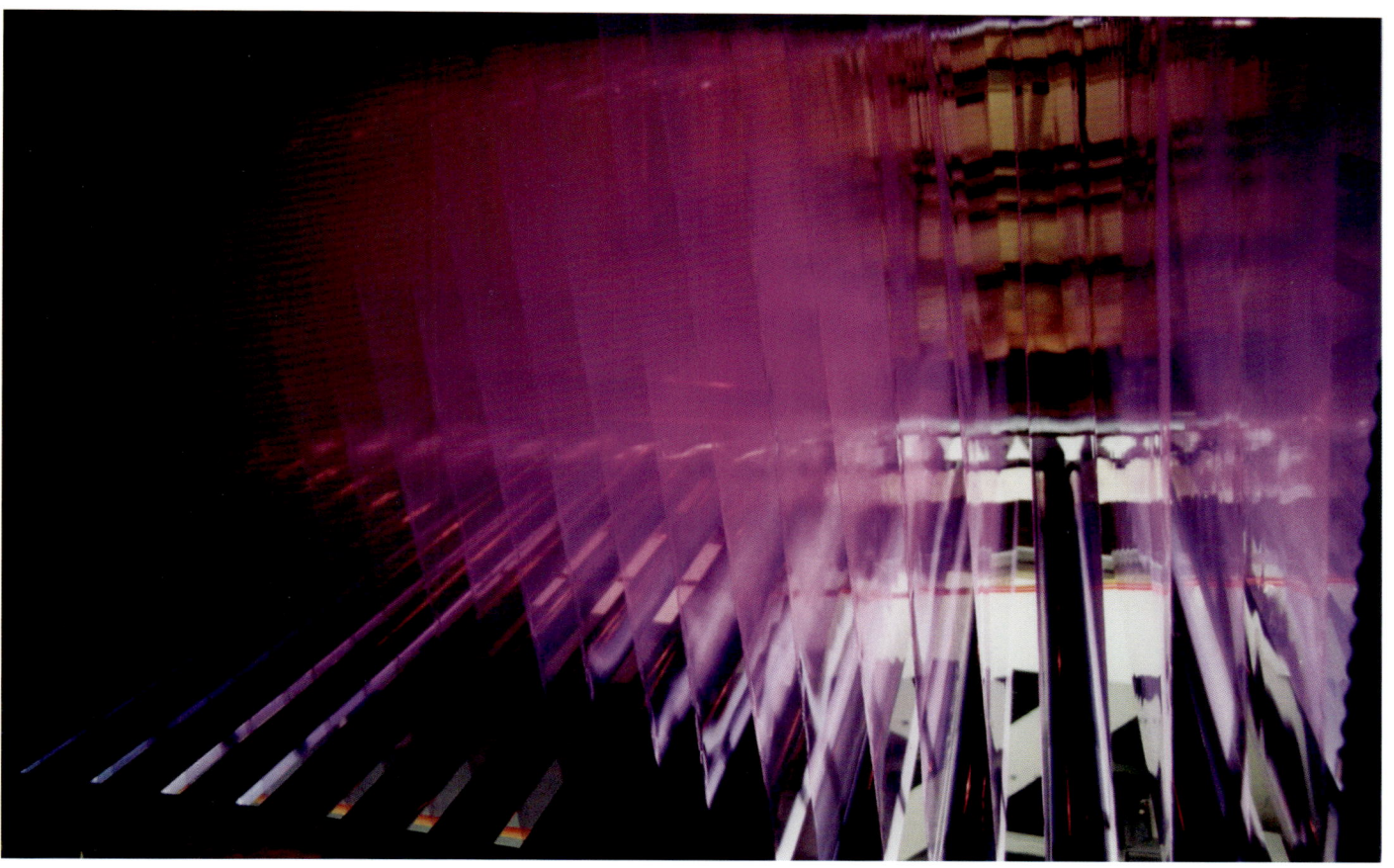

Figure 10. Tacita Dean, *Kodak* (2006; film still), 16 mm color and black and white, optical sound, 44 minutes. Courtesy of the artist, Frith Street Gallery, London, and Marian Goodman Gallery, New York / Paris

Jordan Amirkhani

digital age points to larger forces of change brought on by capitalism, globalization, and the loss of industries and cultural forms shaped by hands as opposed to inanimate devices. A sensitivity to and celebration of the processes and conditions of the photograph is bound up with Pavlović's work as well, who asks what will happen when these traditions of image-making are lost, transformed, and/or replaced by quicker, speedier, slicker modes and what can be learned from these losses in relation to our own history, personal and collective? Photography, like history, is malleable, personal, and often mediated by the conditions of its own making and representation. Pavlović's Hotels images reflect these questions and concern back to us—what do these images and the narratives and nostalgia for the Cold War Era and its trappings signal about a nation's relationship to the past? What is being erased, preserved, imagined, lost as our histories unfold? How might the photograph reveal and conceal these concerns?

By working within the transnational interstices of late twentieth-century photographic traditions, Pavlović's Hotels opens up new territory in contemporary photography and refutes the common narratives that American photography of recent decades was an inherently inward and uninterested discourse with little to no room for international artists to access that generation of strategies due to America's geopolitical dominance and other latent Cold War biases.[*] In Hotels, Pavlović's documentary aesthetic points to the power of photography to uncover the anxieties of an age, a nation, a culture, and makes evident that culture and context itself is neither static nor finished. Just as American photographers of this generation saw the politics of "home" as a viable path for re-presenting the unconscious animus of a nation in tension undergoing a variety of new social transformations, so too does Pavlović give leverage to a national identity alive to its own historical pasts and futures and ask, What becomes of national context when the nation is no longer? Between public and private, leisure and ruin, Serbia and Yugoslavia, photograph and document, Pavlović's commitment to suspending the past in her images reveals a dedication to crafting a sense of time, history, and place that delights in its own unsettlement.

ASSESSMENT AND THE ARCHIVE

While the artist's national past looms heavily across Pavlović's photographic oeuvre, her varied use of archival materials and strategies has created exciting new opportunities to harness time and its accumulations as a material to be manipulated and reified. Again, history is rendered contingent within Pavlović's archive-based projects, allowing for new articulations of contextual and aesthetic "between-ness" to emerge within the origins and staging of her materials and the unfolding of narrative meaning. These issues are powerfully unpacked in Pavlović's recent project Sites of Memory—a proverbial coda of two decades of work in which the artist makes a series of material interventions into existent archival imagery (in this case, the holdings of the Museum of Yugoslav History in Belgrade) using processes of digital printing and hand stitching, which are then turned back into photographs. Pavlović's various transformations of her materials in this work provides a powerful form of re-assessment of the archive as a working tool and vehicle for self-reflection. By complicating our notion of the "original" art object and embracing both handmade and digital strategies, Sites of Memory marks the artist within the accumulations of the archive in an overt and critical way.[*] Thus, it is the

*   See Branislav Dimitrijević's discussion of memory and photographic praxis in Pavlović's recent oeuvre in the exhibition catalogue essay titled "Vesna Pavlović and Lost/Found Memory of Photography," in *Fabrics of Socialism* (Belgrade: MoCAB/KCB, 2019), 32–37. This exhibition catalogue was published in celebration of the presentation of Pavlović's work at The Artget Gallery, Cultural Center of Belgrade, in January 2019.

†   For more on my assessment of Pavlović's engagement with contemporary art's discourse of the "archival turn" see my review "Art History Slide Become Art: Vesna Pavlović at Whitespace" for *Burnaway*, July 8, 2016, burnaway.org/vesna-pavlovic-at-whitespace. For an important essay on "the archival turn," see Okwui Enwezor's "Archive Fever: Photography between History and the Monument" in *Archive Fever: The Uses of the Document in Contemporary Art*, Okwui Enwezor, ed. (New York: International Center for Photography, 2008), 11.

Jordan Amirkhani

archive itself that forms the crux of Pavlović's focus—an institutional apparatus that shapes, creates, and embroiders upon the monumentalization and memorialization of a particular past. By interrupting, reconstructing, and ultimately revising an extant archive with her own creative processes and existing work, Pavlović inscribed her work within the rich territory of contemporary archival praxis, but invited a subversive deconstruction of the historicizing methodologies brought to bear in the processes of collecting, finding, and recontextualizing materials. Incorporating the processes of archival work into her own oeuvre, Pavlović points to the staging of history as a political and personal act, for as we know, archives are not random organizing institutional receptacles of history, but inherently political and ideological entities authored and edited from a particular perspective and representational intent.

While the "archival turn" is writ large in the recent histories of contemporary art praxis, the acknowledgment of archival excavation's dependence upon personal bias and interpretation via the artist is often dimmed.[†] The great strength of Pavlović's recent project is her identification of the relationality between historical and institutional archival practices and their negotiation of psychological and personal strategies of material collection. Made resolutely clear is Pavlović's assertion that our memories, histories, private experiences, and sense of identity are also narratives constructed by gathering, sorting, and editing from the broad continuum of historical time, and are thus deeply connected to processes of spatialization and visualization inherent to archives. For Pavlović, nothing is neutral, and the autonomy of an image is once again proved as an impossibility. As a continuation of "in-between-ness," Pavlović engages her own aesthetic practice as an interstice between a national and personal subjectivity, mining and reconfiguring what marks the political and the private, the historical and the aesthetic, the professional and the individual journeys that shape a life, a way of making, the unfolding of history, the sense of her own project.

This is most acutely articulated in the series' title: Sites of Memory. A project dependent upon gathering and intervening into historical objects, documents, and institutional sites that embody Yugoslavia and the history of the Non-Aligned Movement—a decolonizing movement that sought to decenter the global division of the world into West and East—Sites of Memory mobilizes the title of French historian Pierre Nora's multi-volume collection *Les lieux de mémoire* (1984) to acknowledge the ways in which history is

* See Pierre Nora's *Les lieux de mémoire*, ed. Pierre Nora (Paris: Gallimard, 1984–1992), 3 vols.; in English, see Pierre Nora, *Realms of Memory: The Construction of the French Past*, ed. Lawrence D. Kritzman, trans. Arthur Goldhammer (New York: Columbia University Press, 1996).

not just incumbent upon physical locations such as monuments, institutions, and cities, but intangible even psychic spatialities as well. According to Nora, any adequate conceptualization of a nation would acknowledge that the "stuff" of a nation's collective unconscious—symbols, museums, flags, mythologies—is a coagulation of materiality and memories, the intangible and the physical, which forces us to decode the leftover fragments and detached signs of our experience to "refill our depleted fund of collective memory."* For Nora, both site and memory together contour the conditions of history, with symbols and fragments of the past crystallizing into a substitute "body" of a nation that has lost the community rituals, shared faith, and social practices that had once bound and unified it in an era prior to industrialization and great wars, and the immense destructiveness created in their wake. However, Nora's centering of memory as the connective tissue that animates a nation's sense of identity and remembrance of itself points to a significant aspect of Pavlović's own harnessing of memory: that it is a forgetful, unreliable, and manipulative material, and that its constructed nature is rendered most present in the space of the archive.

Pavlović's mediation between archival and photographic processes as well as her intervention into the material collated for Sites of Memory provides an alter-space for the material and ephemeral conditions of memory to persist, thus embodying Nora's collapse of physical and psychological memory within institutional sites. Connected in their functions to record, gather, and recall images from the past, both photography and archives embrace their relationship to memory. But while archives provide a specific location or "home" for meaning and images where records might be retrieved, photographs remain material "things," discrete documents that register a more individual versus collective identity. Pavlović rightly suggests within this project that memory appears and enacts differently between these two media, oscillating between both the material or physical form of the document and facilitating the negotiations of past and present for remembrance to take place within an archival arrangement. While there are many significant avenues for this new body of work, perhaps most resonant is the way in which Pavlović seeks to acknowledge as well as liberate historical memory from its achievements and failures and allow us to think about how we might remember again, differently, and take agency to re-encounter it for ourselves and others.

Als, Hilton. "Nan Goldin's Life in Progress." *New Yorker*, June 27, 2016. www.newyorker.com/magazine/2016/07/04/nan-goldins-the-ballad-of-sexual-dependency.

Amirkhani, Jordan. "Art History Slide Become Art: Vesna Pavlović at Whitespace." Burnaway, July 8, 2016. burnaway.org/vesna-pavlovic-at-whitespace.

Bhabha, Homi. "After Words: Hybridity." *Artforum* 35, no. 9, May 1997.

Crair, Ben. "I Found Myself Seeing Pictures All the Time." *New Republic*, October 22, 2013. newrepublic.com/article/115243/stephen-shore-photography-american-surfaces-uncommon-places.

Curley, John J. "Curtain Call: History Taking a Bow." In *Vesna Pavlović's Lost Art: Photography, Display, and the Archive*. Edited by Morna O'Neill. Hanes Art Gallery, Wake Forest University, 2018.

Dean, Tacita. *Analogue: Drawings 1991–2006*. Basel: Steidl/Schaulager, 2006.

Dimitrijević, Branislav. "Vesna Pavlović and Lost/Found Memory of Photography." In *Fabrics of Socialism*. Belgrade: MoCAB/KCB, January 2019.

Enwezor, Okwui. "Archive Fever: Photography between History and the Monument." In *Archive Fever: The Uses of the Document in Contemporary Art*, edited by Okwui Enwezor. New York: International Center for Photography, 2008.

Fried, Michael. "Jeff Wall, Wittgenstein, and the Everyday." *Critical Inquiry* 33, no. 3, Spring 2007.

Kulić, Vladimir. "Building Brotherhood and Unity: Architecture and Federalism in Socialist Yugoslavia." In *Toward a Concrete Utopia: Architecture in Yugoslavia, 1948–1980*. Edited by Martino Stierli and Vladimir Kulić. New York: Museum of Modern Art, 2018.

Lauzon, Claudette. *The Unmaking of Home in Contemporary Art*. Toronto: University of Toronto, 2017.

Nora, Pierre. *Les lieux de mémoire*. 3 vols. Edited by Pierre Nora. Paris: Gallimard, 1984–1992.

Nora, Pierre. *Realms of Memory: The Construction of the French Past*. Edited by Lawrence D. Kritzman. Translated by Arthur Goldhammer. New York: Columbia University Press, 1996.

Pasternak, Gil. "Introduction: Photography in Transitioning European Communist and Post-Communist Histories." *Photography & Culture* 12, no. 2, June 2019.

Raqs Media Collective. "An Ephemeris, Corrected for the Longitudes of Tomorrow: Speculations on the Orbit and Motion of Objects and Processes in Contemporary Art Today and Tomorrow." In *Art History in the Wake of the Global Turn*. Edited by Jill H. Casid and Aruna d'Souza. New Haven: Yale University Press, 2014.

Ghosts in the Present Tense
The Photography of Vesna Pavlović

JOHN J. CURLEY

* Wayne Kostenbaum, *Hotel Theory* (New York: Soft Skull Press, 2007), 116. For Sigmund Freud's original text, see *The Uncanny* (1925), translated by David McLintock (New York: Penguin Classics, 2003).

p. 67

Hotels are odd spaces: a temporary home in a place that is not one's home. Described as such, the liminality of hotels align with Sigmund Freud's notion of the *uncanny*, a place that is both homely and unhomely, or as Wayne Kostenbaum has described in his book *Hotel Theory*, "home defamiliarized."* Bars in hotels deepen the unsettling quality of this liminal space by adding alcohol and proximate intimacy with iterant strangers to the mix. It is no wonder these spaces are a staple of spy fiction; hotel bars are anonymous spaces where strangers meet strangers—or acquaintances can pretend they are strangers—just steps away from their temporary beds.

These thoughts come to mind when viewing the empty bar in Vesna Pavlović's *Kasina Hotel* from 2001. The space has an impossible amount of deep red leather, or a vinyl that mimics leather, that covers the boxy chairs and sofa, as well as the facing side of the bar itself. With this distinctive color, this is a self-consciously modern interior, likely from around the early 1970s, designed for a future that never arrived. It is fitting that this saturated red hue recalls the chairs in the lobby of the outer space Hilton Hotel featured in Stanley Kubrick's *2001: A Space Odyssey* from 1968 (Figure 11). But the rich wood of the walls and table in *Kasina Hotel* add warmth and earthly familiarity to the space while also serving as a traditional foil to all that modern red. The result is a *formally* uncanny space—both familiar and strange—within the already uncanny space of the hotel bar. With Pavlović's focus on this jarring design, *Kasina Hotel* expresses that the uncanny, for

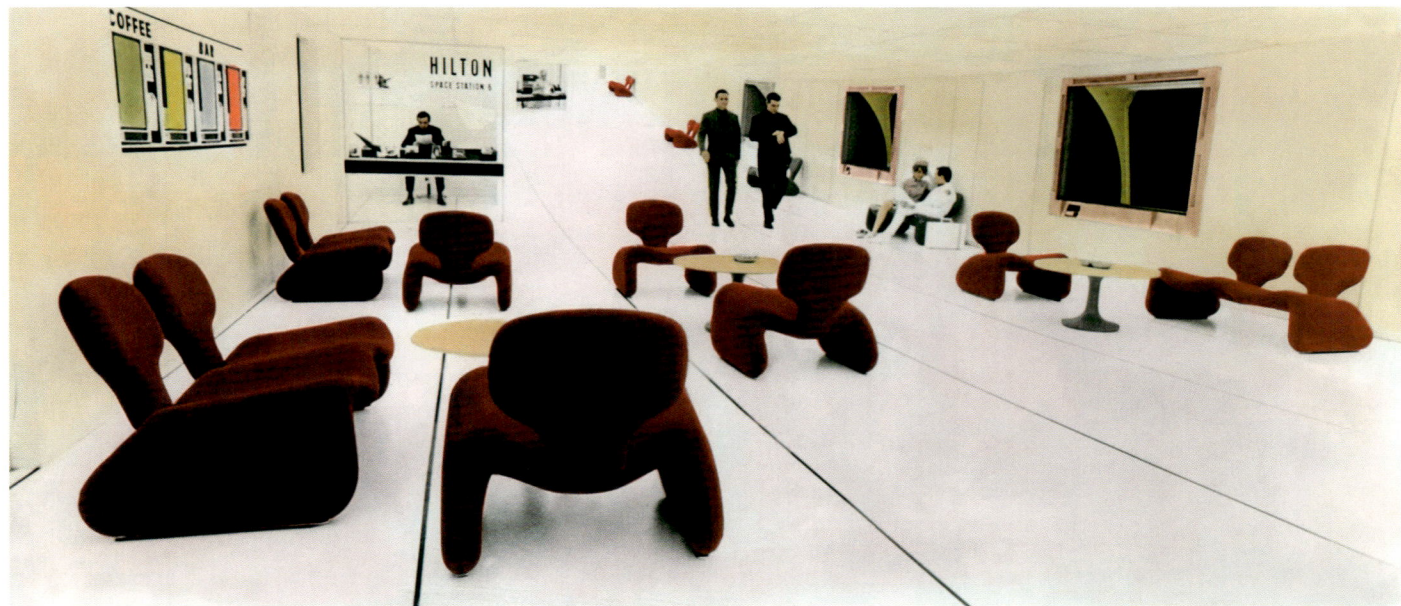

Figure 11. Hilton Hotel scene from *2001: A Space Odyssey* (1968). AF archive / Alamy Stock Photo

* Kostenbaum, *Hotel Theory*, 116.

† See Miško Šuvaković, "Impossible Histories," in *Impossible Histories: Historical Avant-Gardes, Neo-Avant-Gardes, and Post-Avant-Gardes, 1918–1991*, eds. Dubravka Đurić and Miško Šuvaković (Cambridge, MA: MIT Press, 2003), 2–35. I also discuss Tito and Yugoslavia in my *Global Art and the Cold War* (London: Laurence King, 2018), esp. 81–83.

‡ For the quoted passage, see Martino Stierli and Vladimir Kulić, "Introduction," in *Toward a Concrete Utopia*, ed. Stephanie Emerson (New York: Museum of Modern Art, 2018), 8. This show featured a number of hotels as exemplars of Yugoslav architecture.

Freud, was not only a psychological sensation, but also an *aesthetic* one. As Kostenbaum paraphrases, "Hotels in their uncanniness belong to aesthetic theory, not merely to tourism."[*]

Kasina Hotel is also politically uncanny. Pavlović photographed this bar in Majdanpek, a coalmining town in Eastern Serbia. If we assume the design is from the early 1970s, then it was taken during Yugoslavia's non-aligned period during the Cold War. Yugoslav autocrat Josip Broz Tito broke with Josef Stalin and the Soviets in 1948 and forged a "third way" between the United States and the Soviet Union that became an example to other nations like Brazil and Egypt in the 1950s and many others for the remainder of the conflict. Yugoslavia thus situated itself both geographically and ideologically between the two Blocs during the Cold War, with each side viewing it with paranoid suspicion as favoring the *other* superpower.[†]

Scholars have argued that Yugoslavian architecture gave "material shape" to Yugoslavia's "larger social project" of political nonalignment and managing ethnic difference in the Balkans through radical modernist forms that subscribed to neither the International Style of American midcentury architecture nor the Socialist Realism associated with the built environment of the Soviet Union and the Eastern Bloc.[‡] Might the same be true for the interior design of important spaces in Yugoslavia—especially those that foreign dignitaries might encounter, for example—like hotels? By this logic, *Kasina Hotel*'s uncanny quality is reinforced many times over: a home away from home that also functioned, de facto, as a medial political space away the "homes" of stable Cold War ideologies. As such, one can easily imagine agents from opposite Cold War sides populating this "neutral" hotel bar, sharing a drink and possibly more.

When Pavlović took this picture in 2001, the interior had become something else entirely: a reminder of the utopian dreams of Yugoslavia, circa 1970, in the aftermath of civil wars that left the Balkans devastated both physically and psychologically. The bar had become a relic of the past, but also, perhaps, had transformed into an igniter of contemporary consumer desire. The fact that this photograph could have easily appeared in period magazines like *Wallpaper* that depended precisely on fetishizing modernist forms that fell outside of the late-1990s generic globalization only attests to this photograph's contradictory and complex power.

Other photographs from Pavlović's Hotels series are not as alluring as hotel spaces, however. *Srbija Hotel, Zaječar, II*, also

p. 103

* Information about *Die Zeit* from email exchange with artist, November 2019.

from 2001, pictures a claustrophobic hallway, whose walls seem to close in upon a tiny window covered by a white translucent curtain. The stained carpet below and harsh florescent light above only adds to the photograph's disquiet and dismal claustrophobia. Today, one might find a photo like *Srbija Hotel, Zaječar* accompanying a negative hotel review on TripAdvisor or in an Instagram post from backpackers in central Europe that functions to show the horrors they survived.

These two photographs from Pavlović's *Hotels*—one aesthetically appealing, the other not—have different layers of meaning. As I suggested, they each could function as a document (producing desire in slick magazines or its opposite in other registers), but, as art, they work dialectically to engage the complexities of remembering Yugoslavia in a post–Cold War and post–civil war landscape. Is Yugoslavia something to remember fondly—disparate populations linked through a socialist ideology of "brotherhood and unity," trying to escape the violent binaries of the Cold War? Or a time to forget, considering Tito's dictatorship—although benevolent when compared to Soviet and other regimes—that nonetheless curtailed individual freedom and violently squashed opposition? When the civil wars of the 1990s are added to this history, the politics of memory become even more complicated: does resurrecting ideas of Yugoslavia—thereby leapfrogging backward over the 1990s—operate as a means to repress the trauma of these years, including the conflict's mass atrocities and ethnic cleansing? The bar pictured in *Kasina Hotel* welcomed guests from the periods of Tito's Yugoslavia, the dissolution of the nation, and the subsequent 1990s wars. The hallway in *Srbija Hotel, Zaječar, II* had its own foot traffic during these years. Under these historical pressures, the political uncanniness of Pavlović's photographs becomes even more palpable and urgent, layering over the psychological and aesthetic varieties already present.

Pavlović began her career as a photojournalist—a job that requires producing compelling images that are able to convey information in a succinct fashion. So in addition to her art photographs doubling as reporting—*Kasina Hotel* approaching the condition of an image in a design magazine, for instance—her photojournalism, when read outside of a press context, can also moonlight as art. Her work from the period of the civil wars exhibits this duality, especially a series of 1999 photographs taken for the German newspaper *Die Zeit* inside the Hyatt Hotel where journalists were staying during bombing of Belgrade.* In fact, the

John J. Curley

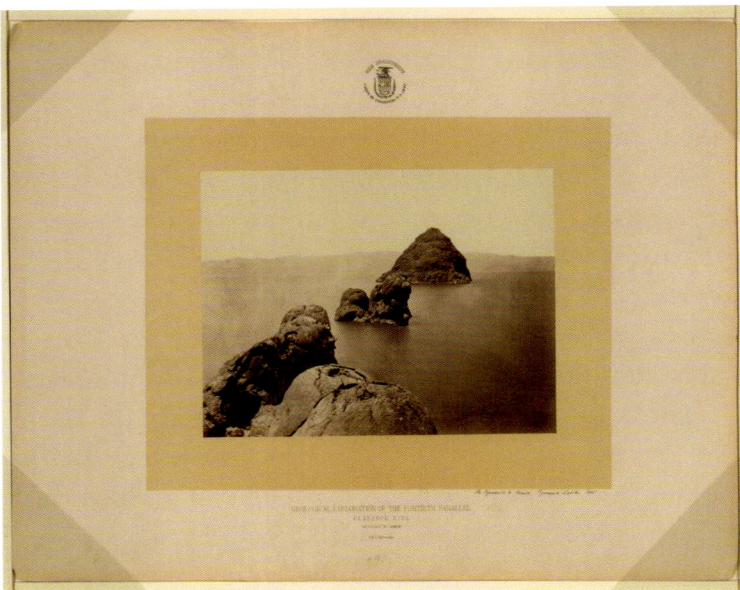

Figure 12. *The Pyramid and Domes, Pyramid Lake, Nev. / T.H. O'Sullivan, phot.* Library of Congress Prints and Photographs Division, LC-DIG-ppmsca-11875

* Rosalind Krauss, "Photography's Discursive Spaces" (1982), in *The Originality of the Avant-Garde and Other Modernist Myths* (Cambridge, MA: MIT Press, 1985), 134.

† See John Szarkowski, ed., *From the Picture Press* (New York: Museum of Modern Art, 1973). I discuss Szarkowski's formal strategies in "Controlling Doubt: Abstract Painting and Photography," in Sabine T. Kriebel and Andrés Mario Zervigón, eds., *Photography and Doubt* (London: Routledge, 2017), 201–19.

image of a journalist lounging poolside while looking at his mobile phone has become one of Pavlović's most iconic works of art, selected for numerous group shows and as the poster image for at least one of her solo shows. Suggesting the very mobility of guests in hotels, Pavlović's photographs move from context to context, never really finding a comfortable home.

Rosalind Krauss has discussed the ways that this discursive fluidity is the heart of photography.* Citing the photographs of the American West taken by Timothy O'Sullivan, like *Tufa Domes* from 1867, Krauss demonstrates how the meaning of a photograph is transformed when its display context changes. O'Sullivan took *Tufa Domes* as part of a government survey of topography, led by geologist Clarence King, and not as a work of art whose flat lake anticipates the ambiguity in paintings by Cézanne (Figure 12). But when this photograph is ripped from its geological context— literally excised from a book produced as the product of the survey, framed, and hung on a white wall—the image can accept a whole range of other meanings, including a dialogue with the traits of modernist painting. John Szarkowski, the curator of photography at the Museum of Modern Art for nearly thirty years (1962–1991) even staged some exhibitions that transformed press photographs into works of formal interest, if not art. The most significant show in this regard was *From the Picture Press* in 1973, which featured photographs from the archives of New York's *Daily News* hung on white walls without captions. Szarkowski's curatorial strategy even tried to transform Nick Ut's famous photograph of napalmed children from the Vietnam War into an aesthetic object.†

While this discursive mobility governs the entire medium of photography, Pavlović's images call explicit attention to this condition. Indeed, Pavlović's movement between photojournalism and art can add yet another layer of uncanniness to some of her work. While *Kasina Hotel* certainly feels at home in an art gallery, its affinities with photojournalism endow the image with a subtle unruliness, as if it would be equally comfortable somewhere else. But in a gallery setting, a place where viewers are conditioned to approach photographs both allegorically and formally, *Kasina Hotel* can express, among other things, the ways design helped forge a distinctive, nonaligned Yugoslavian national identity in the midst of the Cold War. In other words, its ideological significance can hide behind journalistic fact and function. As Roland Barthes wrote in the late 1950s, the political power of a press photograph resides in how its constructed message—its ideological meaning—is naturalized through

Figure 13. Vesna Pavlović, Fototeka (Projection Stills V, IV, II, VI, and I; all 2015), from *Lost Art* at Zeitgeist Gallery, Nashville, 2015. Courtesy of Zeitgeist Gallery

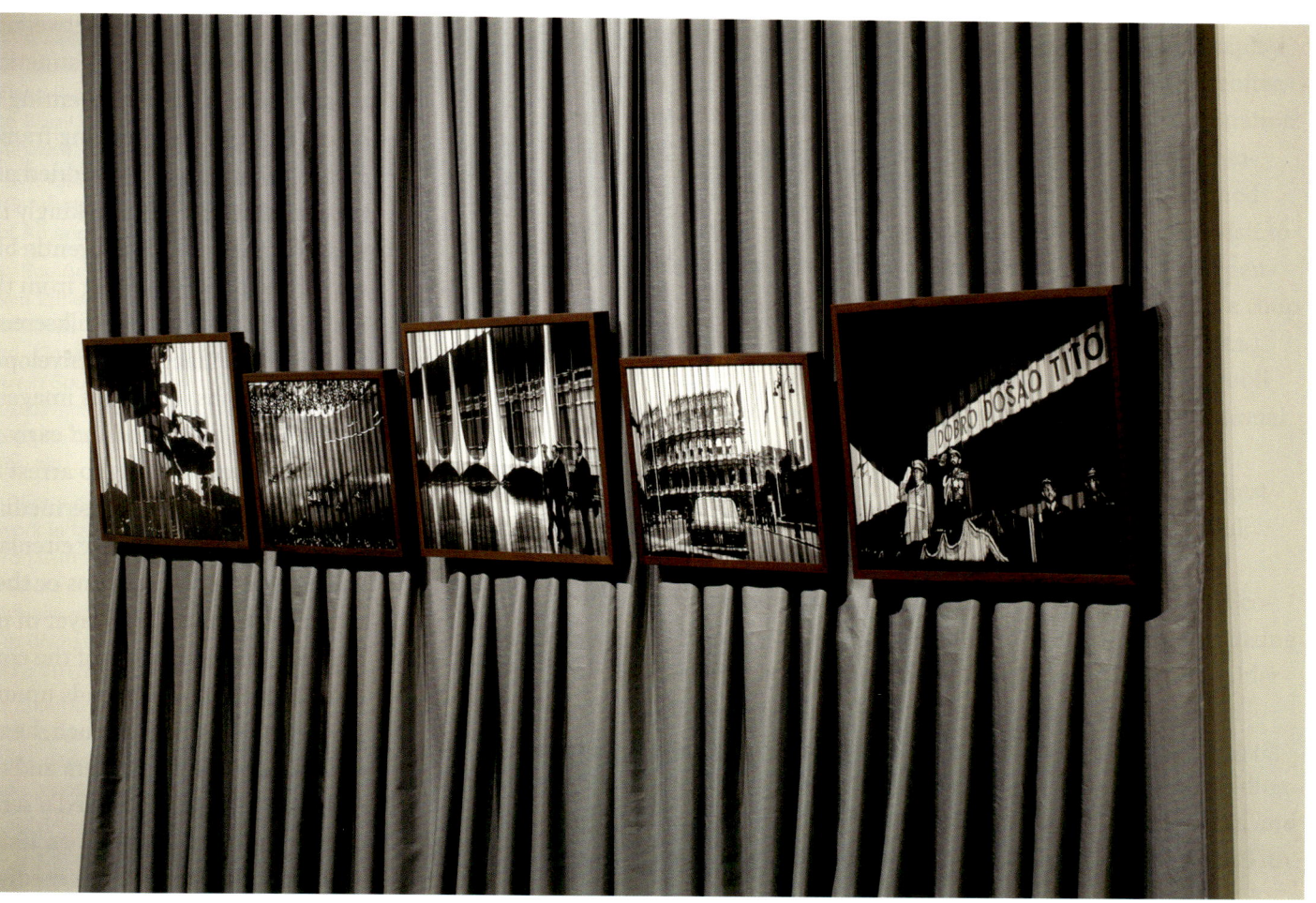

* Roland Barthes, "The Photographic Message" (1961), in *Image-Music-Text*, trans. Stephen Heath (New York: Hill and Wang, 1977), 15–31.

John J. Curley

the objective quality of the newspaper and the camera itself.* Put another way, the discursive uncanny is the primary engine of photography's political power, shaping and constructing ideology beneath the surface of what seems to be a non-partisan and indexical document. Pavlović lays bare his process.

In her series Fabrics of Socialism, Pavlović finds a formal strategy that allegorizes photography's multiple uncanny aspects: she projects photographic slides onto curtains. The pleated and rough fabric of a curtain blurs and scrambles the projected image, compelling viewers to pause, take a step closer, and decipher what exactly is on view. This visual confusion is evident in a 2015 installation photograph of this body of work: the vertical folds of the curtain, which would have also subtly moved and billowed in the ambient air of the gallery, both reinforce and work against the architectural elements of the modern building pictured in the installation's central image (Figure 13). Pavlović thus

* W. J. T. Mitchell, *The Reconfigured Eye: Visual Truth in the Post-Photographic Era* (Cambridge, MA: MIT Press, 1994), 35.

† For a useful discussion of this in terms of the work of Marcel Broodthaers, see Rosalind Krauss, *"A Voyage on the North Sea": Art in the Age of the Post-Medium Condition*

to the viewer: is this a picture of some kind of socialist alternative—a lost moment of unity and independence—that could be a model to fight the rampant capitalism and tribal nationalism of the present moment? Or, alternatively, does it represent some kind of rose-colored nostalgia for Yugoslavia's importance on the world stage, despite the repression associated with Tito as dictator? Or, does it leap backward over the horrors of the 1990s? Pavlović's works thus negotiate the complex terrain of the Cold War and the civil wars of the 1990s without didacticism or plodding ideology; rather she lets her photographs of spaces and concrete archival materials—ghosts from the past—speak in the present tense.

But what of those who approach Pavlović's work with no knowledge of Yugoslavia and its Cold War and 1990s histories? How do her projections and photos function outside of this particular context? They certainly transport viewers to a different moment. For young viewers, it might be their first encounter with a slide projector, for instance. Furthermore, just the experience of looking at unfamiliar images through an unfamiliar technology opens viewers up to something we might identify as the analog uncanny. Slide projections (and photographs of these projections) might resemble images found on screens, but they are ontologically different. W. J. T. Mitchell has argued that the rise of digital photography will be viewed as culturally and politically momentous as the introduction of photography itself in 1839.* The digital image represents a break with the analog past, not a continuation. Not only do Pavlović's works have a material presence, but they also do not appear on hand-held devices and are not networked. Viewers cannot double-click to reveal a caption or merely slide her images aside. If images on iPhones are alive and responsive, Pavlović, to return to Levine, produces ghosts of online images: plodding, mysterious, and unruly.

Walter Benjamin has discussed the ways that outmoded technologies possess a revolutionary potential—once liberated from usefulness, they can force viewers to reconceptualize historical change.† What might have happened differently at that interstitial moment just before obsolescence? As such, it is somehow fitting that in 1992 both Yugoslavia disappeared as a nation and *Photoshop* was first used as a verb. To think about the rise of the digital through the analog—as Pavlović compels her viewers to do—provides an urgent mode of counterfactual thinking: imaging a different past as a means to realize a better future. Utopia is in the archive, but no one knows where.

Barthes, Roland. "The Photographic Message." In *Image-Music-Text*. Translated by Stephen Heath. New York: Hill and Wang, 1977.

Bryson, Norman. "The Gaze in the Expanded Field." In *Vision and Visuality*. Discussions in Contemporary Culture, no. 2. Seattle: Dia Art Foundation and Bay Press, 1988.

Curley, John. *A Conspiracy of Images: Andy Warhol, Gerhard Richter, and the Cold War*. New Haven: Yale University Press, 2013.

Curley, John. "Controlling Doubt: Abstract Painting and Photography." In *Photography and Doubt*. Edited by Sabine T. Kriebel and Andrés Mario Zervigón. London: Routledge, 2017.

Curley, John. "Curtain Call: History Takes a Bow." In *Vesna Pavlović's Lost Art*. Edited by Morna O'Neill. Winston-Salem: Hanes Art Gallery, 2017.

Curley, John. *Global Art and the Cold War*. London: Laurence King, 2018.

Freud, Sigmund. *The Uncanny*. Translated by David McLintock. New York: Penguin Classics, 2003.

Joselit, David. *American Art since 1945*. New York: Thames and Hudson, 2003.

Kostenbaum, Wayne. *Hotel Theory*. New York: Soft Skull Press, 2007.

Krauss, Rosalind. "Photography's Discursive Spaces." In *The Originality of the Avant-Garde and Other Modernist Myths*, Cambridge, MA: MIT Press, 1985.

Krauss, Rosalind. *"A Voyage on the North Sea": Art in the Age of the Post-Medium Condition*. New York: Thames and Hudson, 1999.

Lester, Robert E, ed. *National Security Files, 1961–1963*. Bethesda: University Publications of America, 1987.

Mitchell, W. J. T. *The Reconfigured Eye: Visual Truth in the PostPhotographic Era*. Cambridge, MA: MIT Press, 1994.

Nelson, Adele. "Monumental and Ephemeral: The Early Sao Paulo Biennial." In *Constructive Spirit: Abstract Art in South and North America, 1920s–50s*. Edited by Mary Kate O'Hare. Petaluma, CA: Pomegranate Communications, 2010.

Stierli, Martino, and Kulić, Vladimir. "Introduction." In *Toward a Concrete Utopia: Architecture in Yugoslavia, 1948–1980*. Edited by Stephanie Emerson. New York: Museum of Modern Art, 2018.

Šuvaković, Miško. "Impossible Histories." In *Impossible Histories: Historical Avant-Gardes, Neo-Avant-Gardes, and Post-Avant-Gardes, 1918–1991*. Edited by Dubravka Đurić and Miško Šuvaković, Cambridge, MA: MIT Press, 2003.

Szarkowski, John, ed. *From the Picture Press*. New York: Museum of Modern Art, 1973.

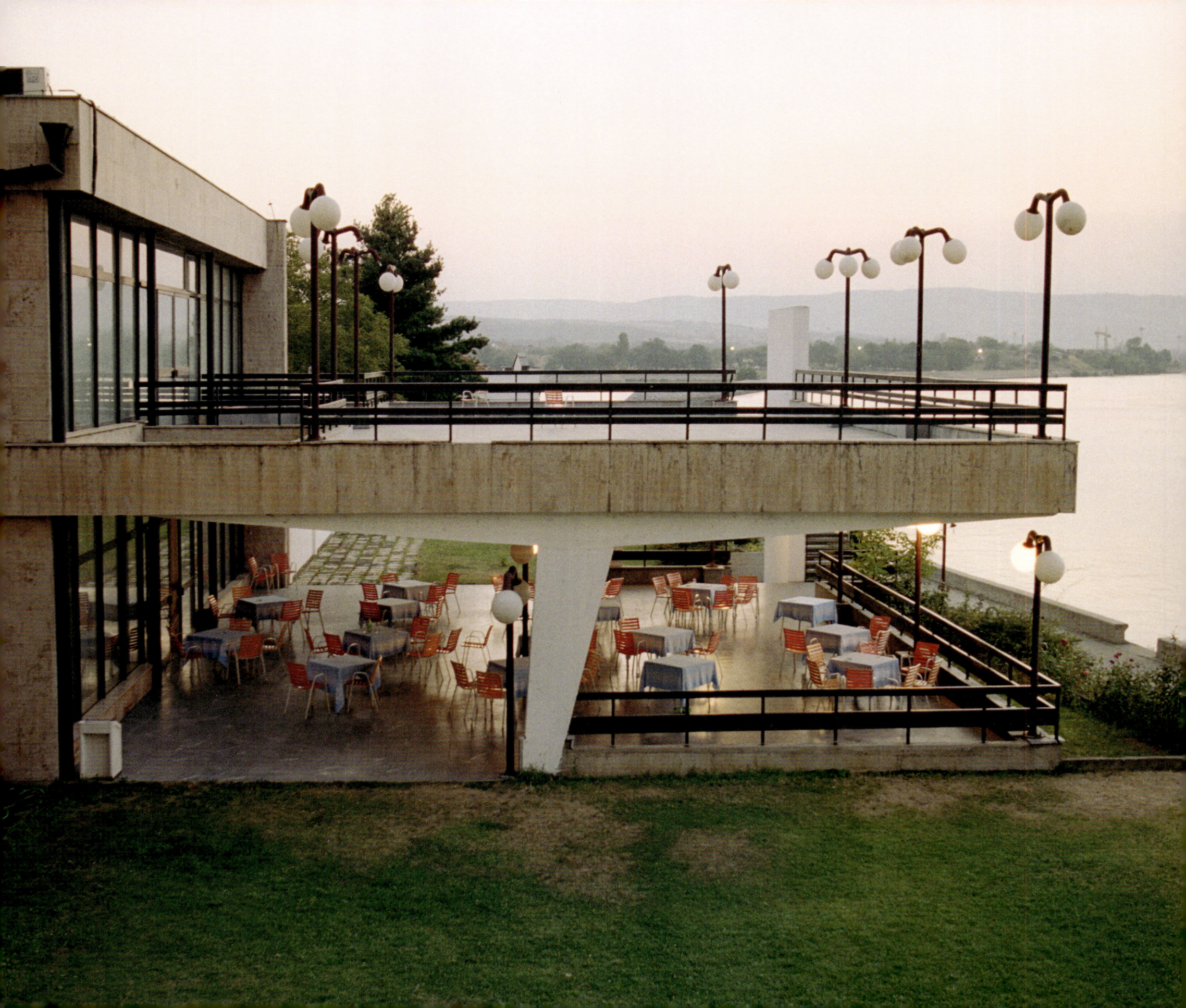

IMAGES

Herzlich willkommen im Hotel Hyatt Belgrad, April 1999. I, 1999

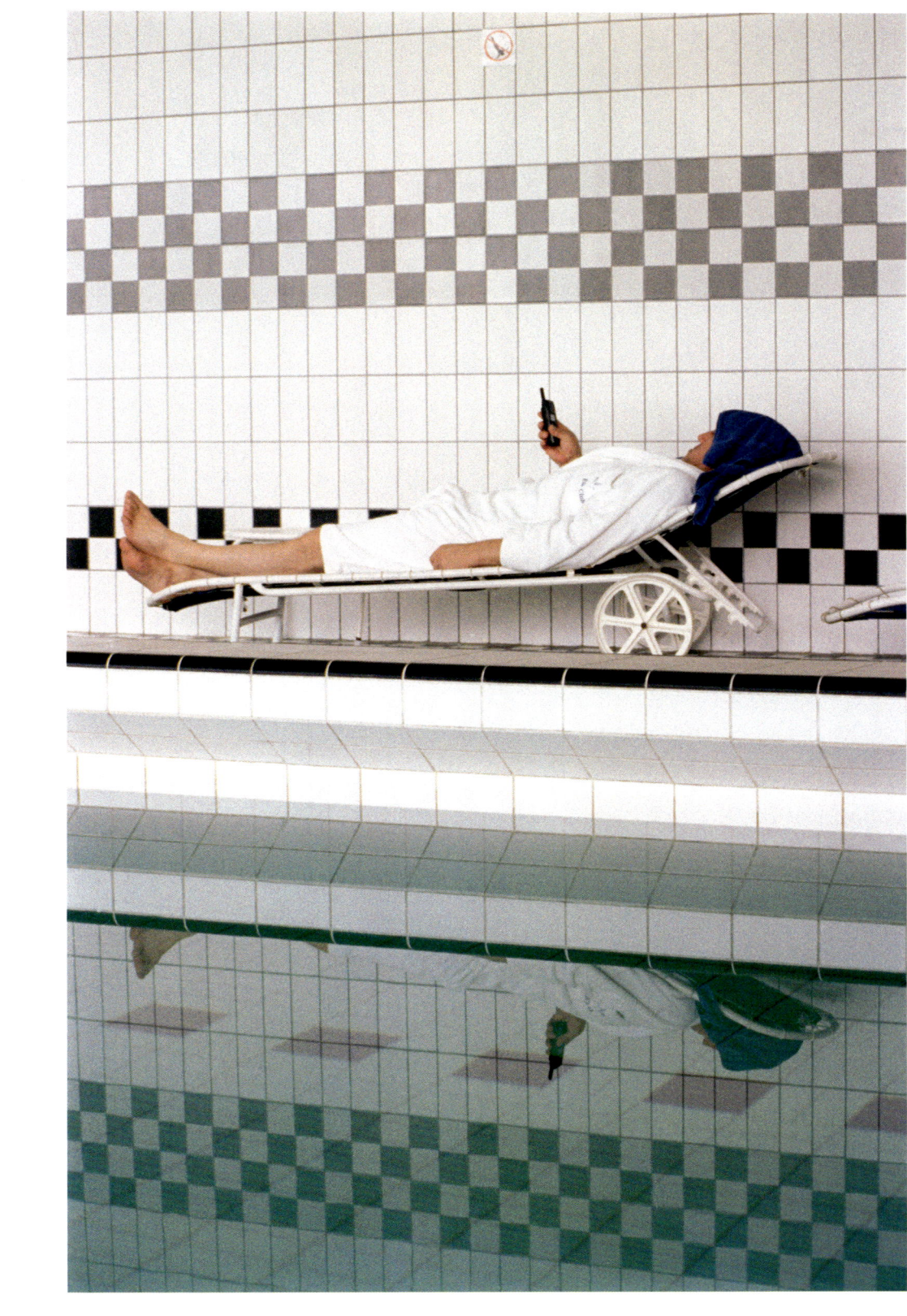

Herzlich willkommen im Hotel Hyatt Belgrad, April 1999. III, 1999

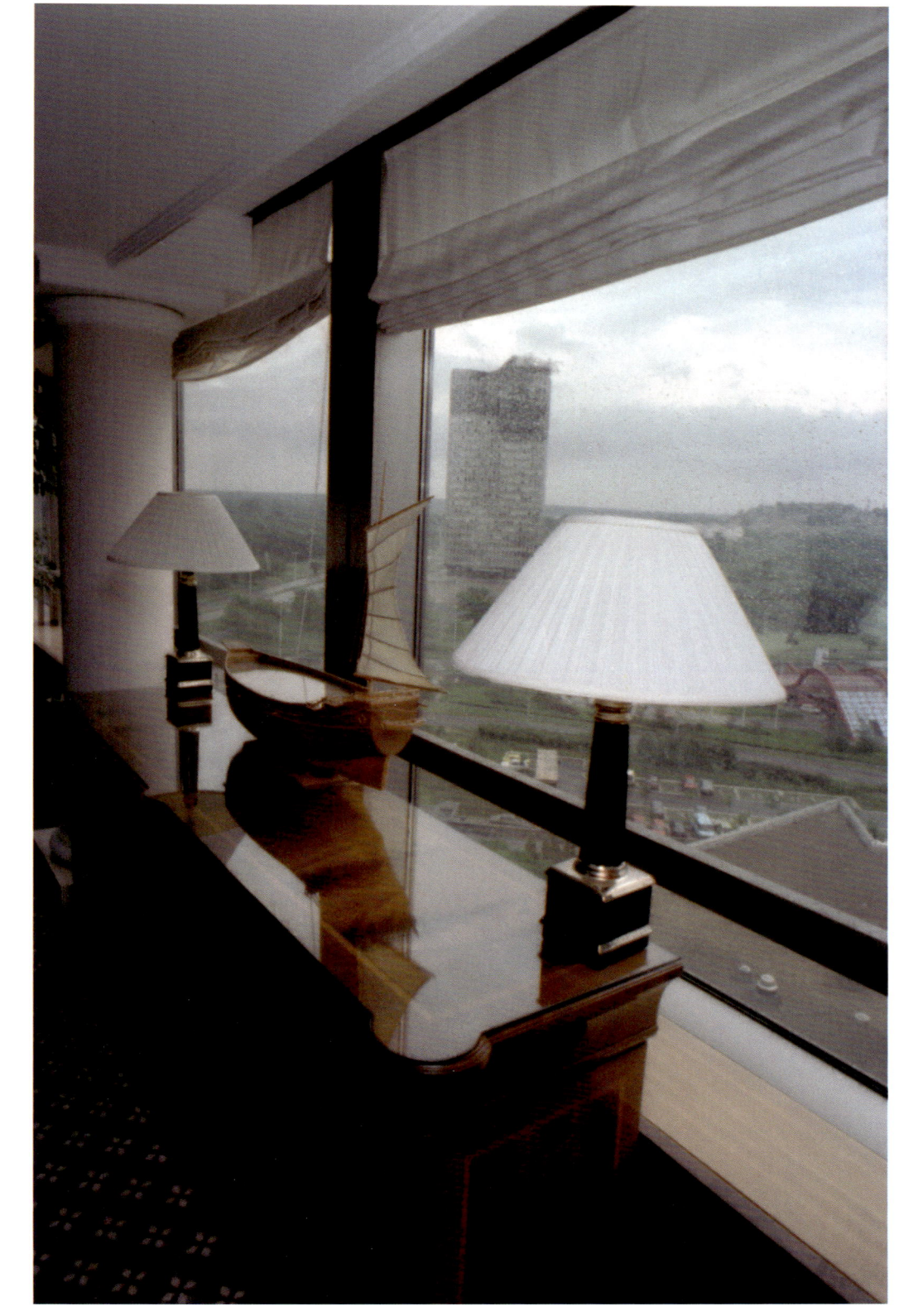

Herzlich willkommen im Hotel Hyatt Belgrad, April 1999. II, 1999

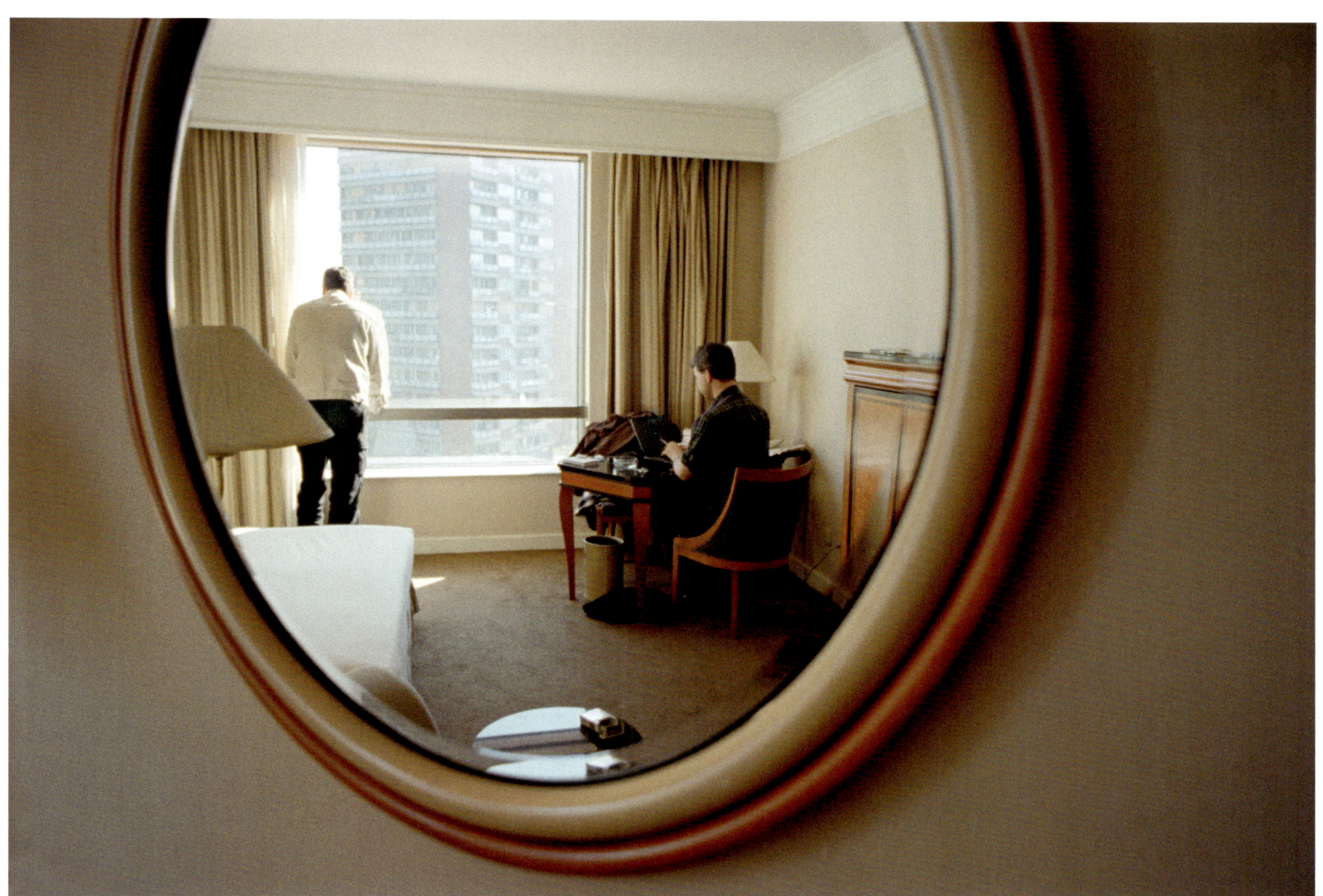

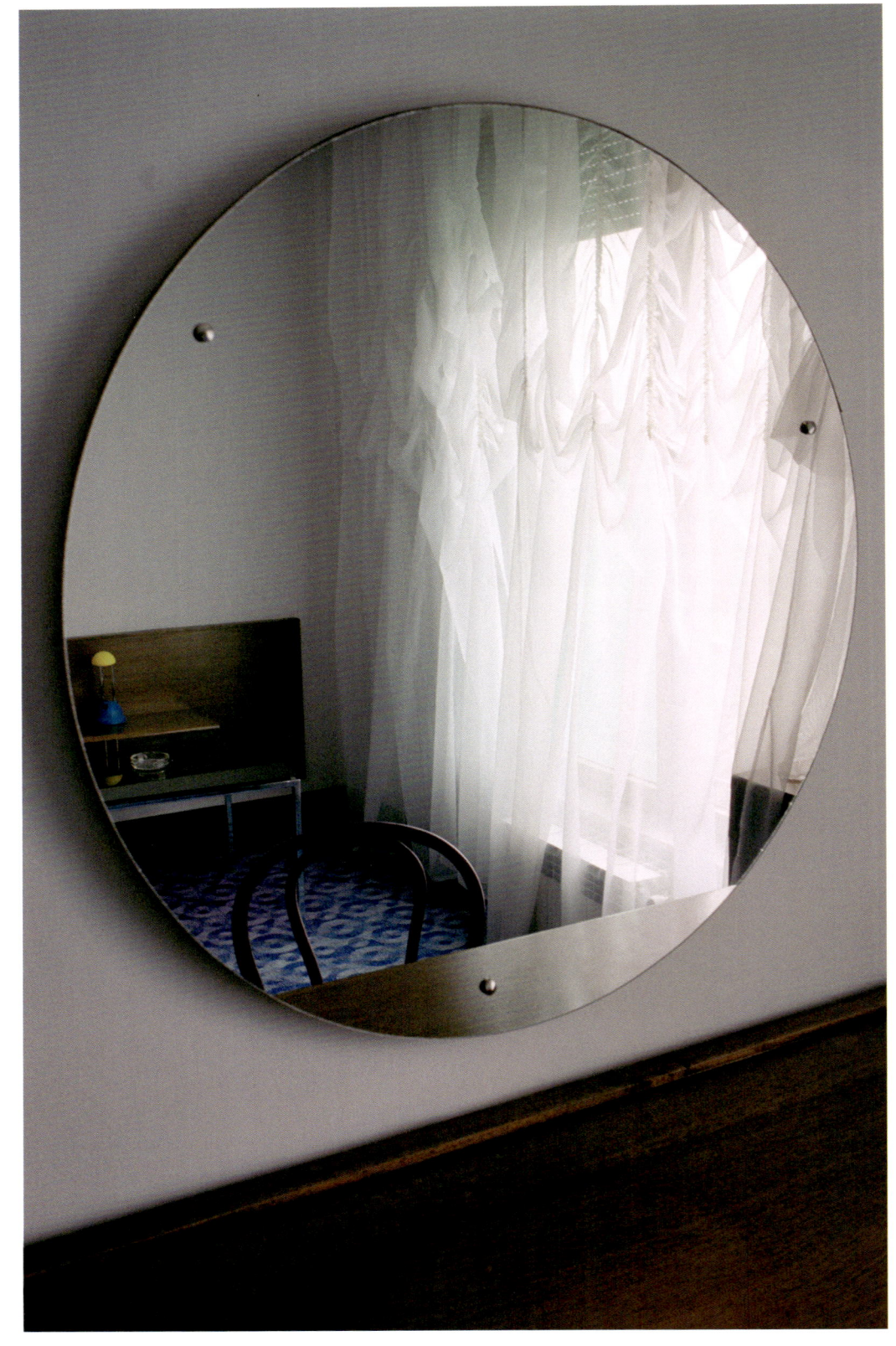

Narvik Hotel, Kikinda III, 2002

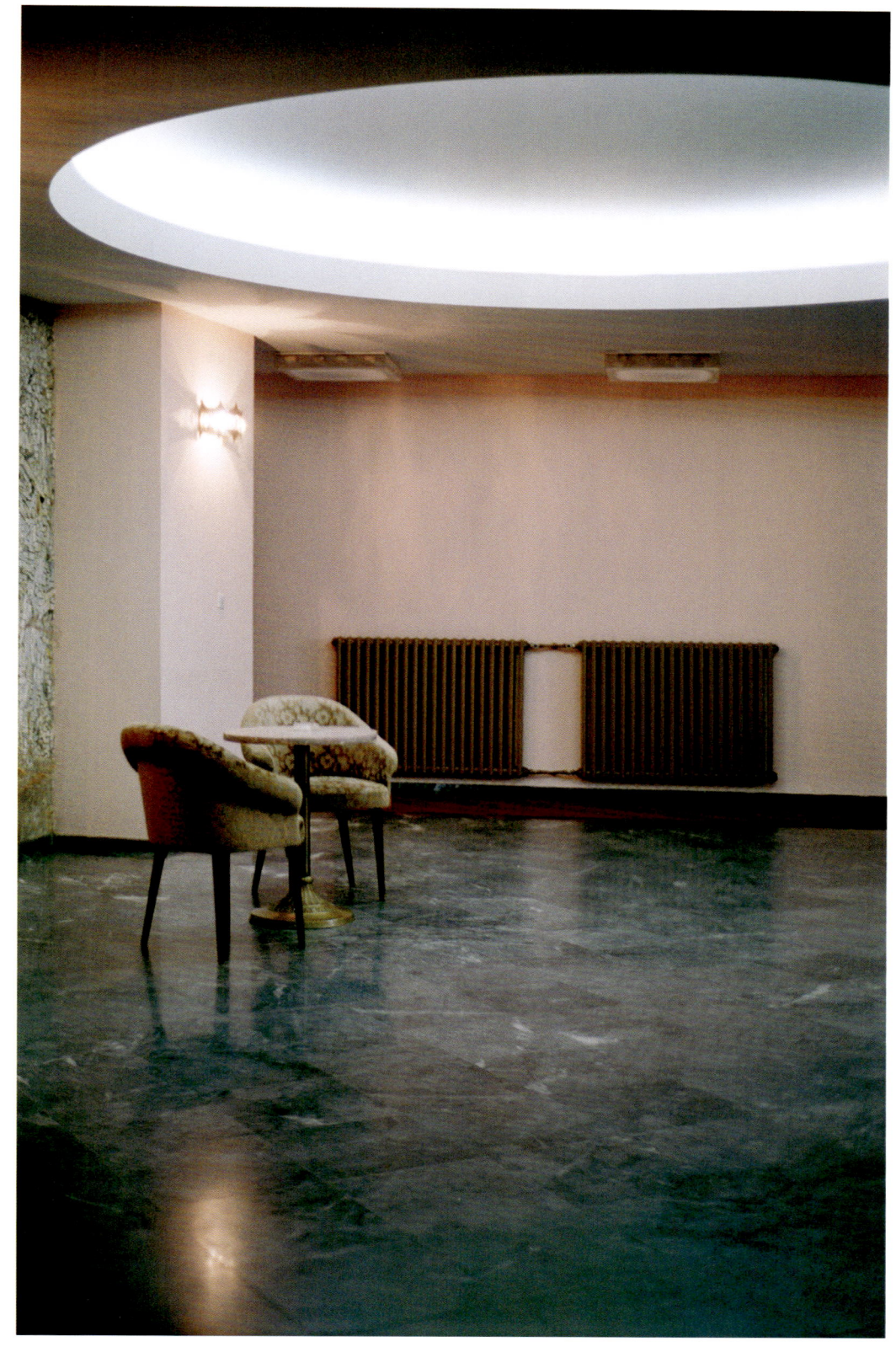

Moskva Hotel, Beograd IV, 2001

Small Stage, Radio Belgrade, 2019

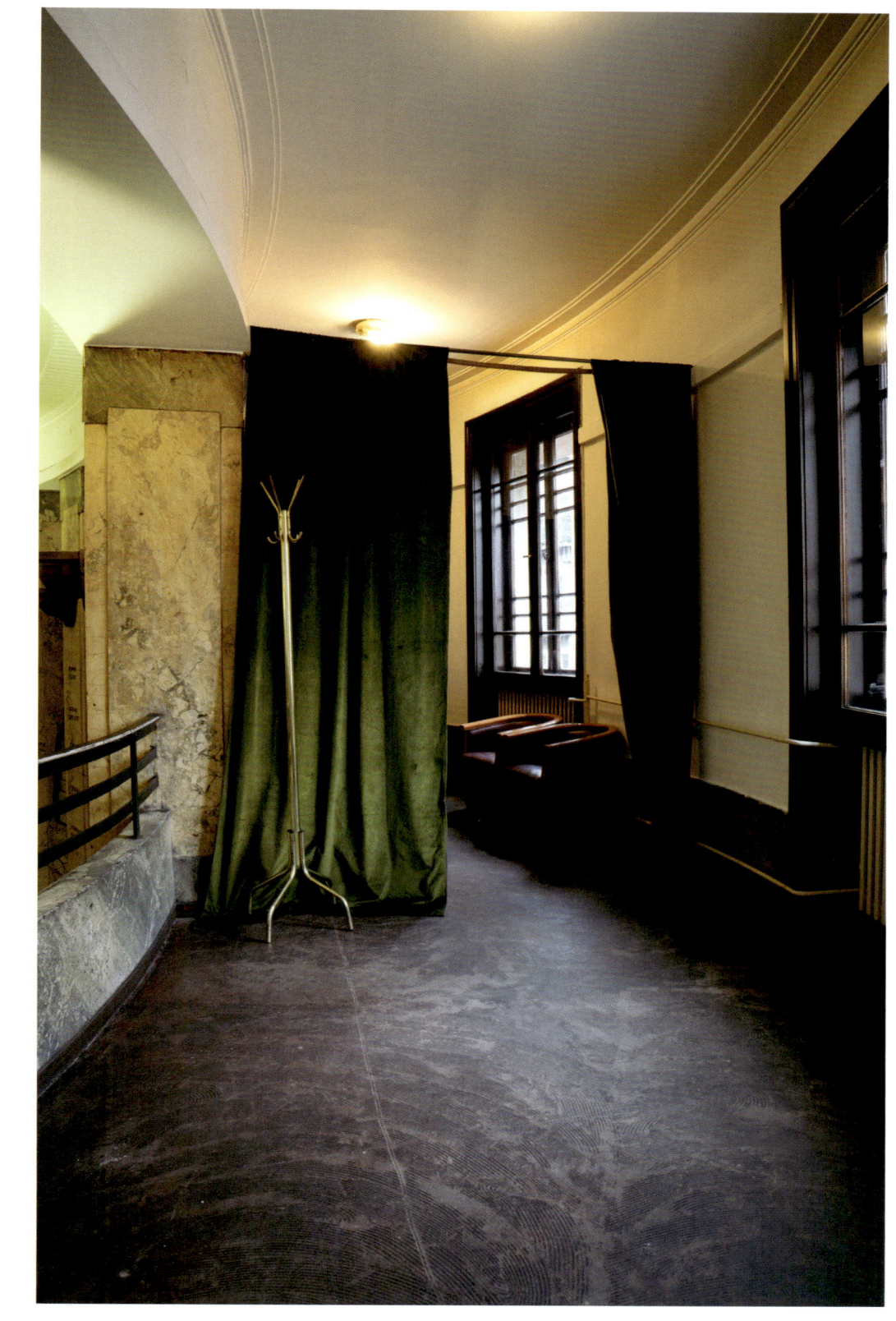

Đerdap Hotel, Kladovo II, 2001

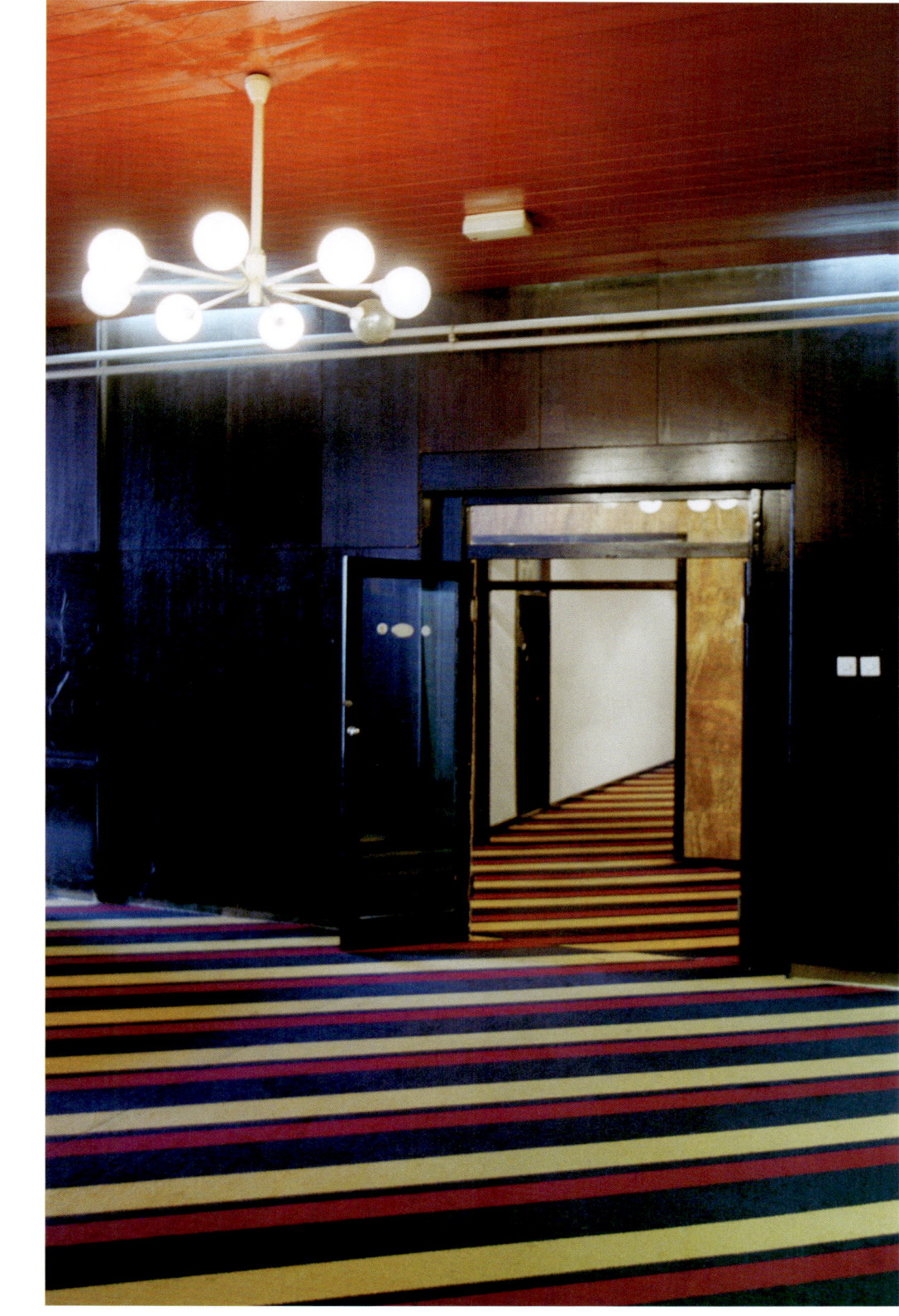

Jagodina Hotel, Jagodina III, 2002

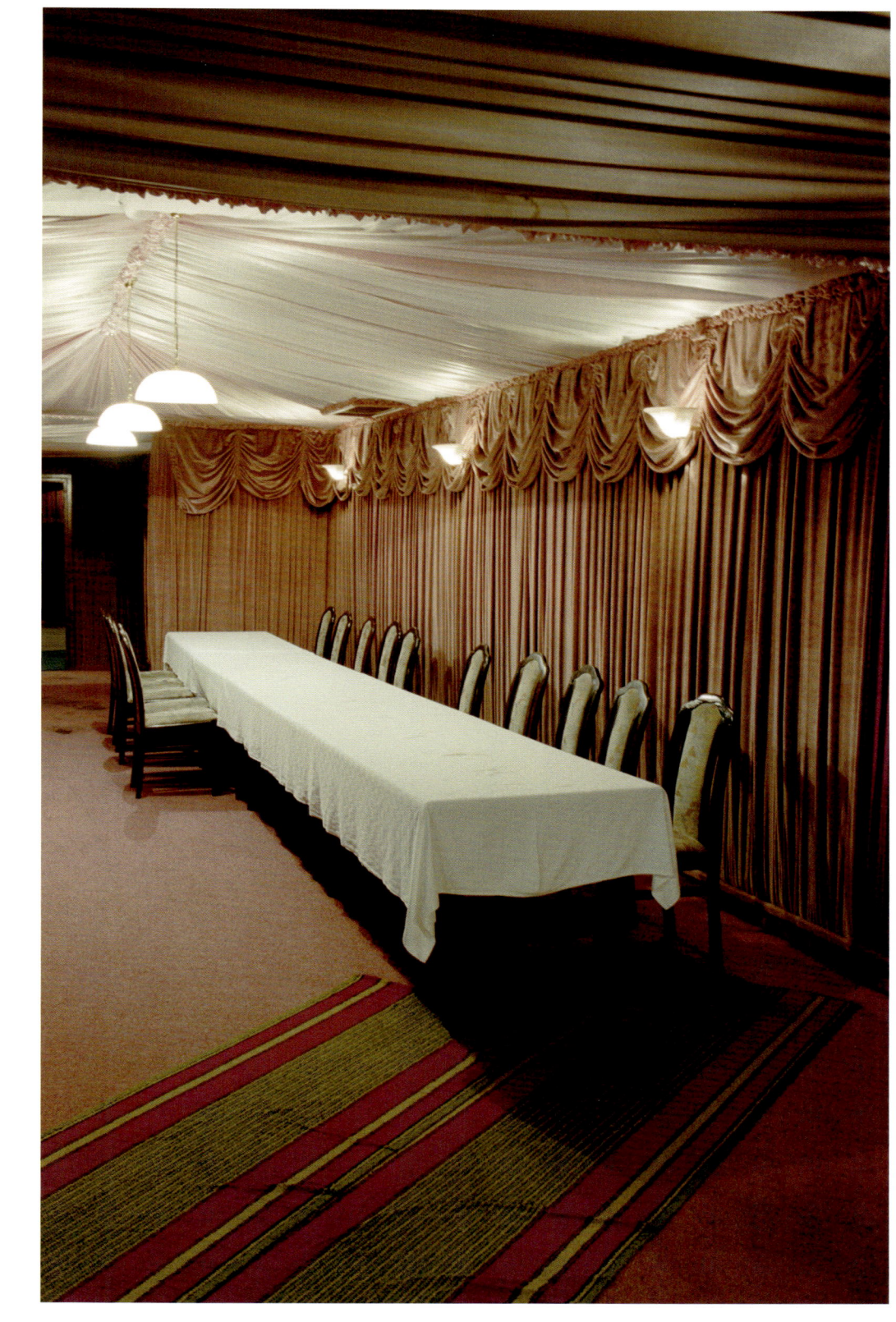

Jagodina Hotel, Jagodina I, 2002

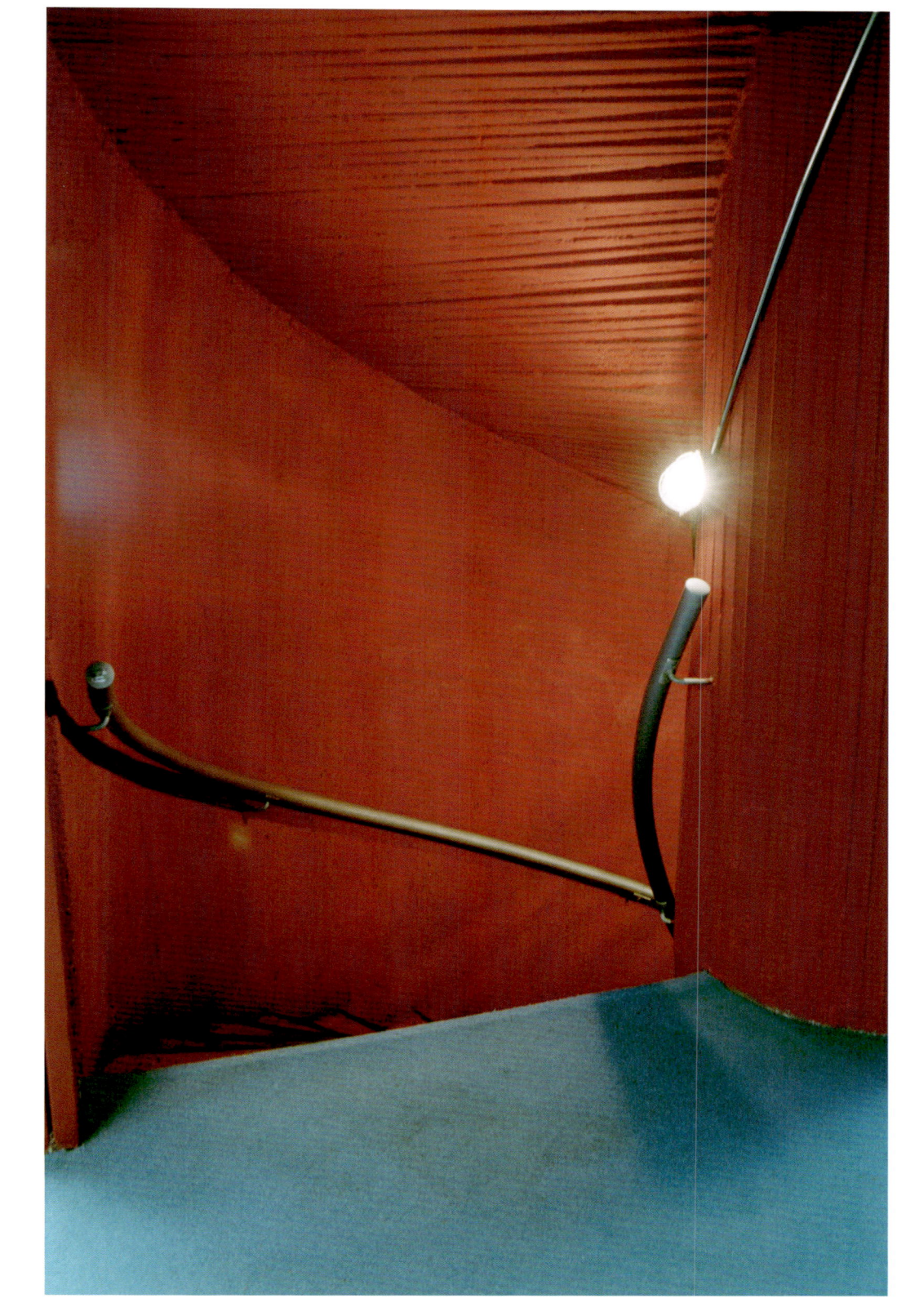

Kasina Hotel, Majdanpek, 2001

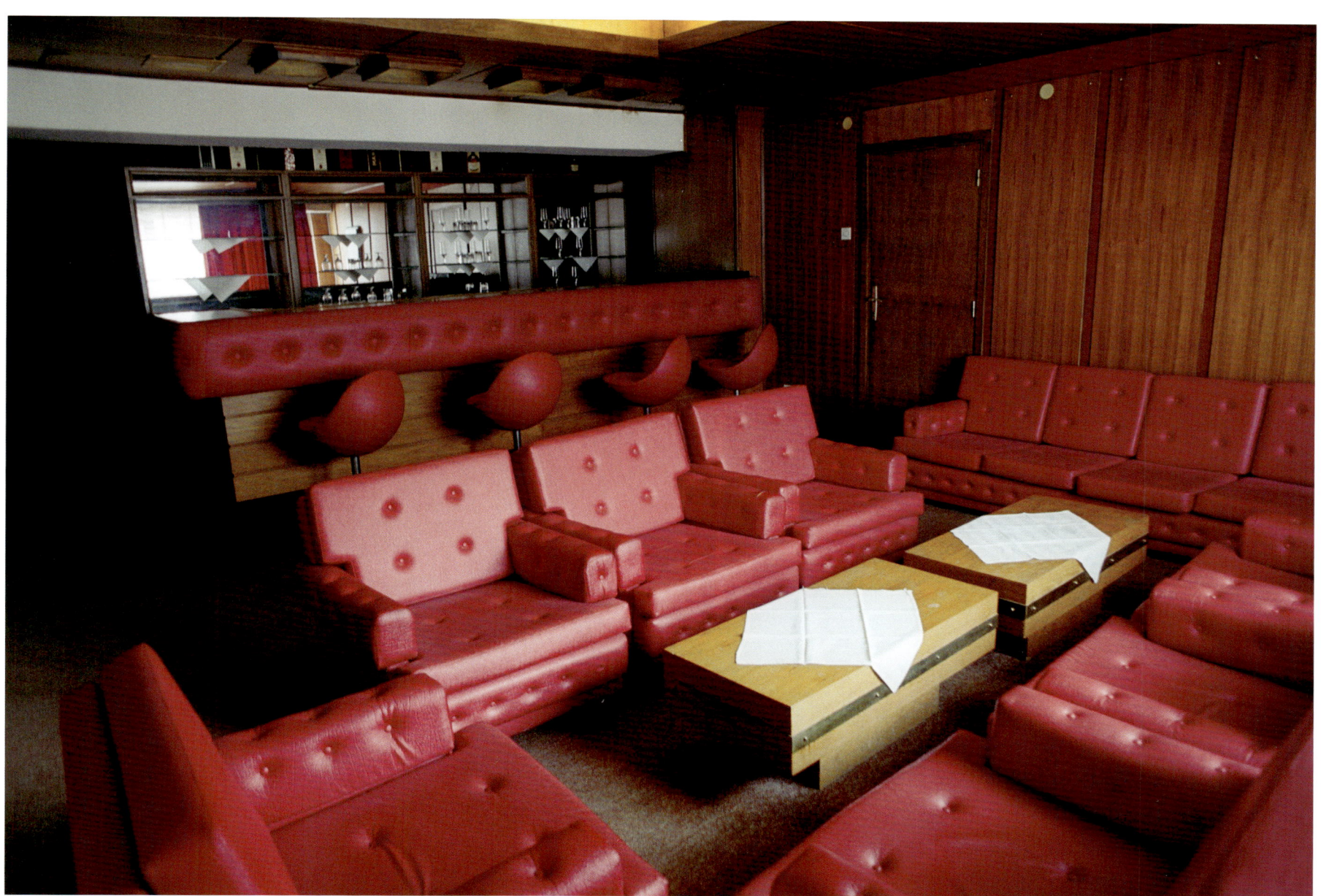

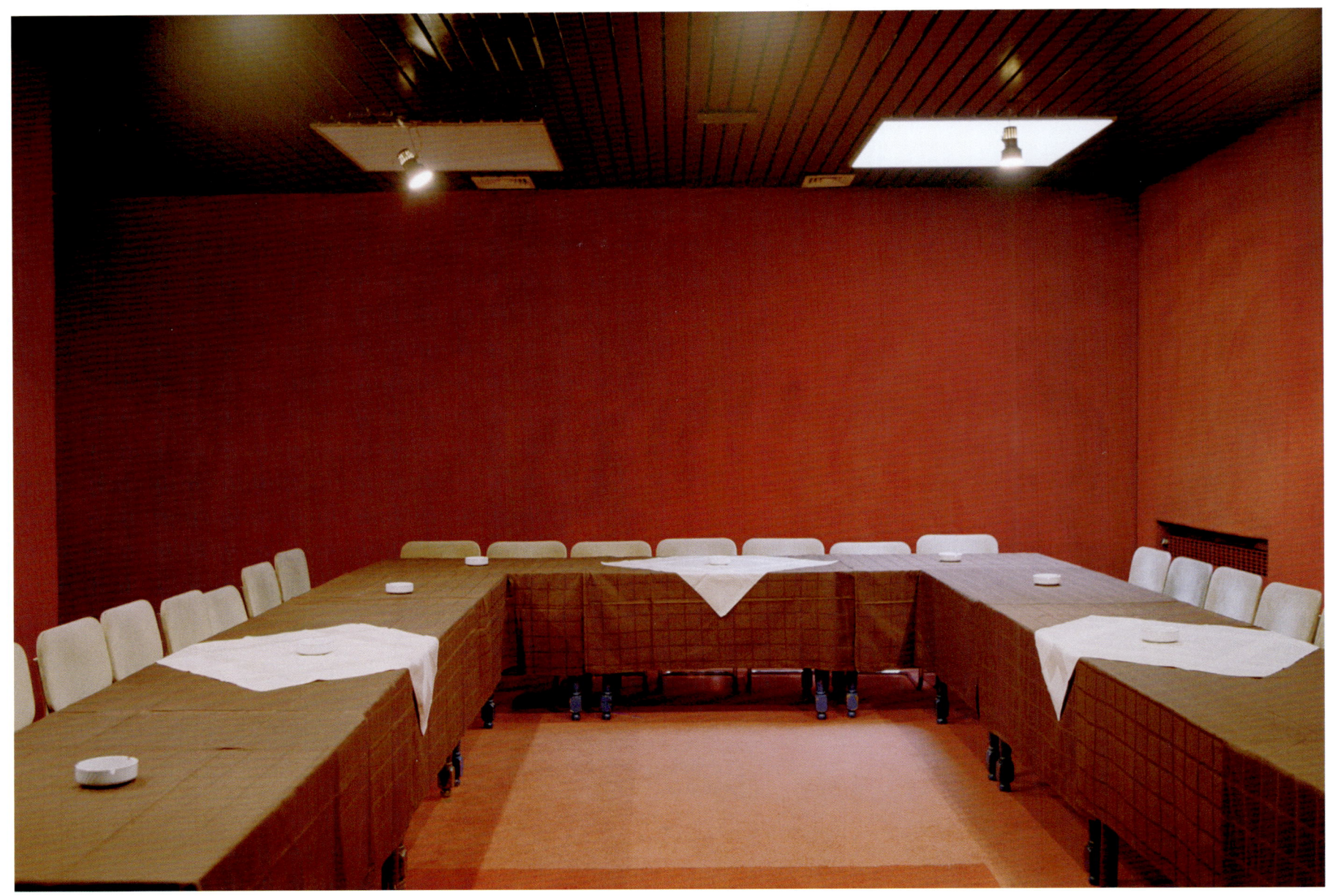

Jagodina Hotel, Jagodina II, 2002

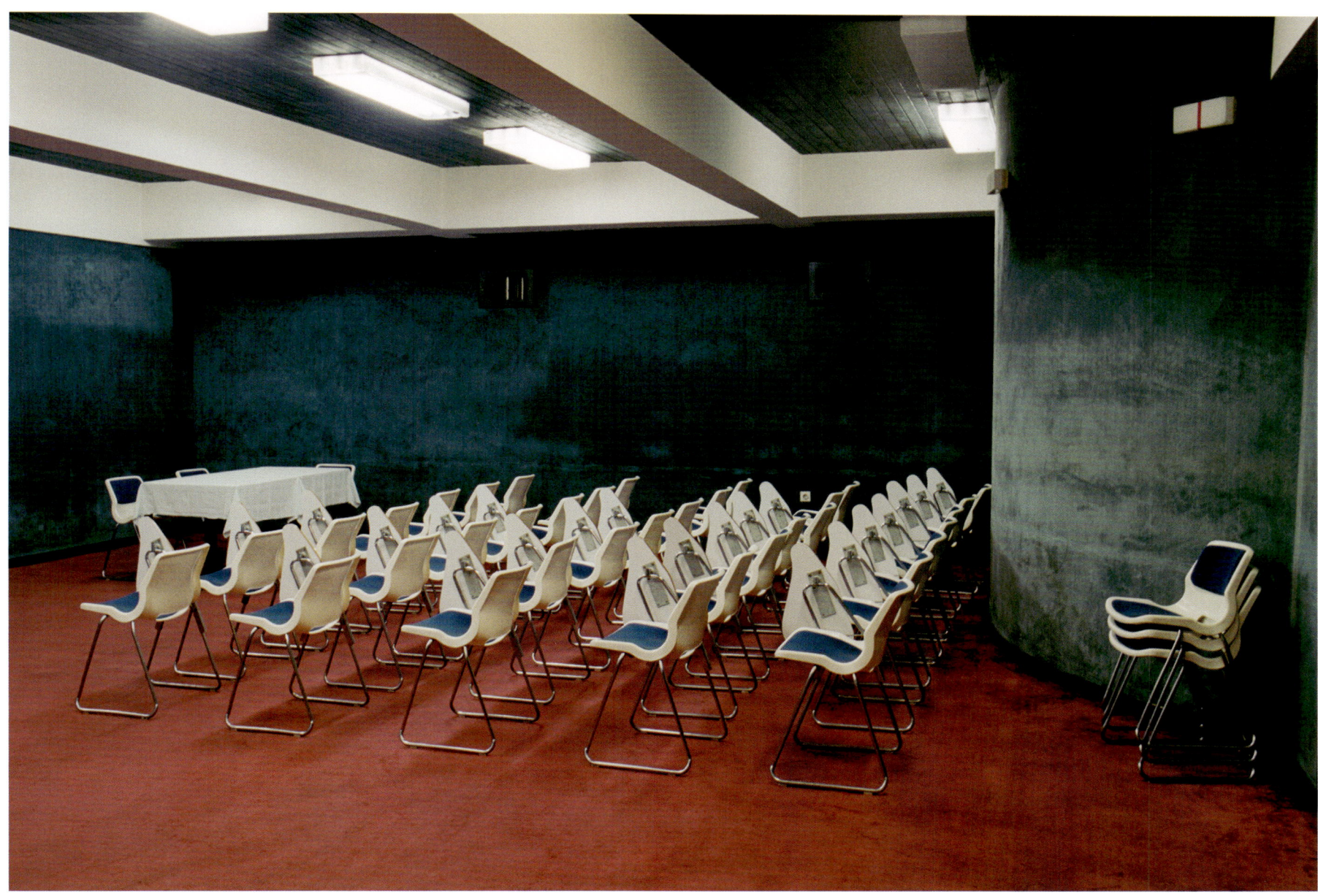

Podrinje Hotel, Banja Koviljača, 2002

Drina Hotel, Bajina Bašta, 2002

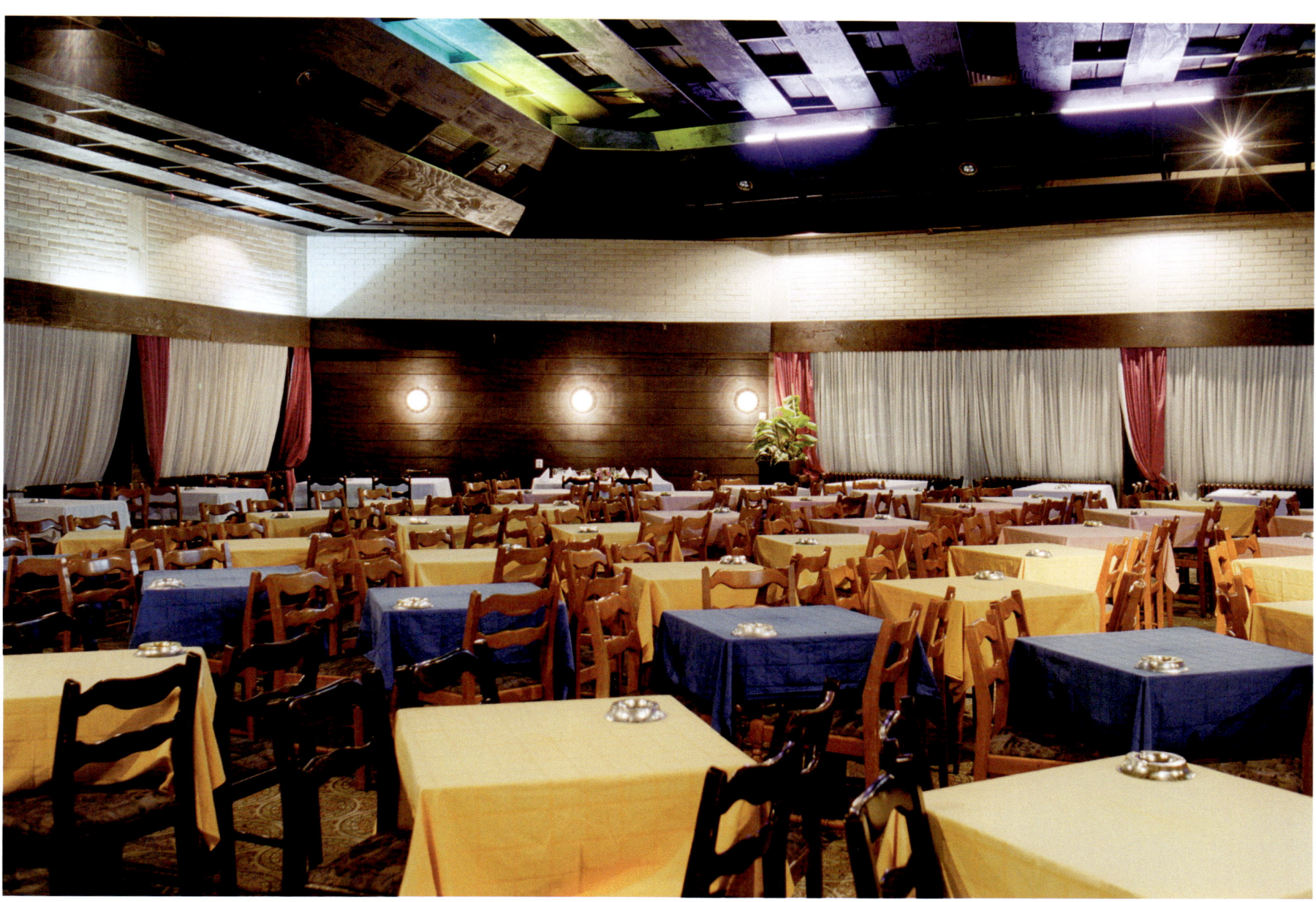

Vrbak Hotel, Novi Pazar I, 2002

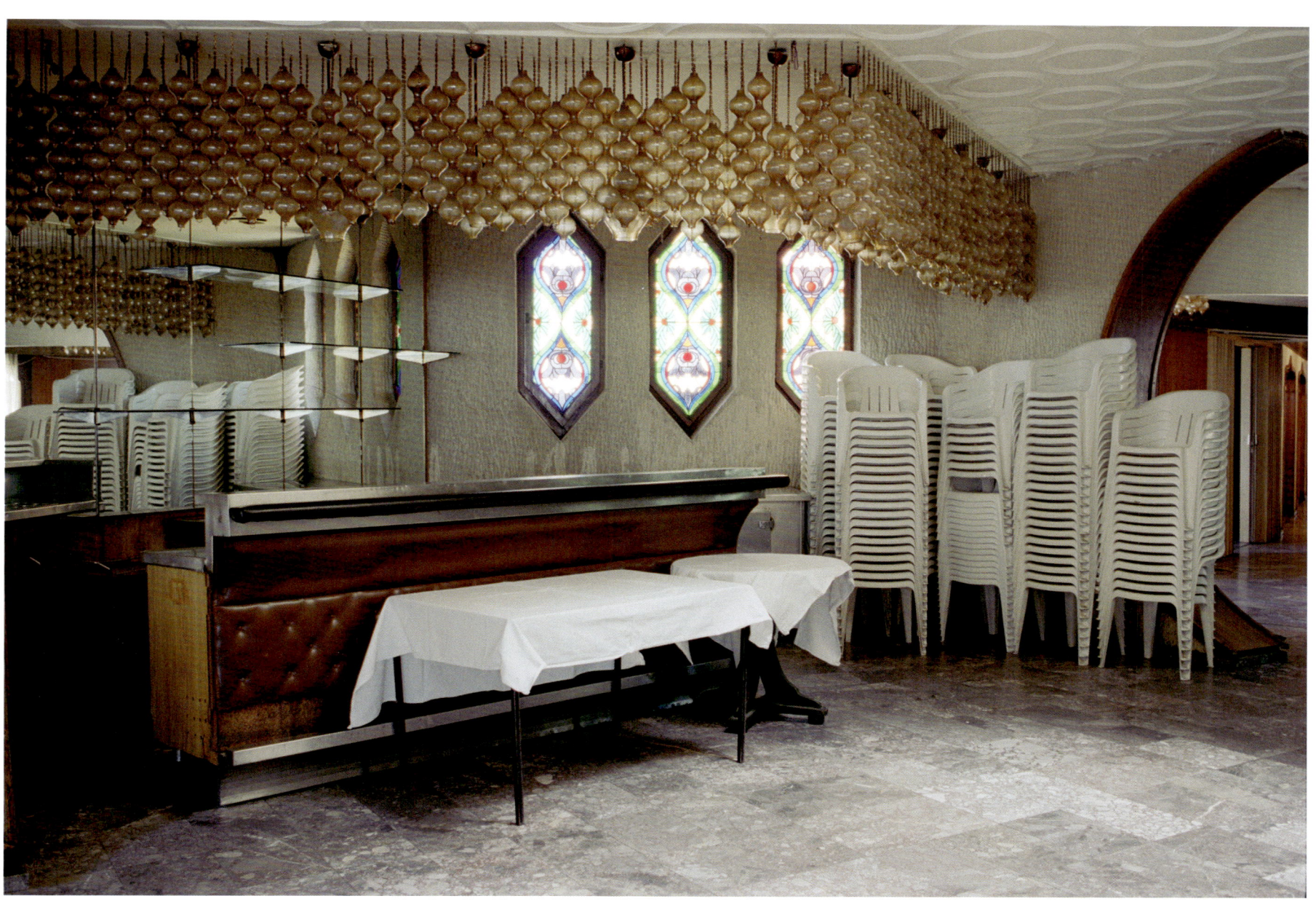

Srbija Hotel, Zaječar III, 2001

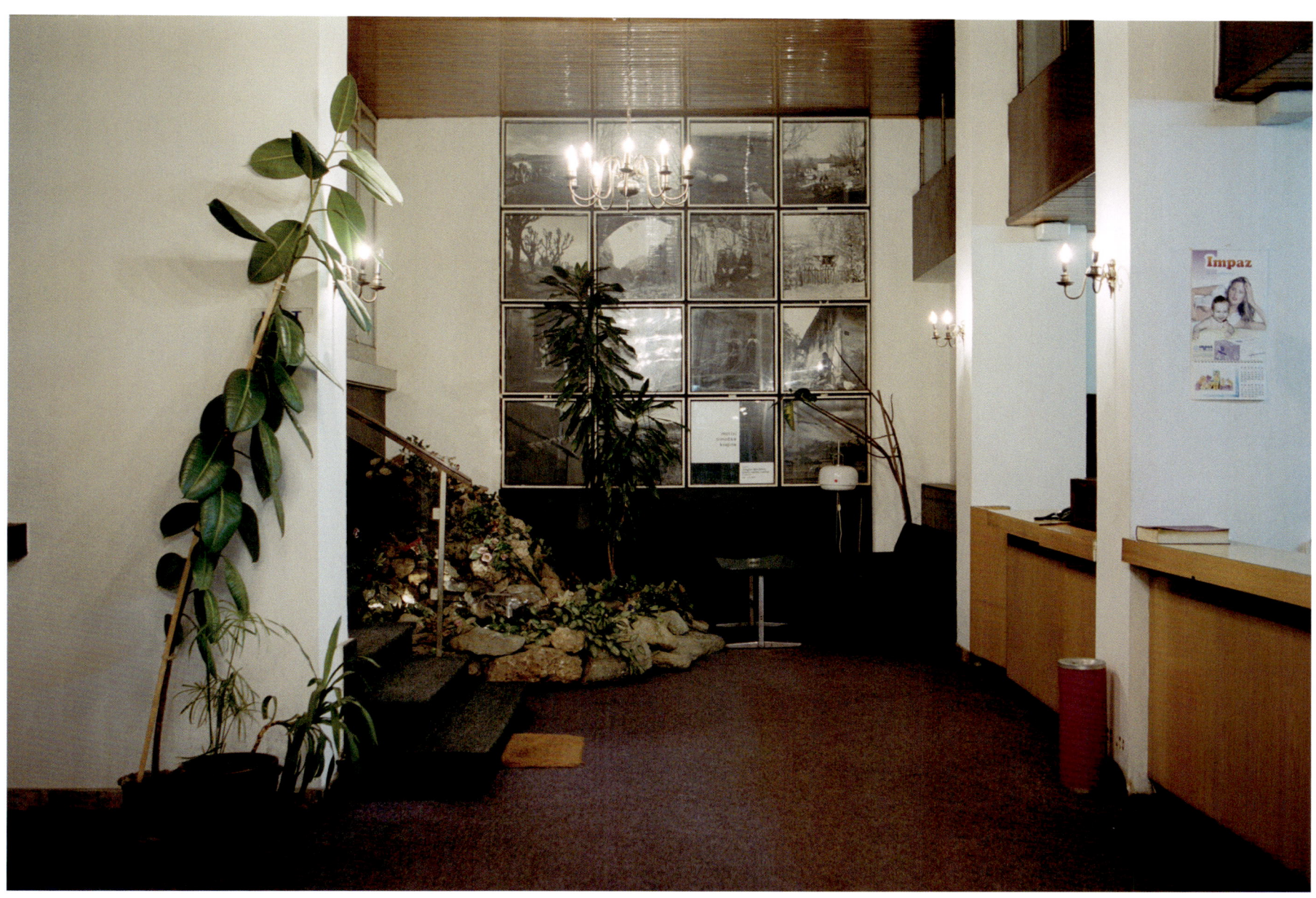

Narvik Hotel, Kikinda II, 2002

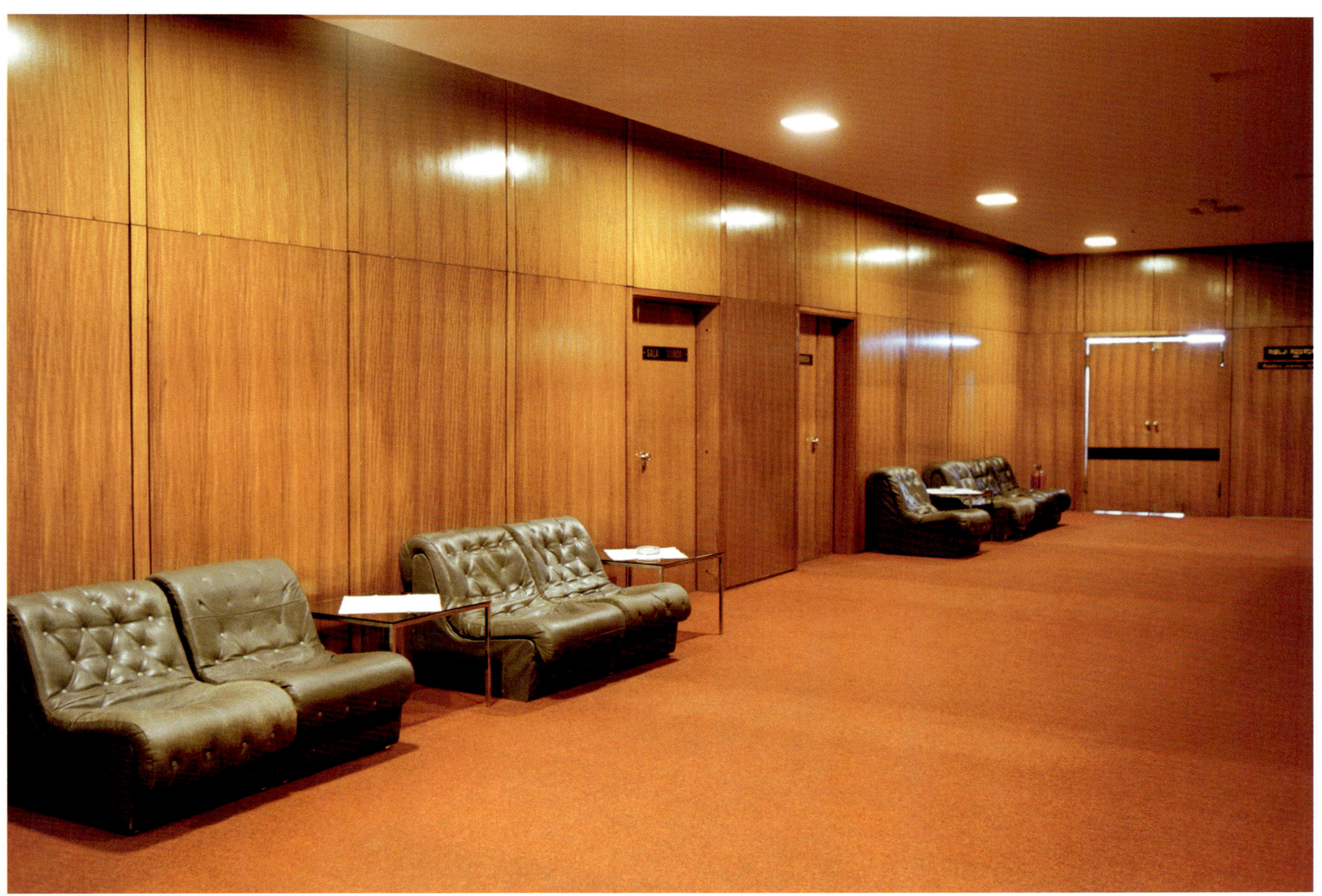

Srbija Hotel, Zaječar I, 2001

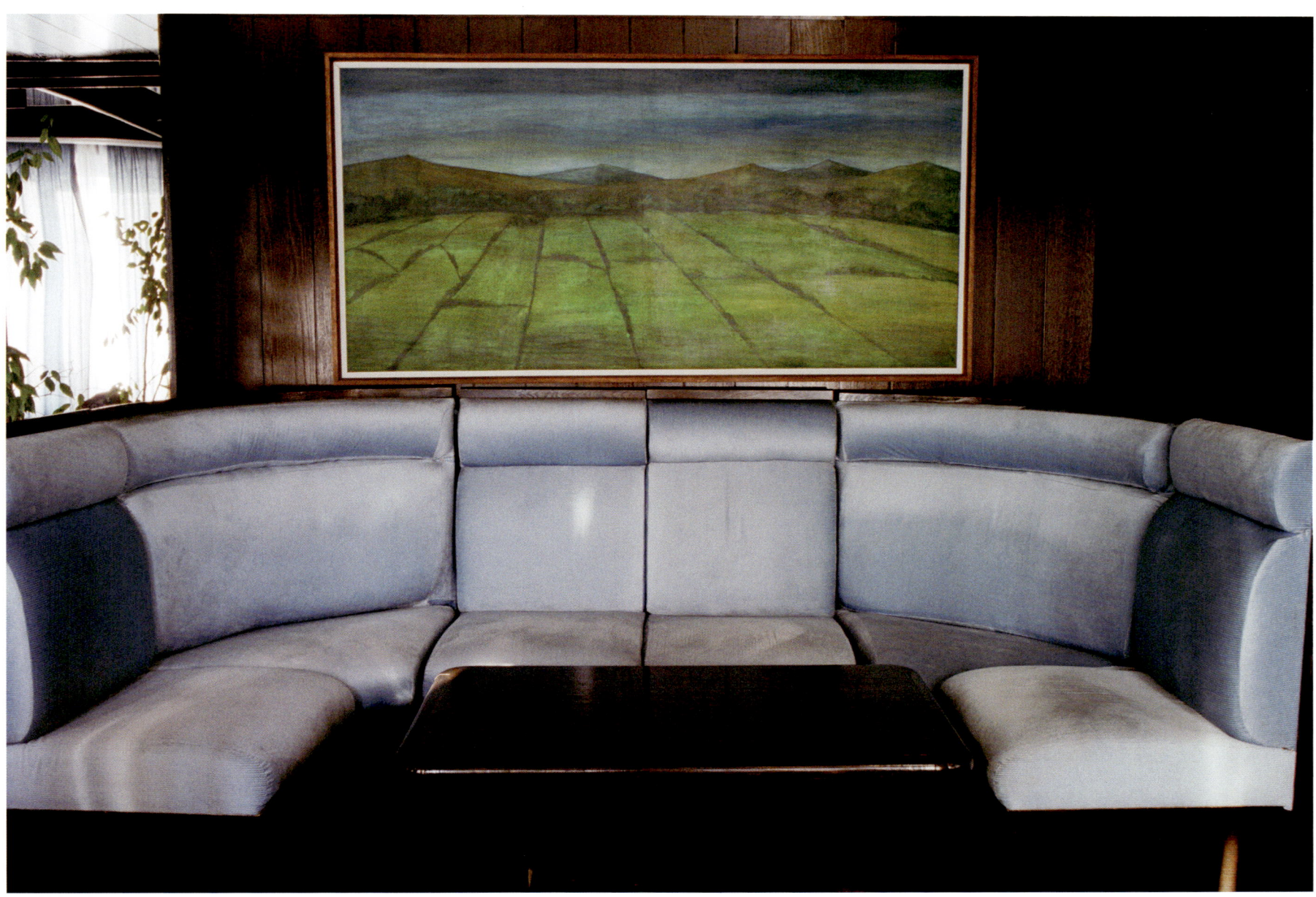

Institute for Testing of Materials Belgrade IMS, 2019

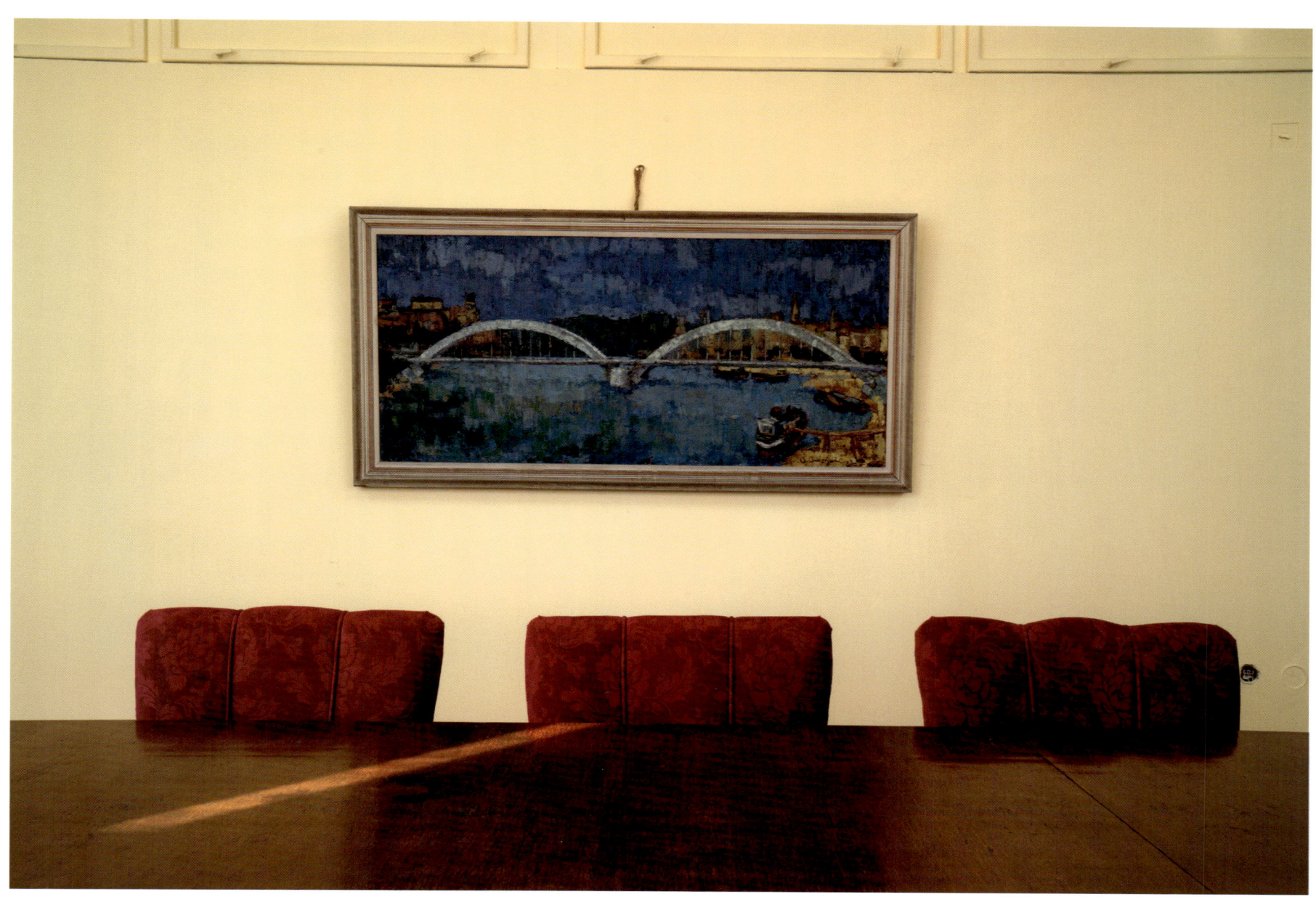

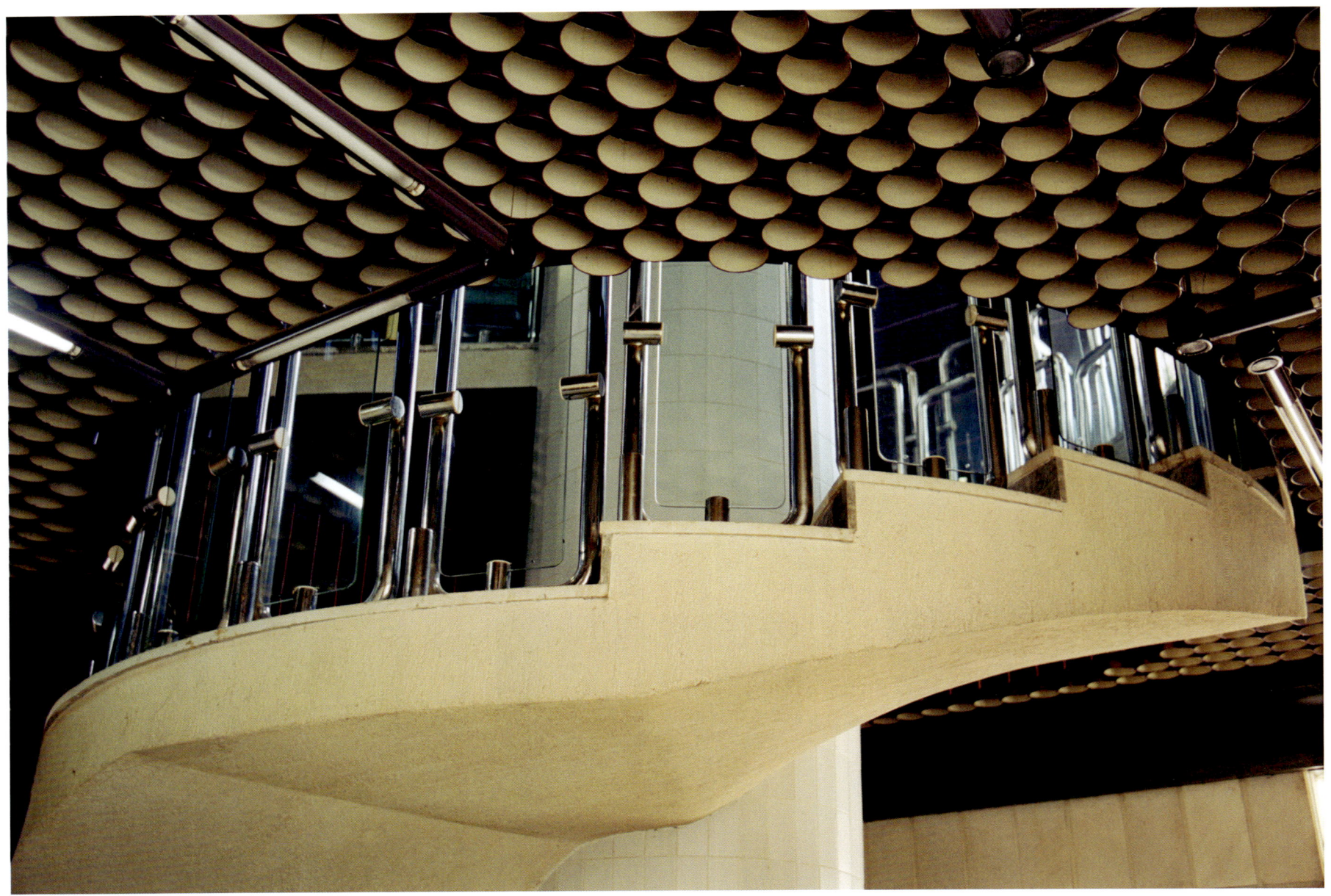

Lim Hotel, Priboj, 2002

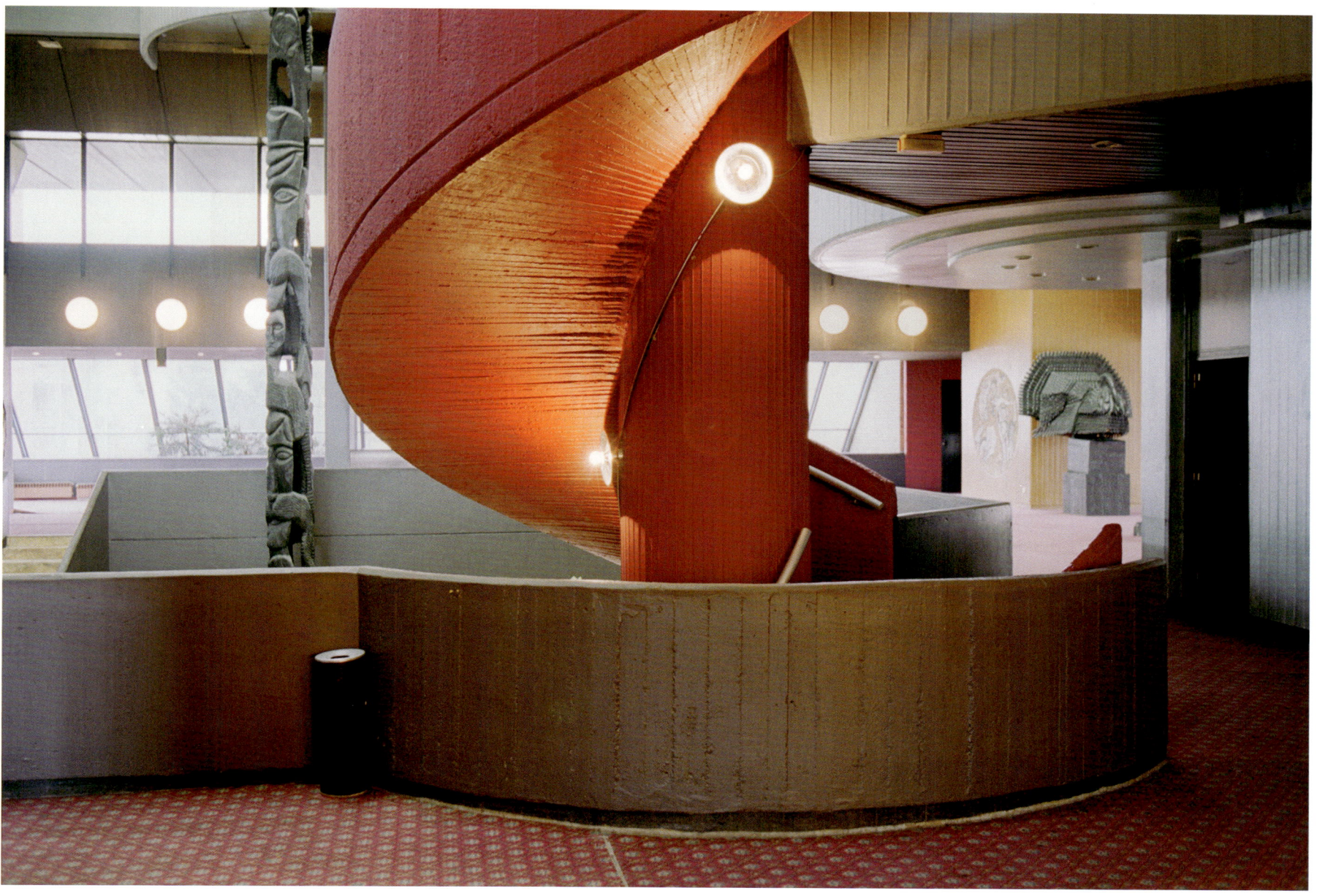

Jagodina Hotel, Jagodina V, 2002

Slavija Hotel, Vrnjačka Banja, 2001

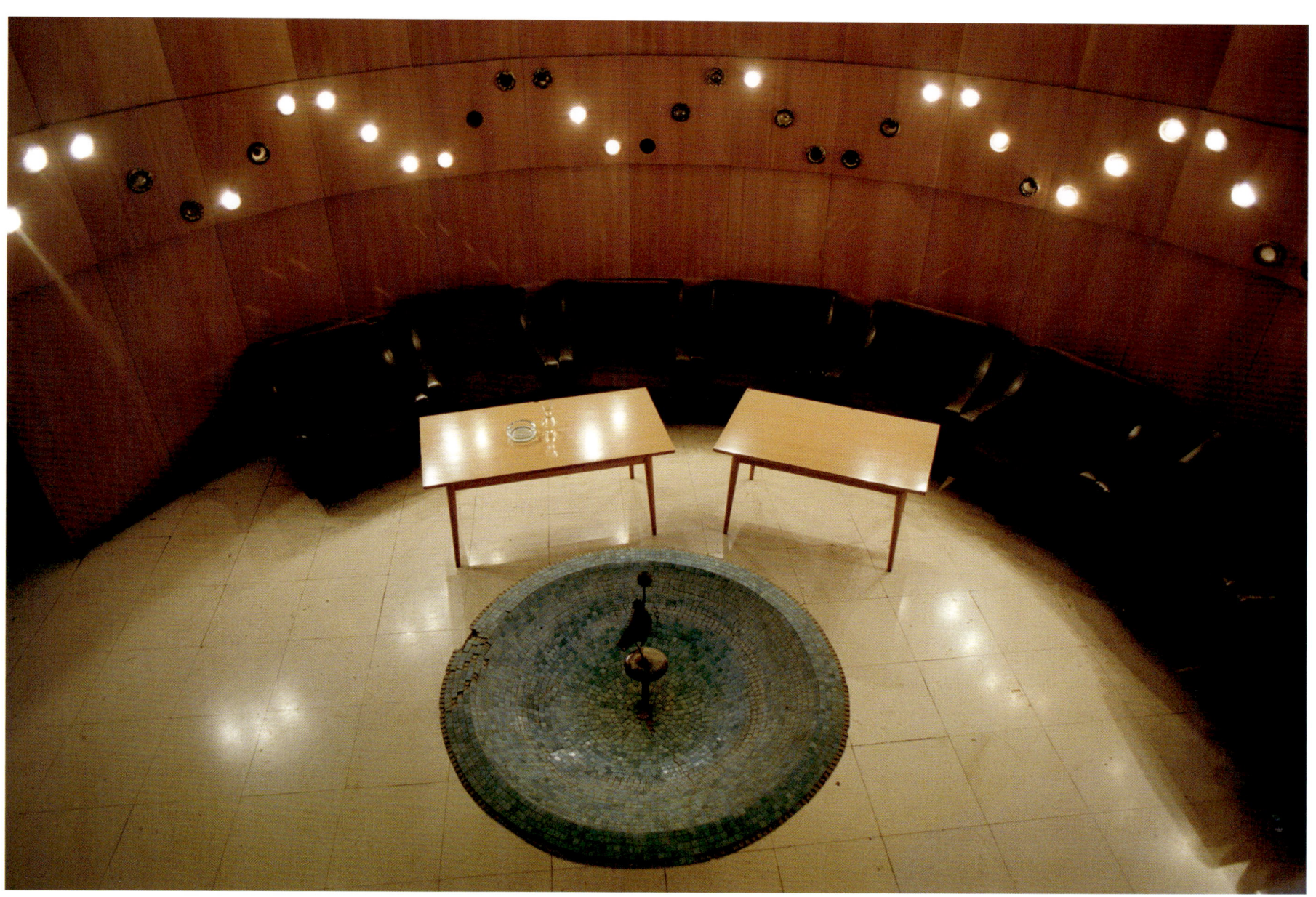

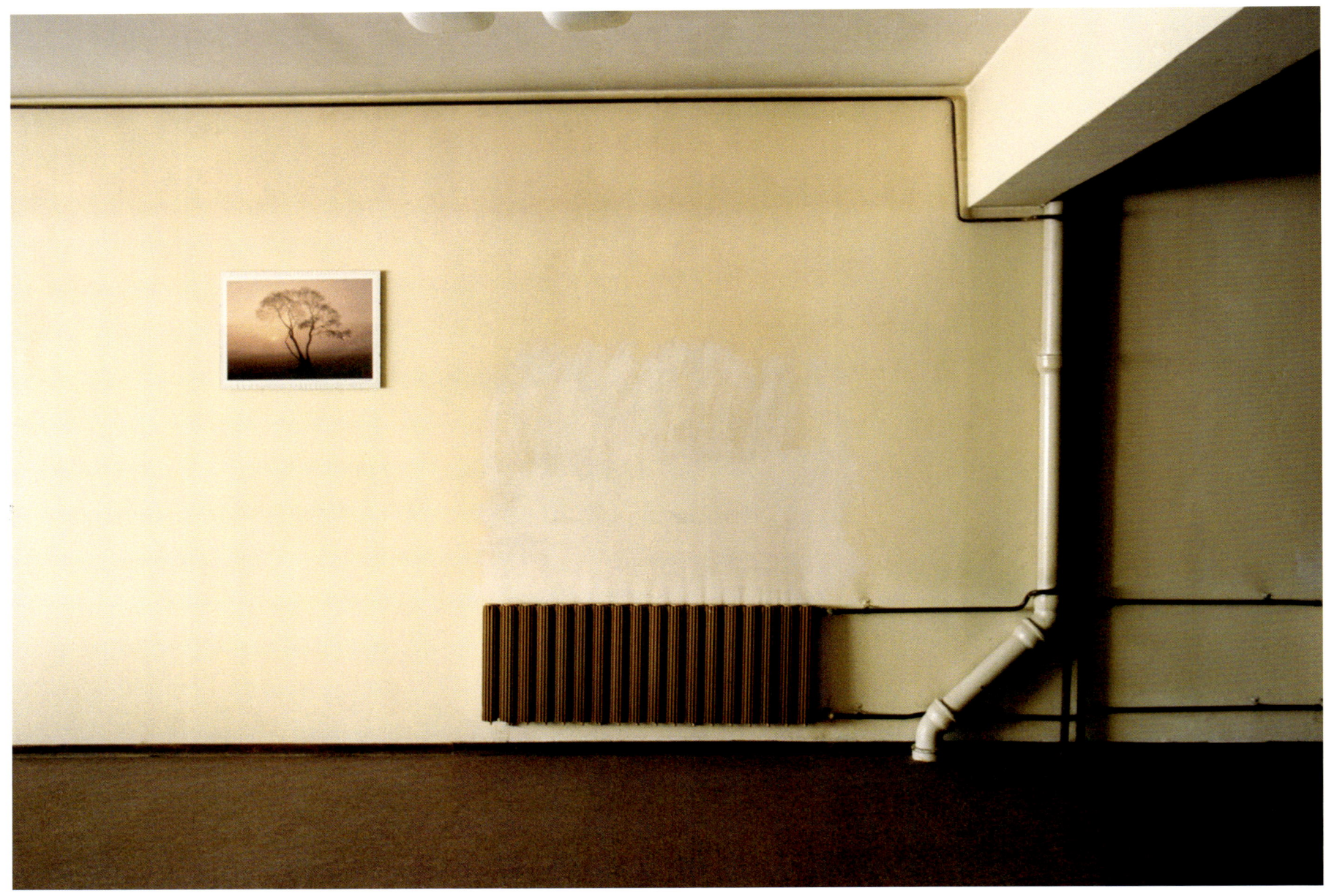

Zvezda Hotel, Vrnjačka Banja I, 2000

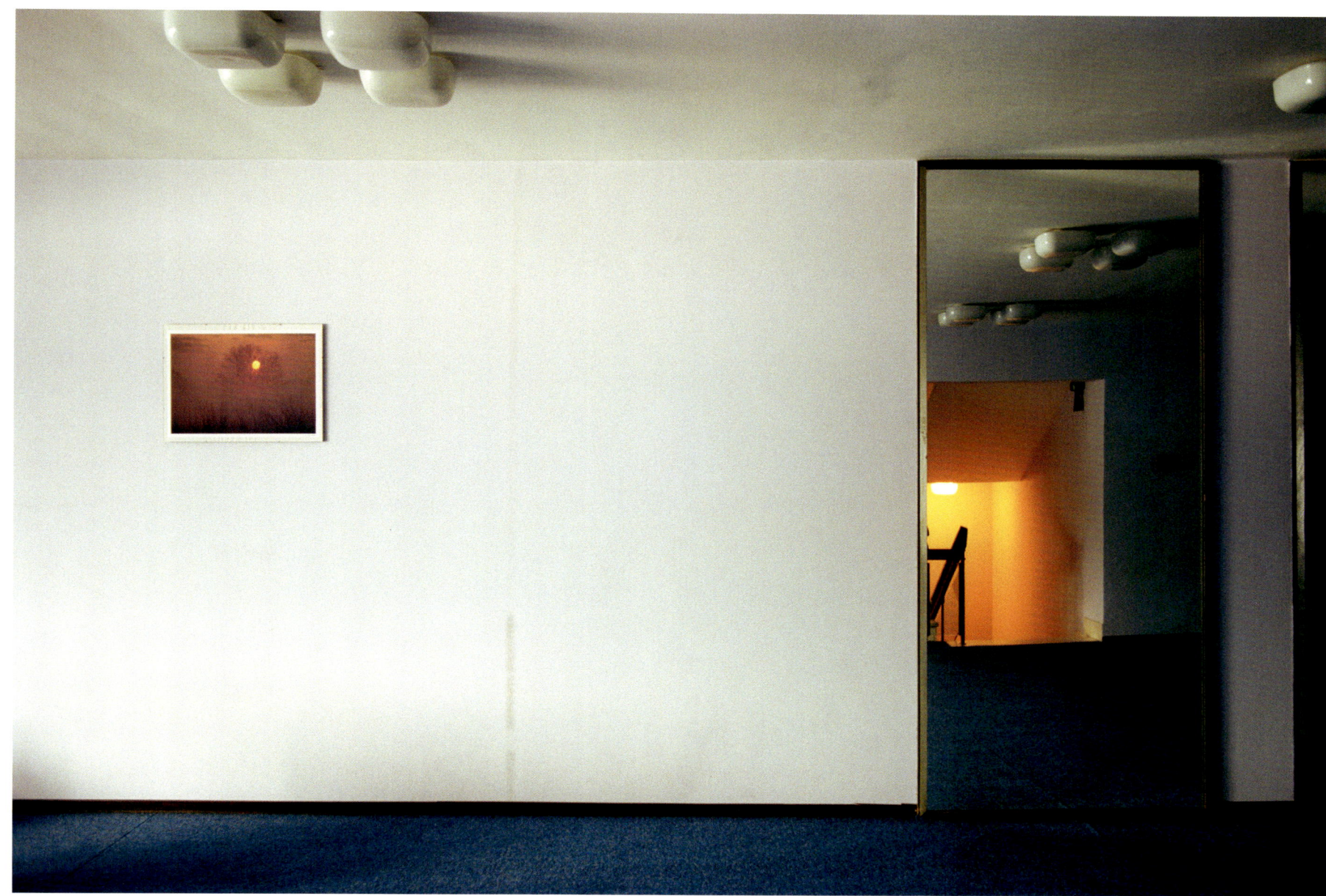

Zvezda Hotel, Vrnjačka Banja III, 2000

Vranje Hotel, Vranje, 2002

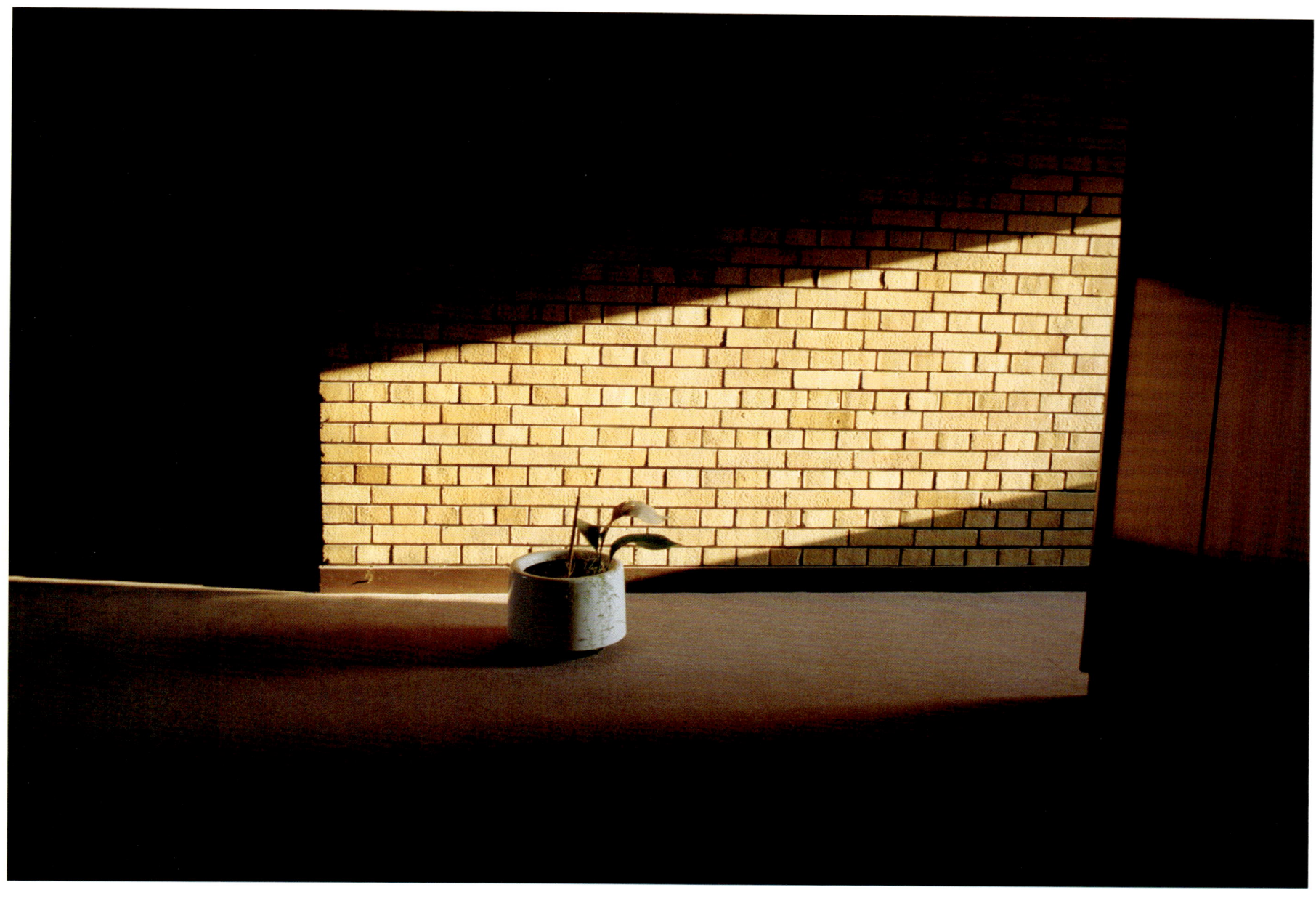

Narvik Hotel, Kikinda, 2002

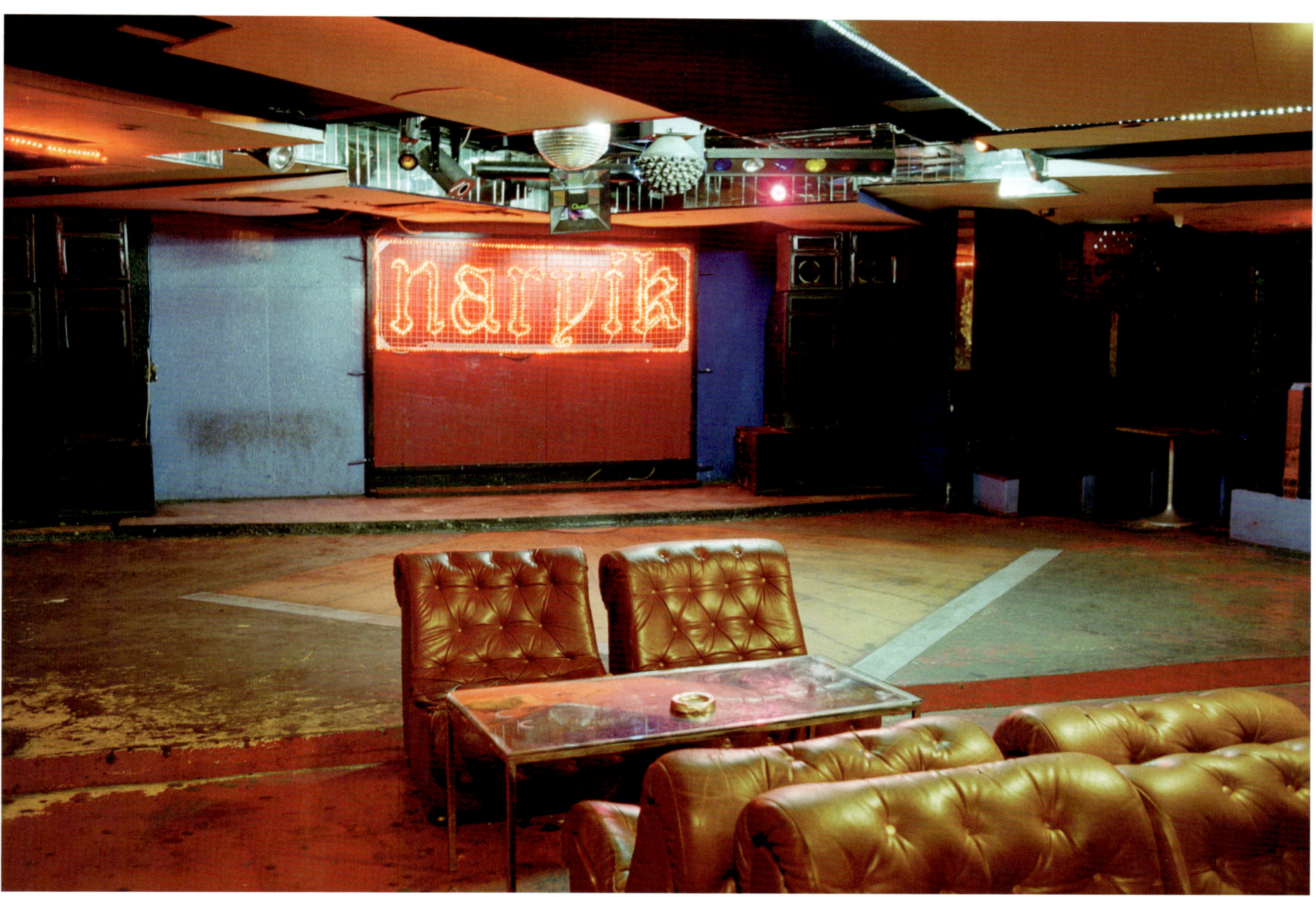

Direction of Light, 2019

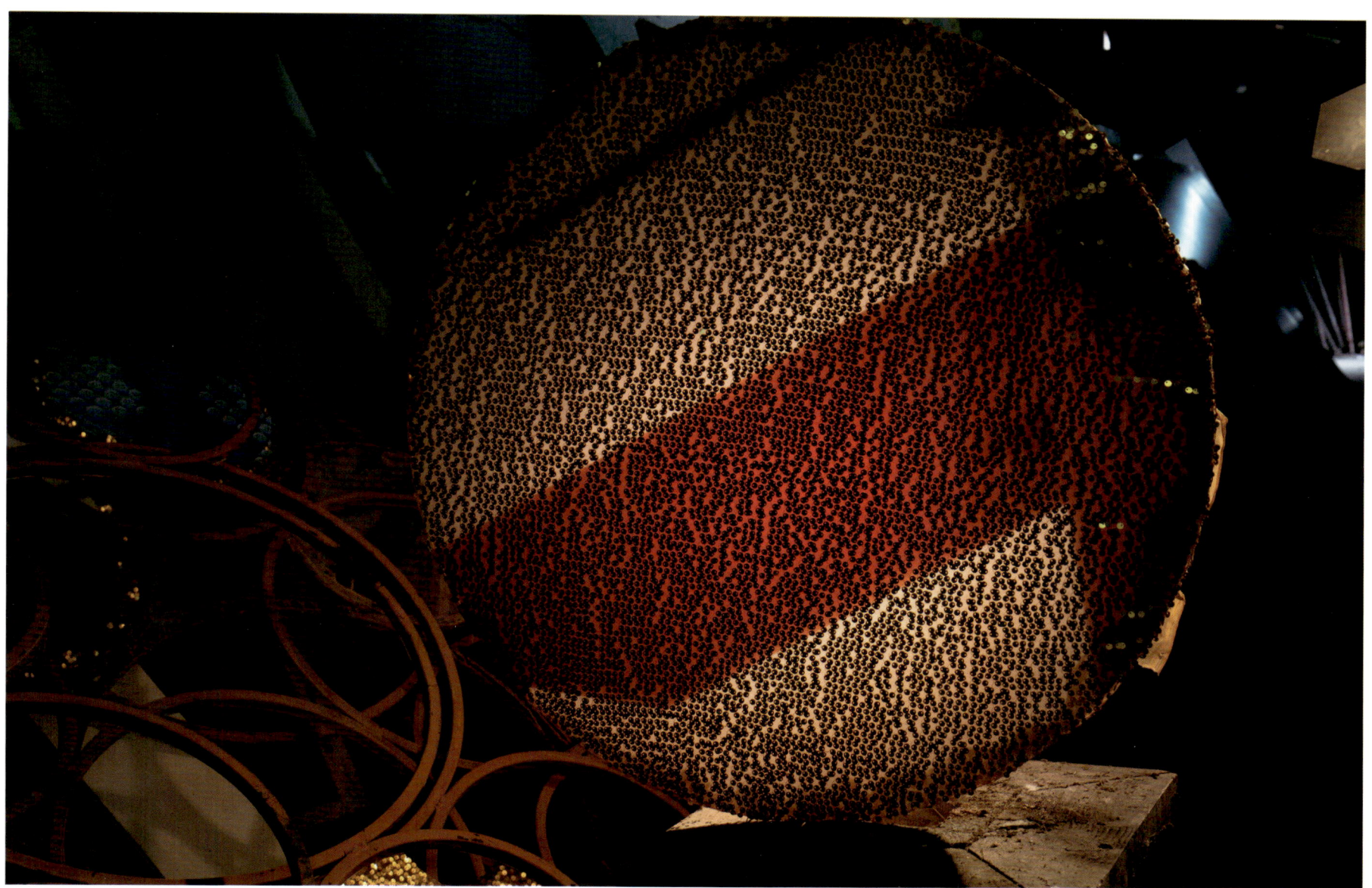

Moskva Hotel, Beograd II, 2001

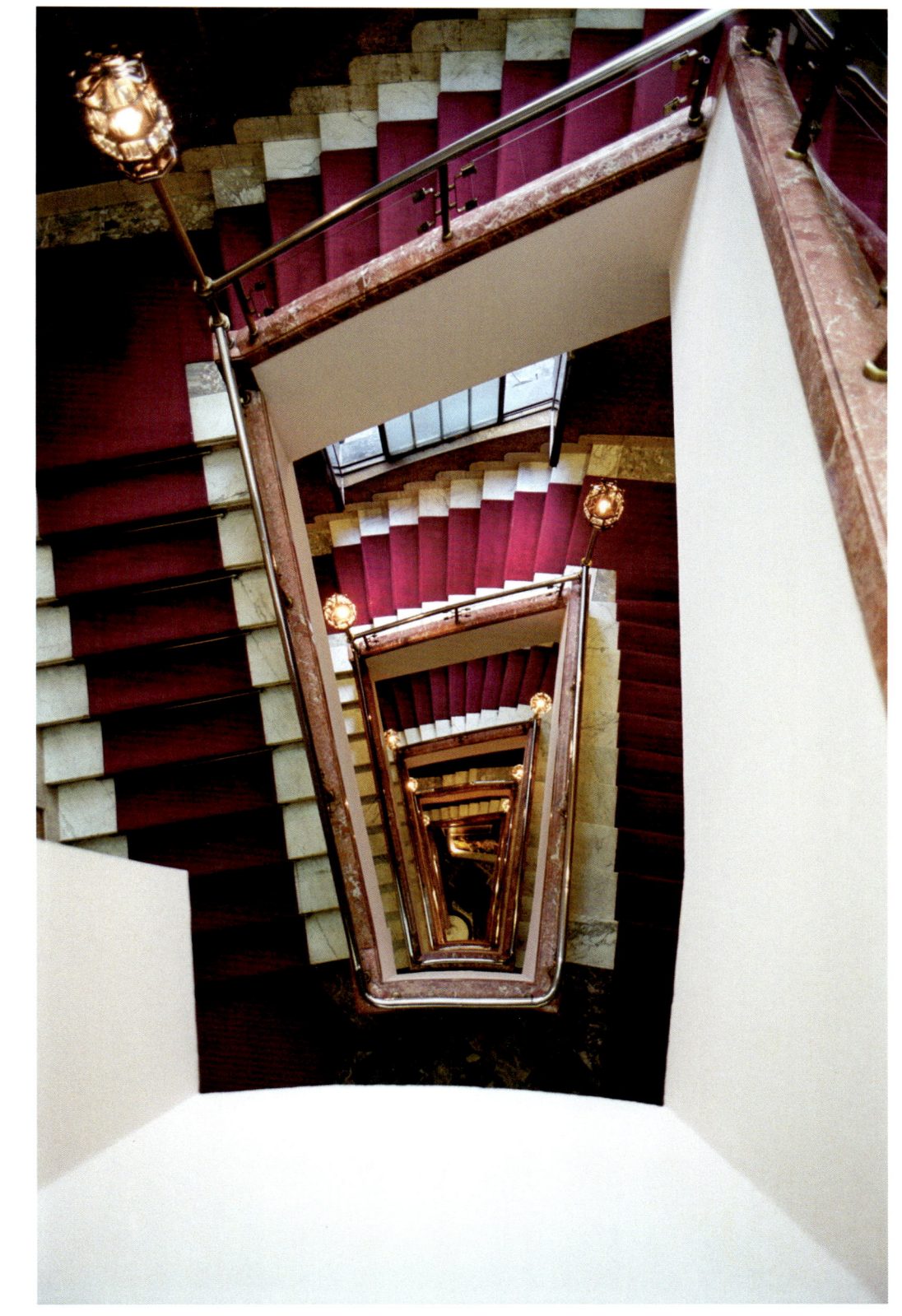

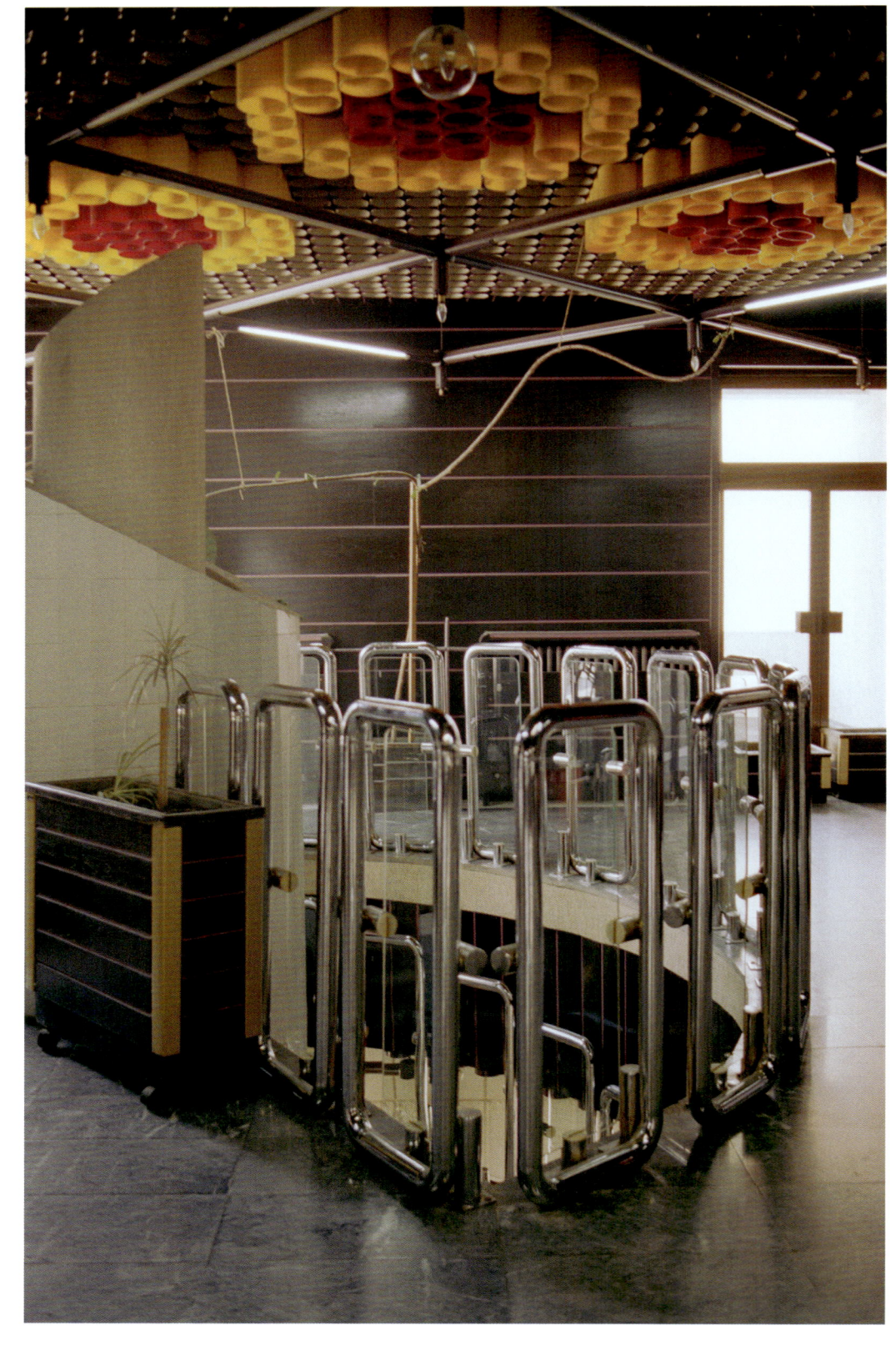

Lim Hotel, Priboj II, 2002

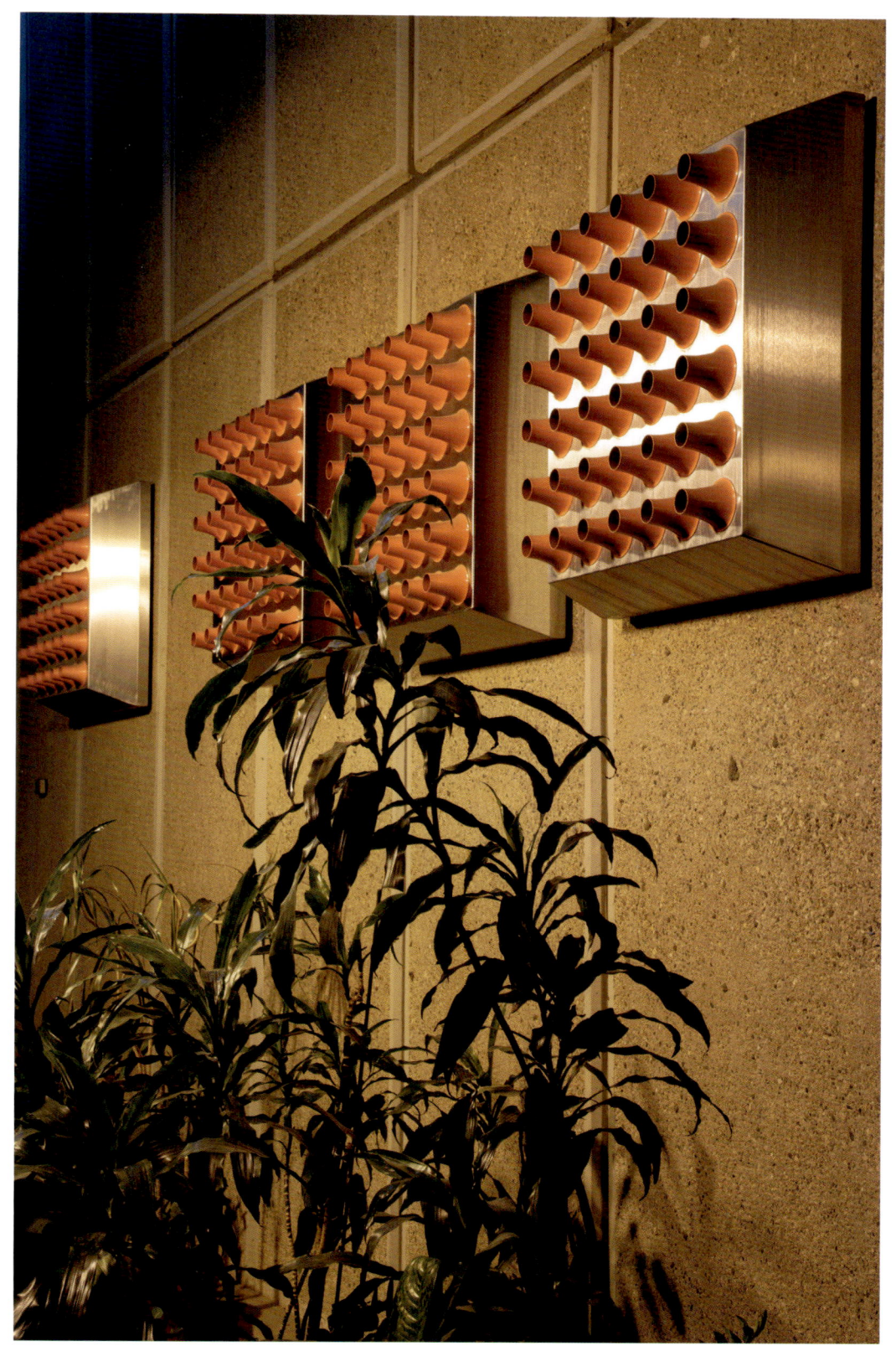

Color Temperature Orange (CTO), 2019

Krajina Hotel, Negotin, 2001

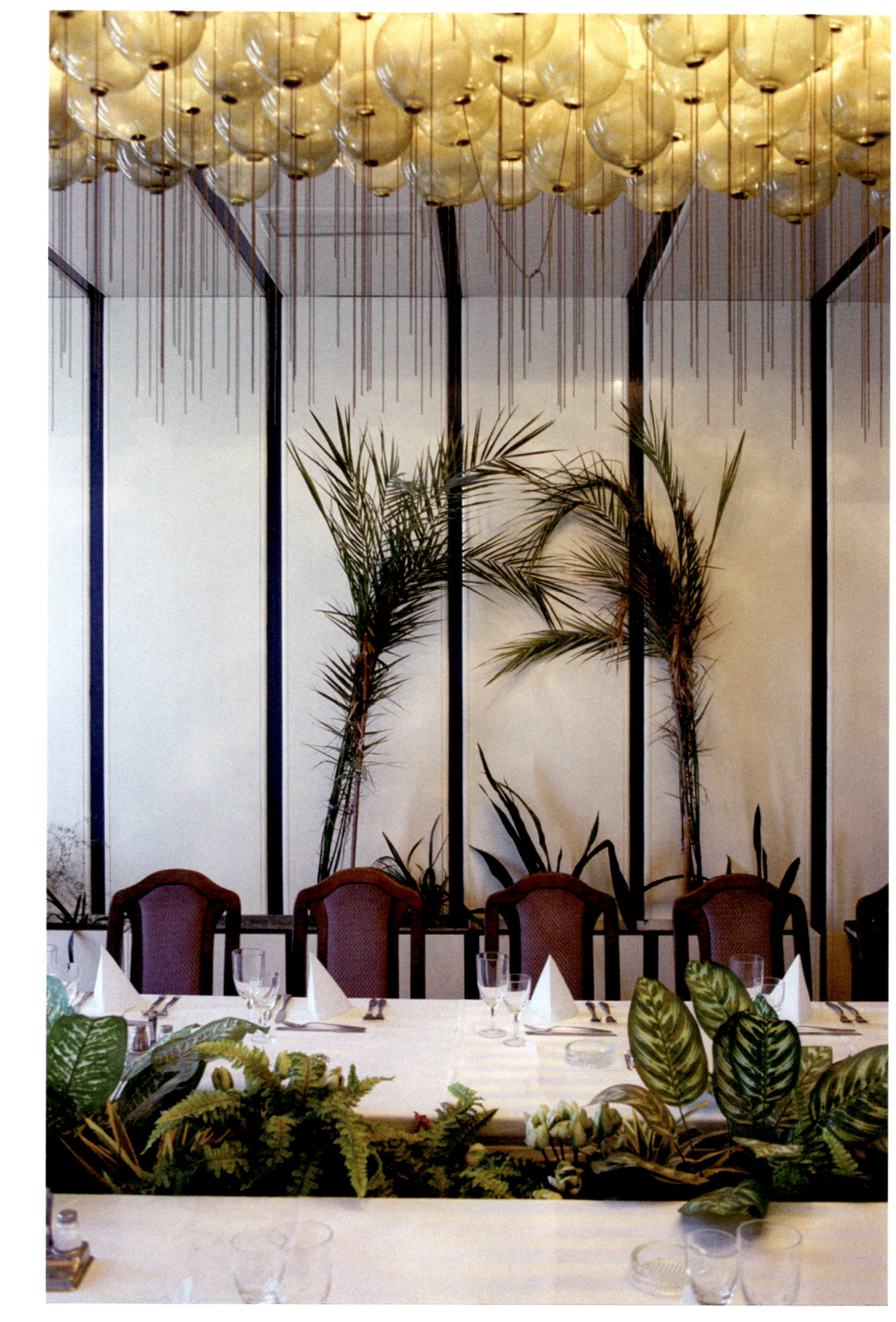

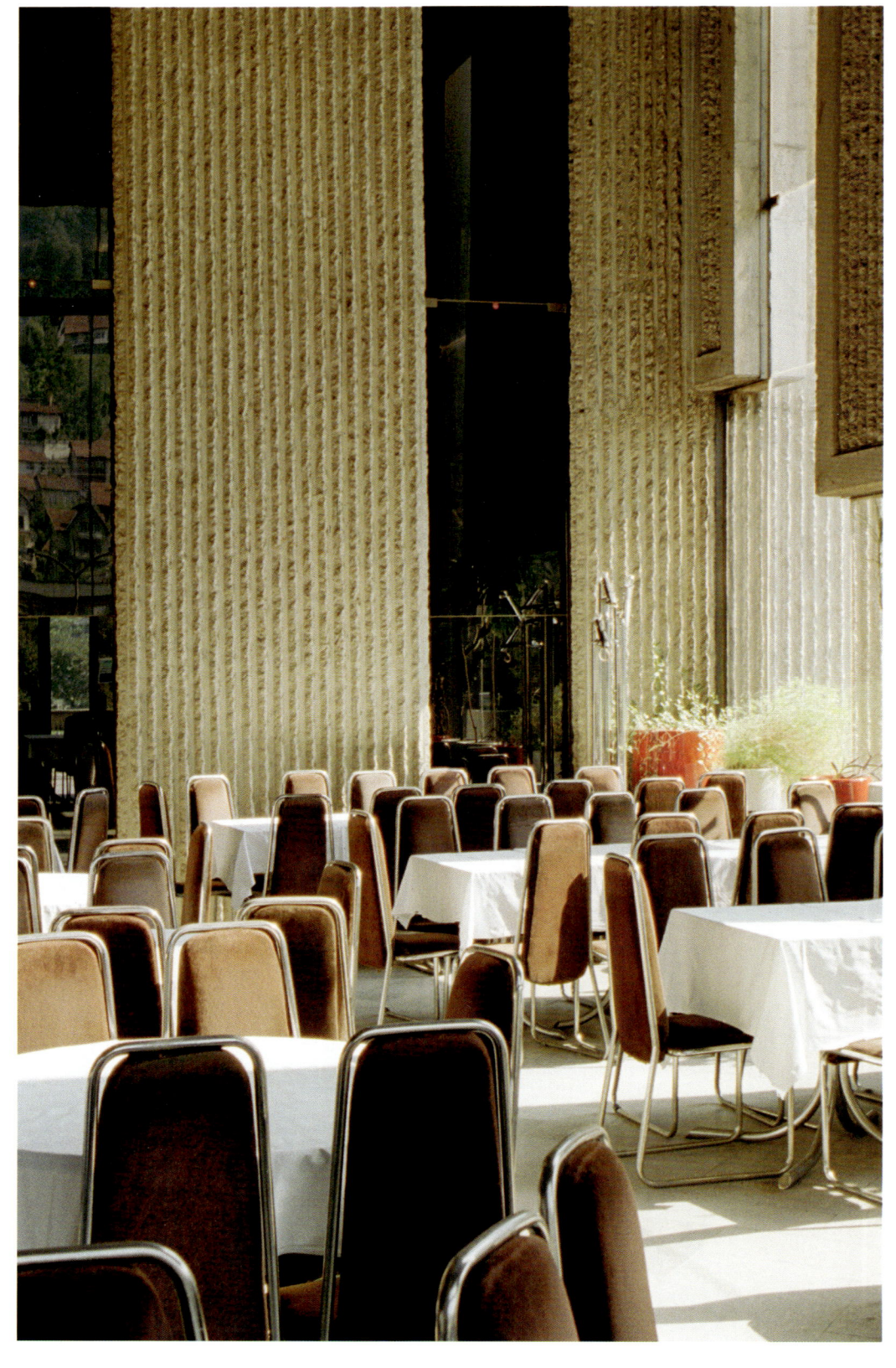

Zlatibor Hotel, Užice II, 2002

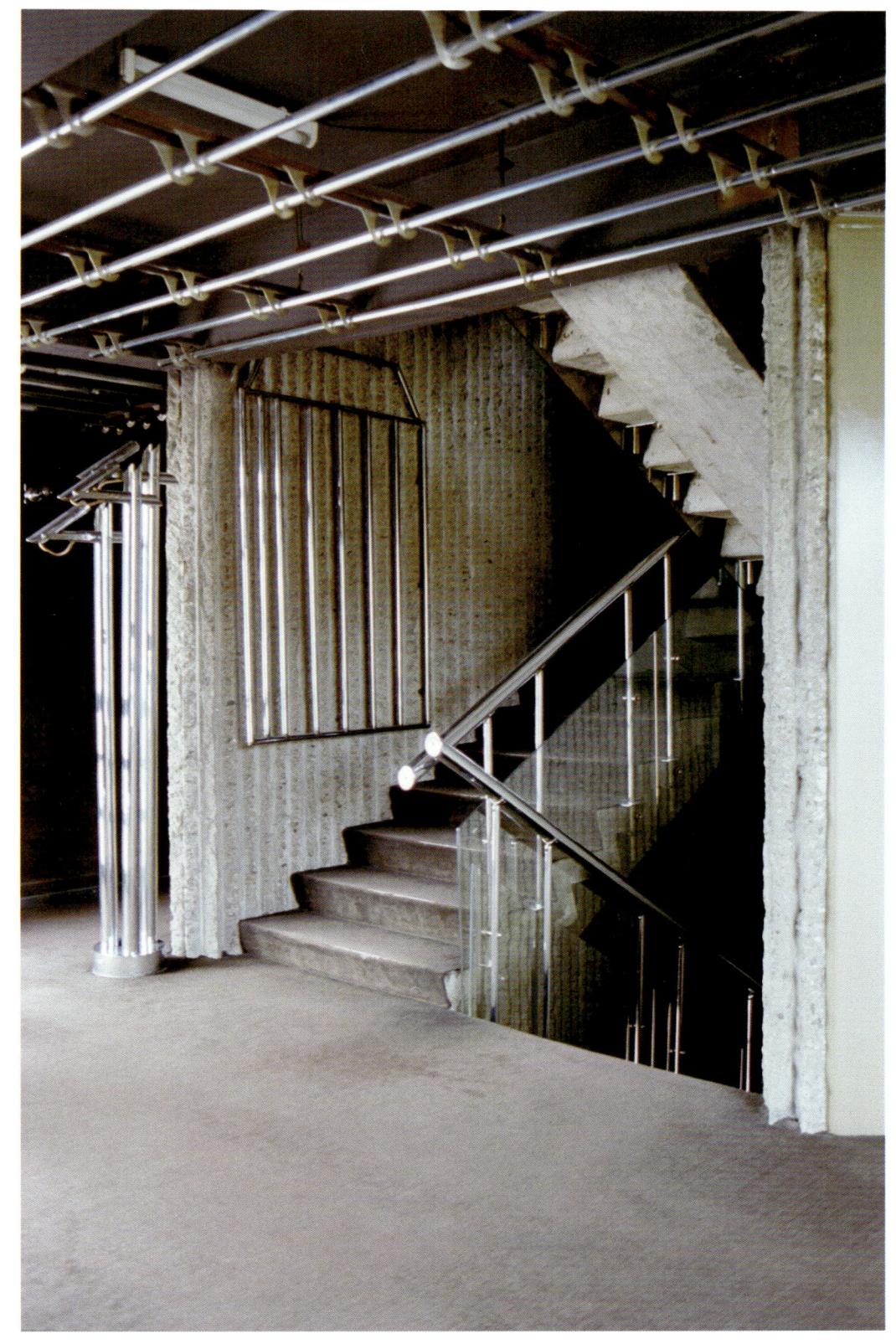

Zlatibor Hotel, Užice I, 2002

Srbija Hotel, Zaječar, II, 2001

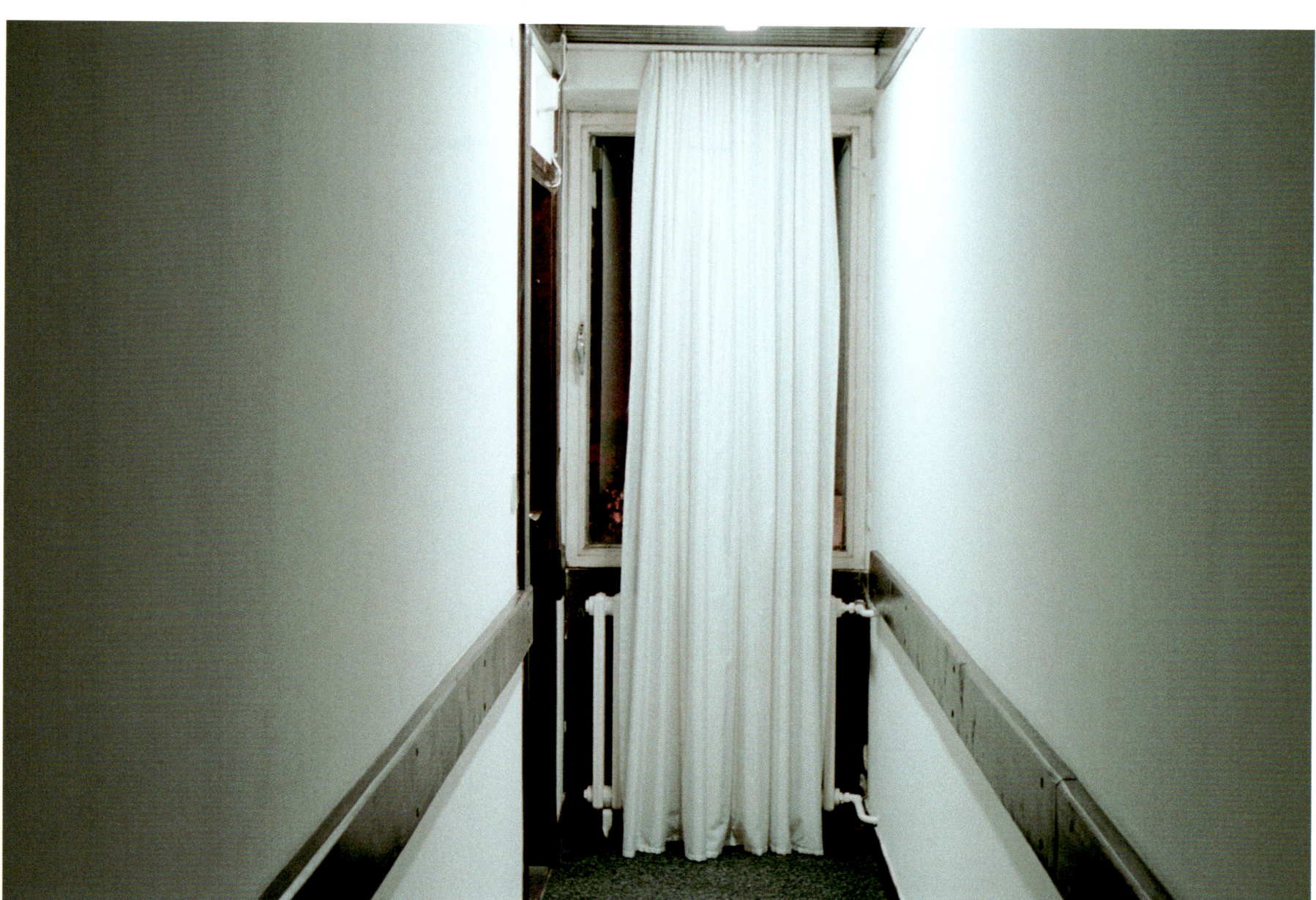

Zvezda Hotel, Vrnjačka Banja IV, 2001

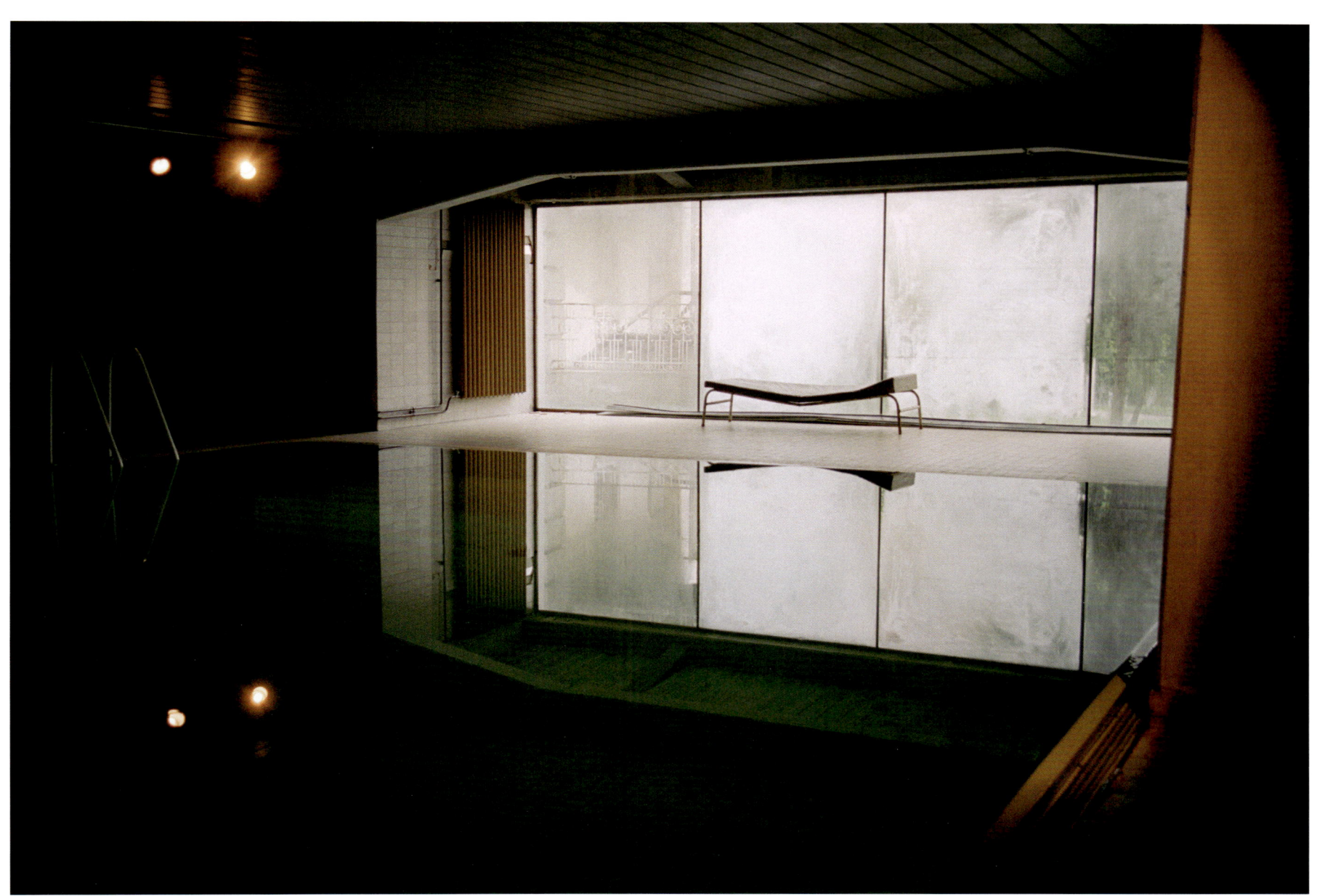

Jagodina Hotel, Jagodina IV, 2002

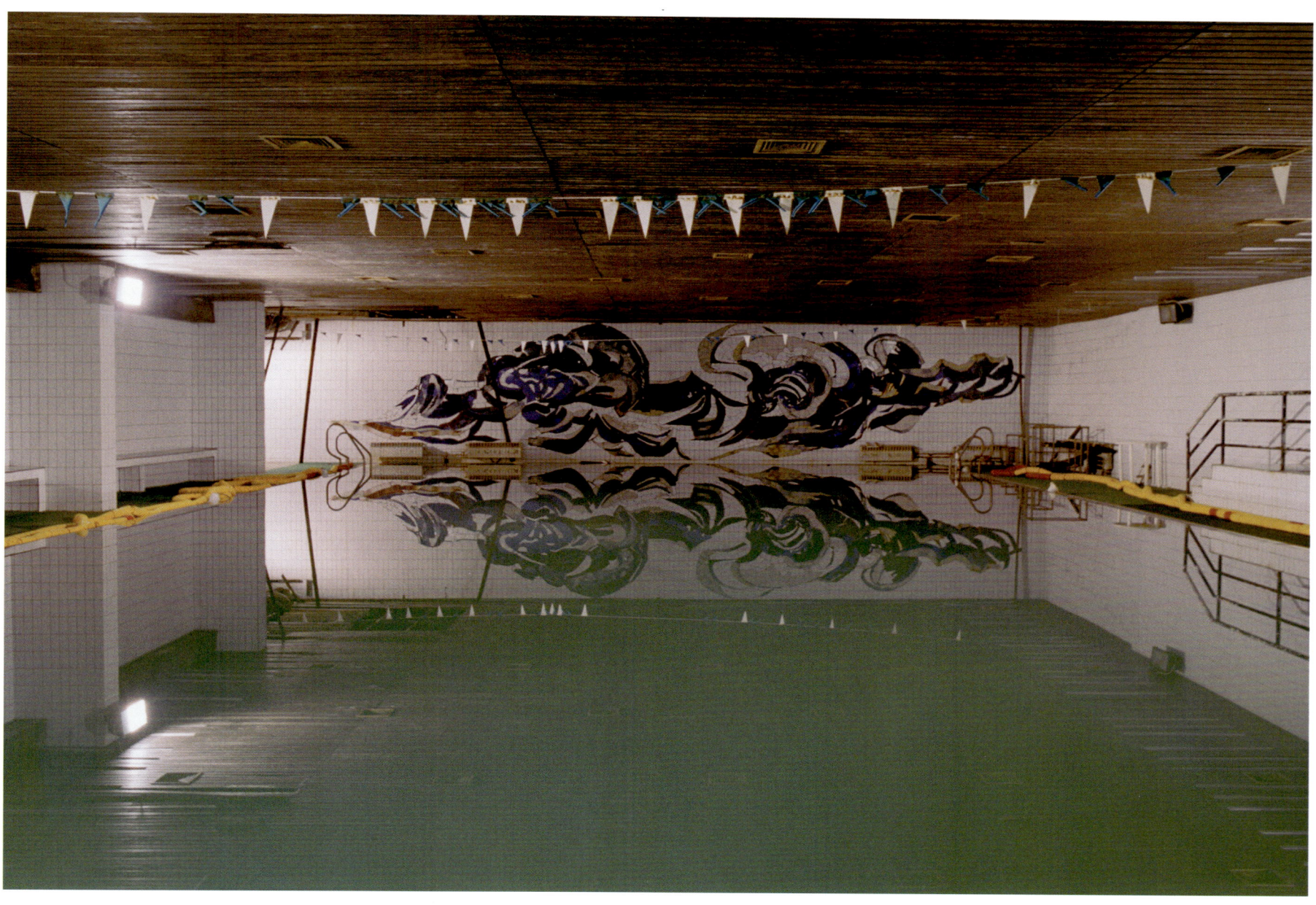

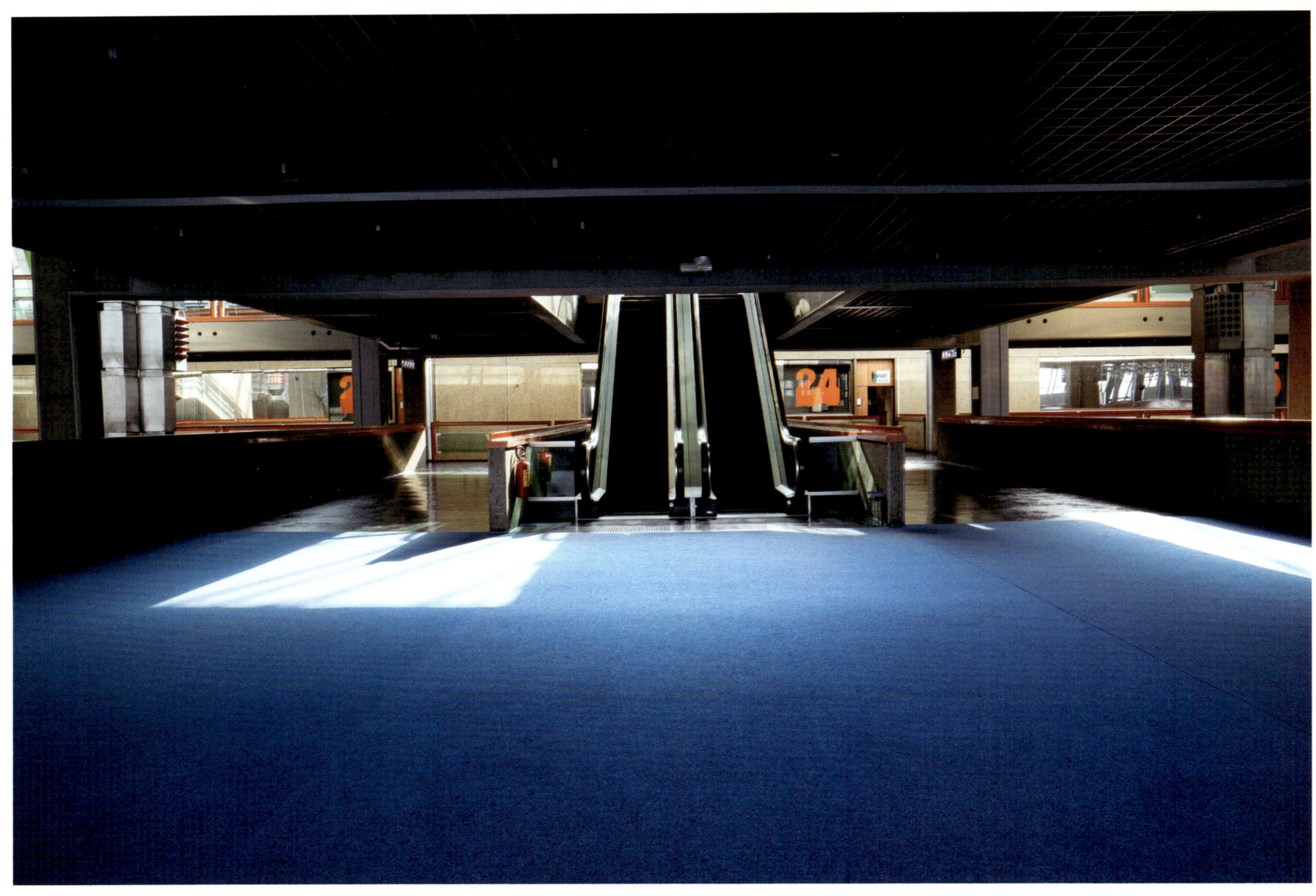

La Jetée (After Chris Marker), 2019

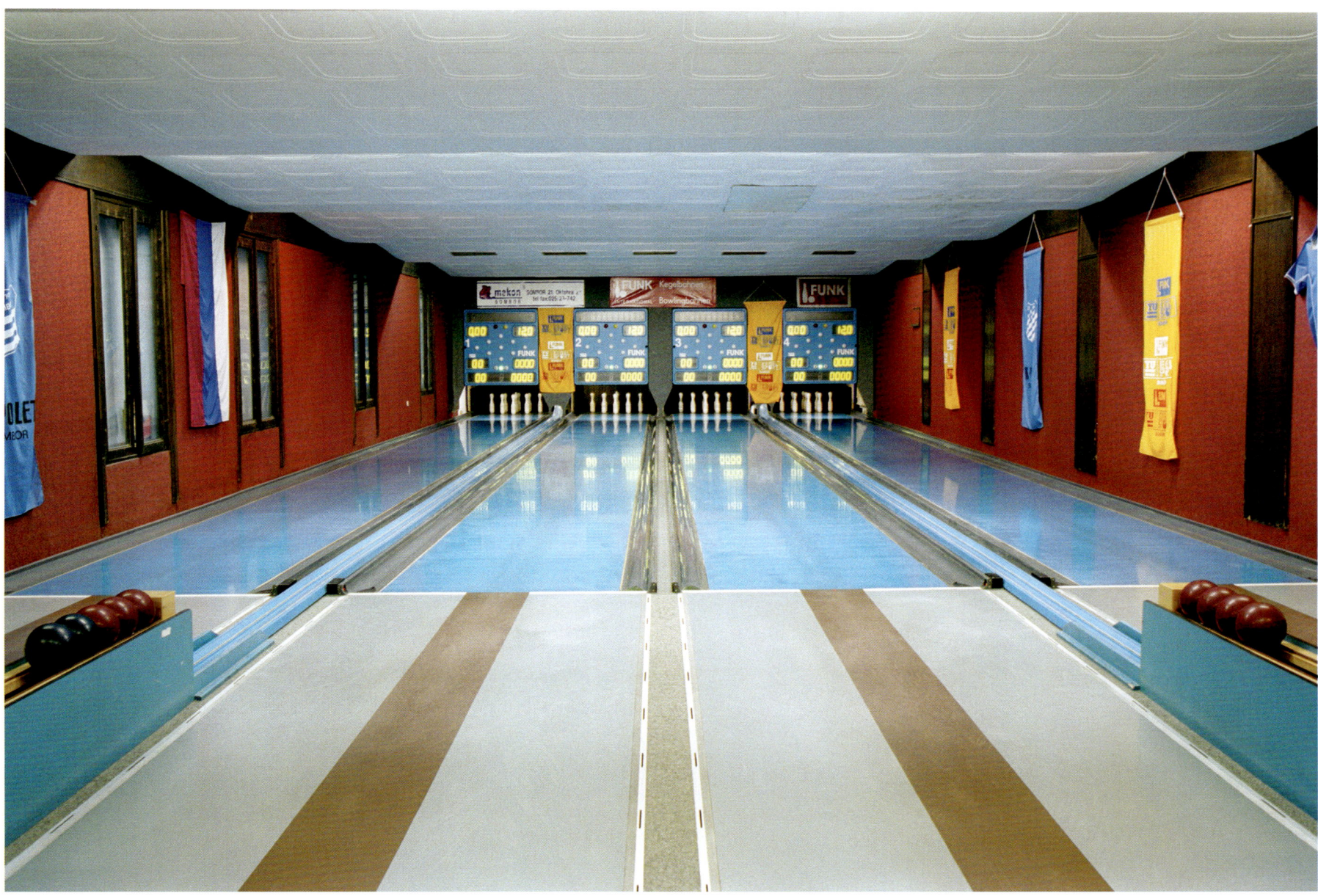

Sloboda Hotel, Sombor, 2002

Đerdap Hotel, Kladovo III, 2001

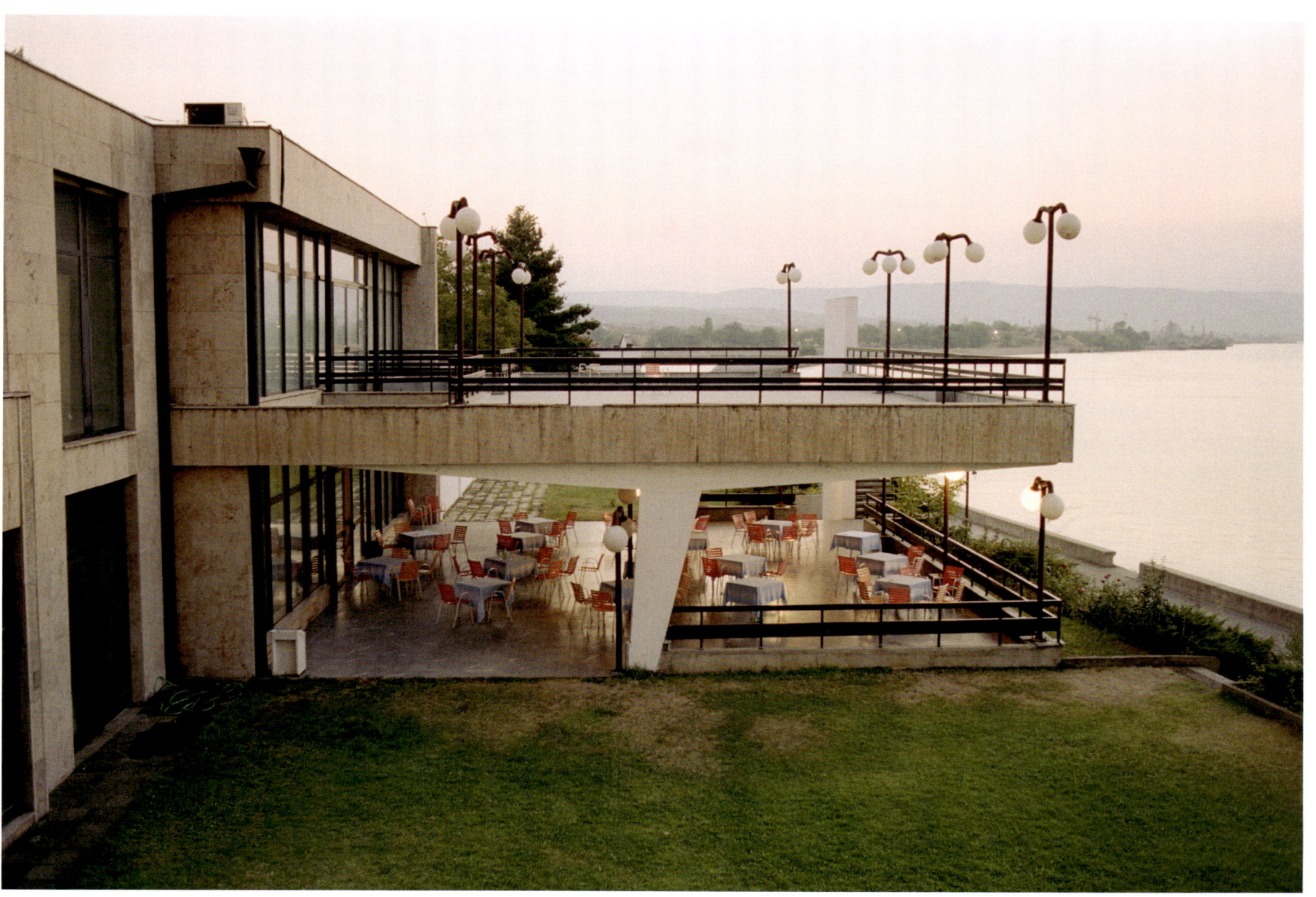

Entrance Hall. Inside the Federal Executive Council Building, Belgrade, Serbia

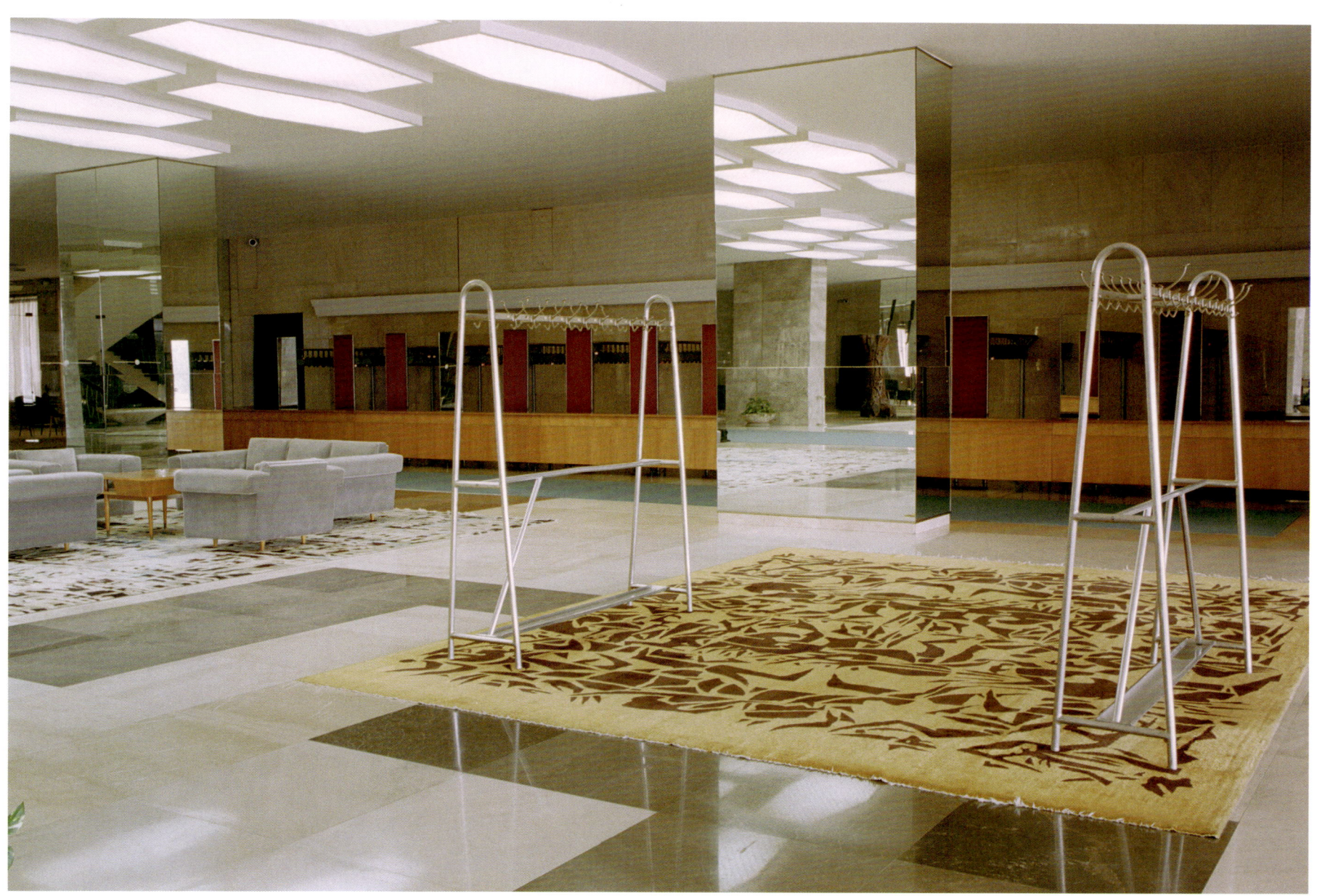

Ocher. Inside the Federal Executive Council Building, Belgrade, Serbia

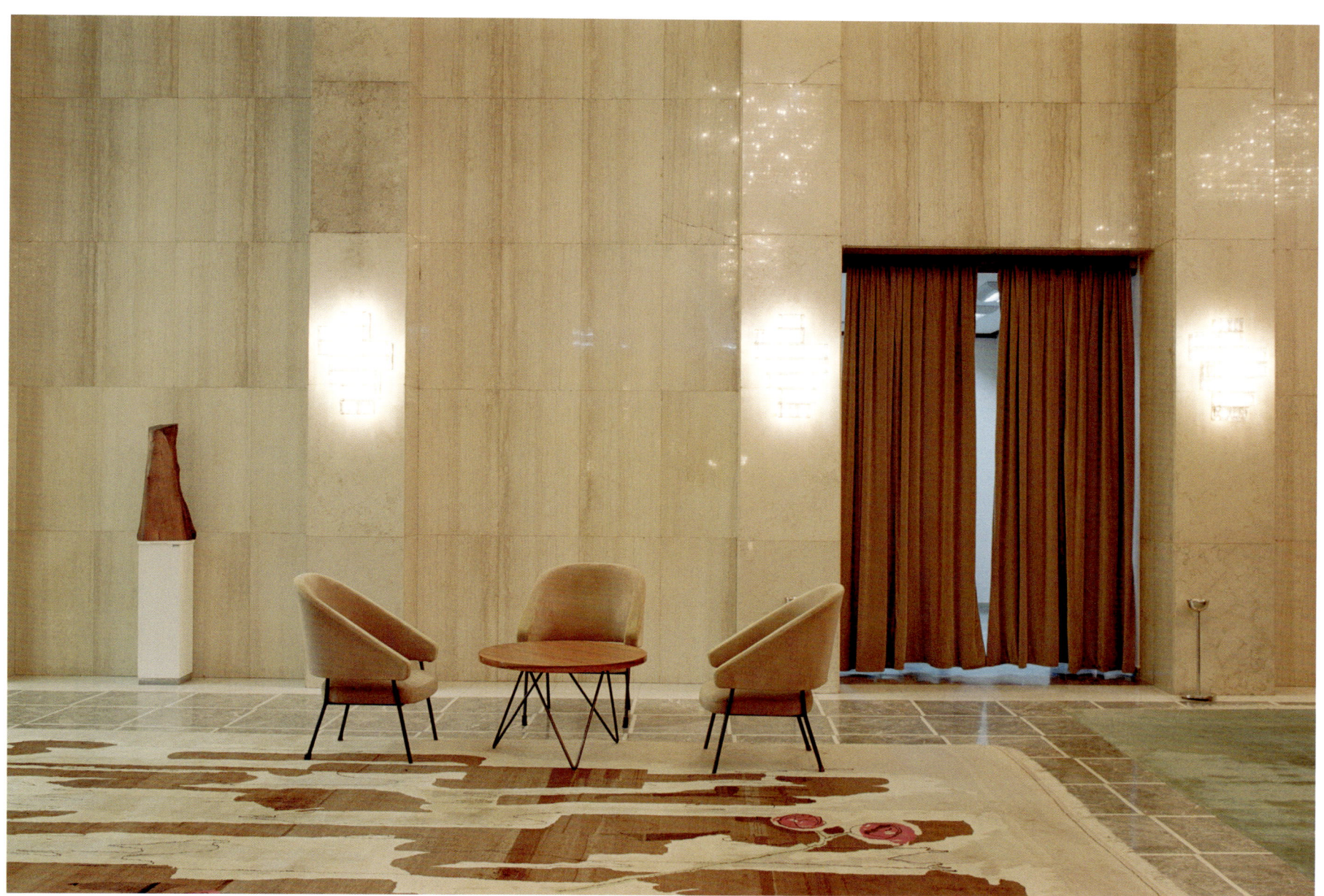

Seating Area with Fluorescent Reflection. Inside the Federal Executive Council Building, Belgrade, Serbia

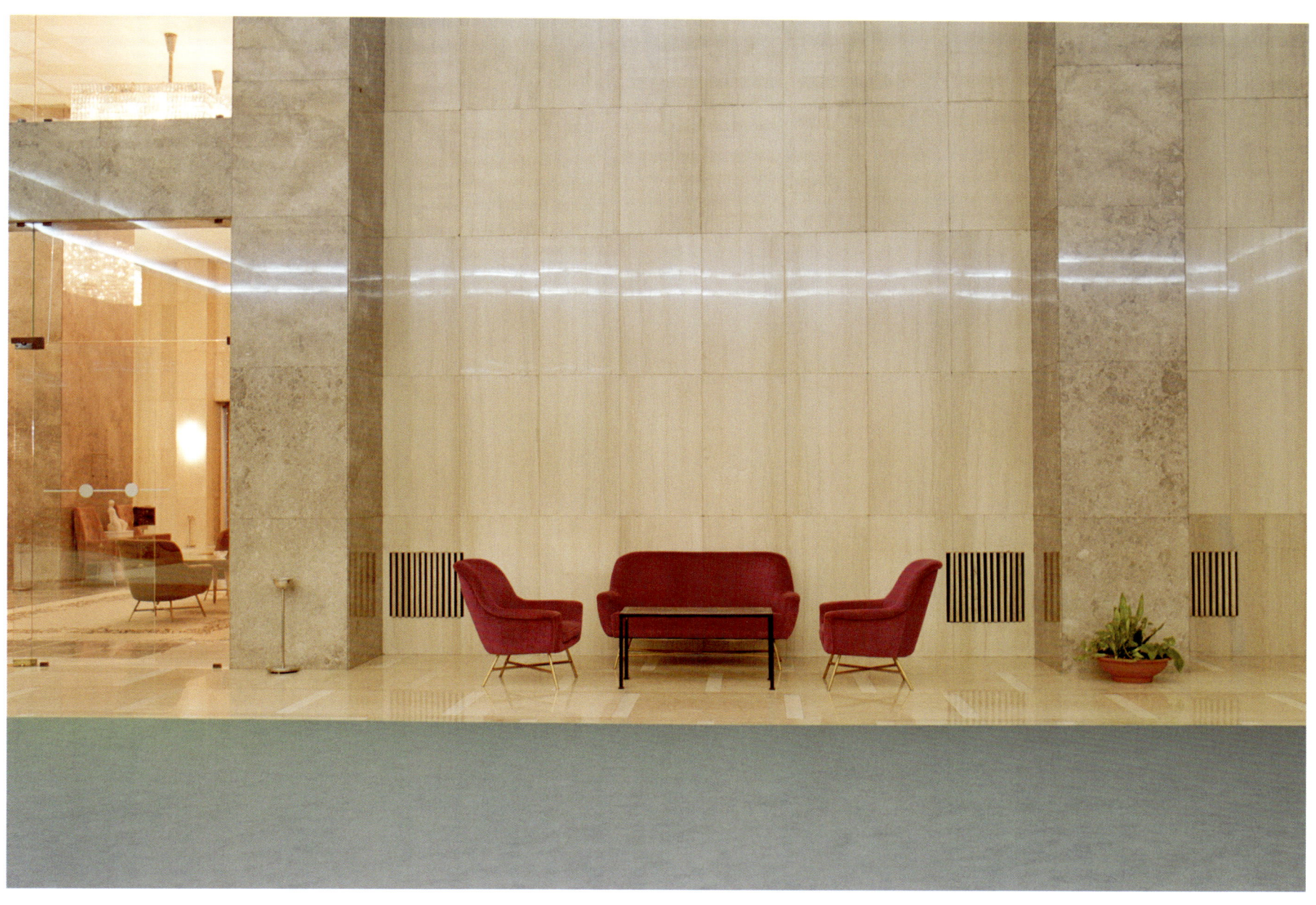

Double Doors. Inside the Federal Executive Council Building, Belgrade, Serbia

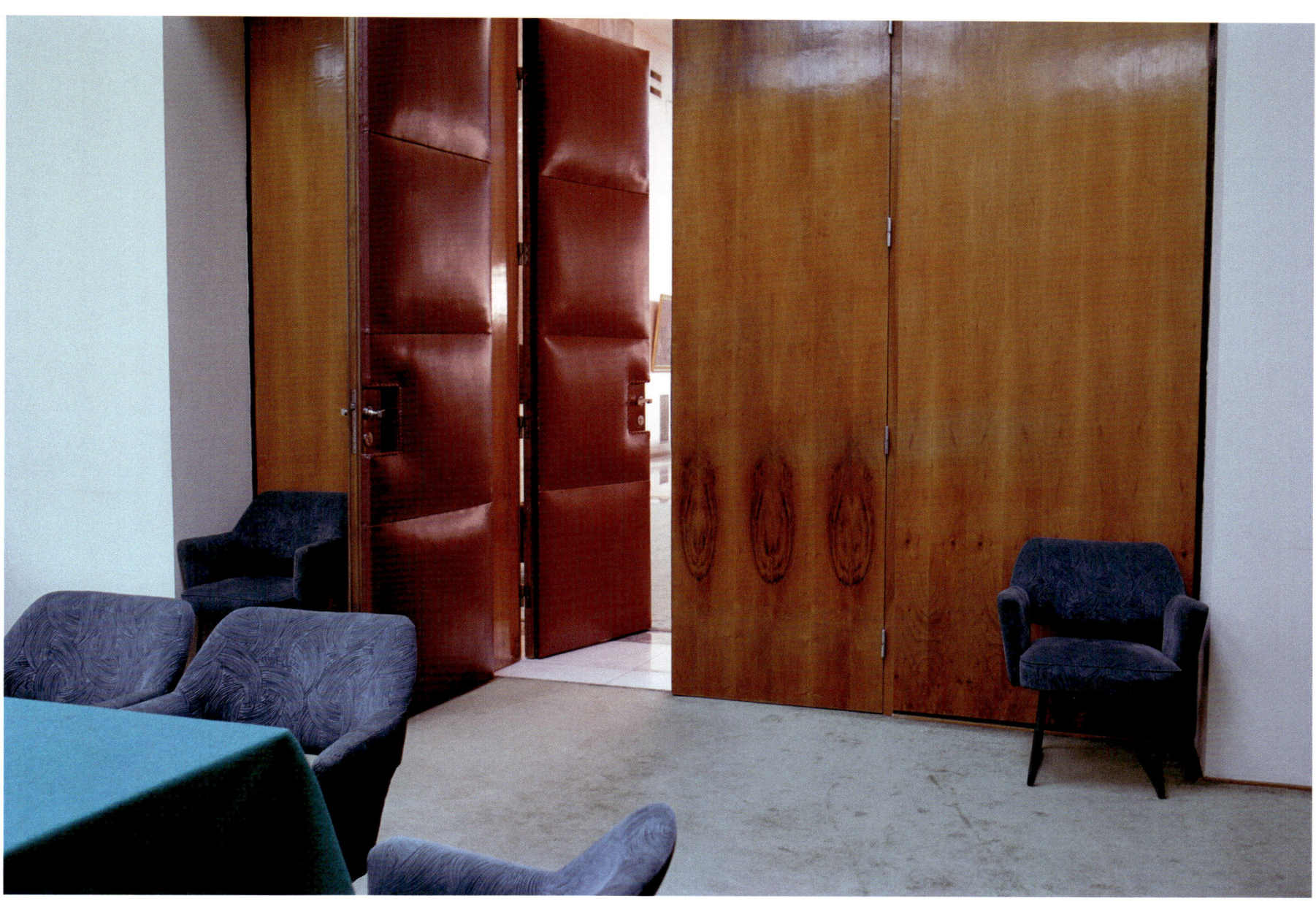

The Salon of the Socialist Republic of Serbia. Inside the Federal Executive Council Building, Belgrade, Serbia

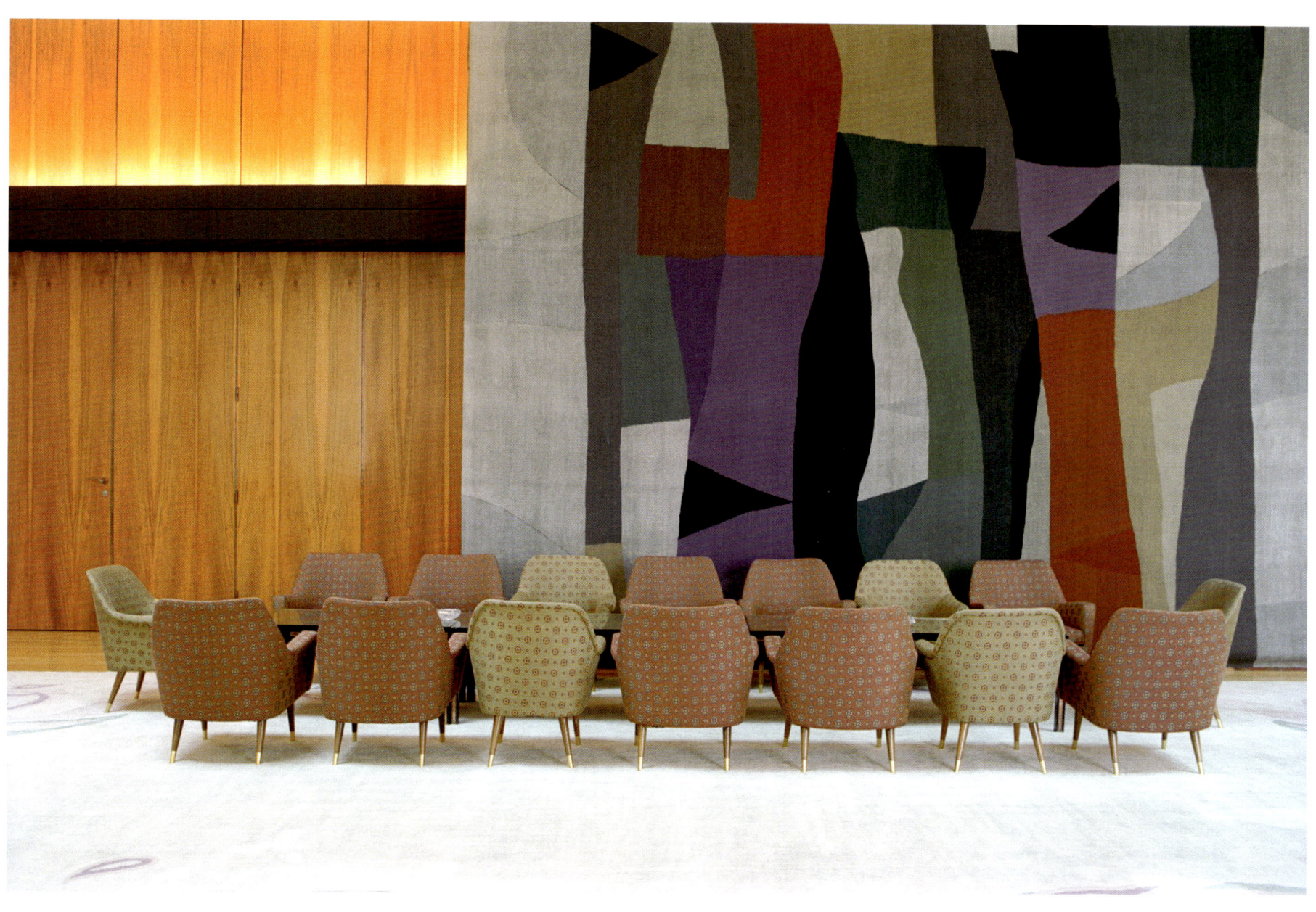

Lobby. Inside the Chase One Plaza Building, Manhattan, NY

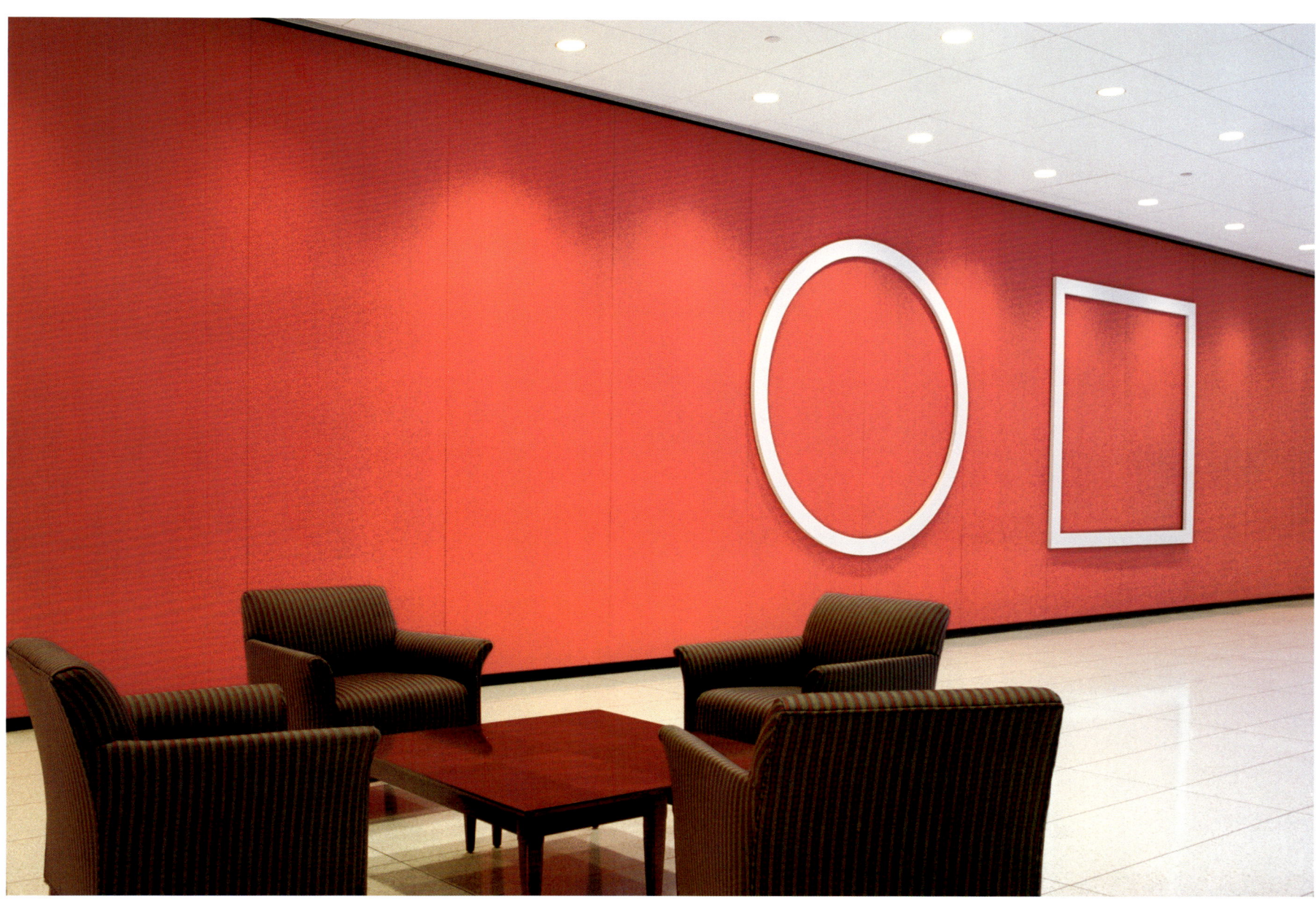

The President's Cabinet. Inside the Federal Executive Council Building, Belgrade, Serbia, 2019

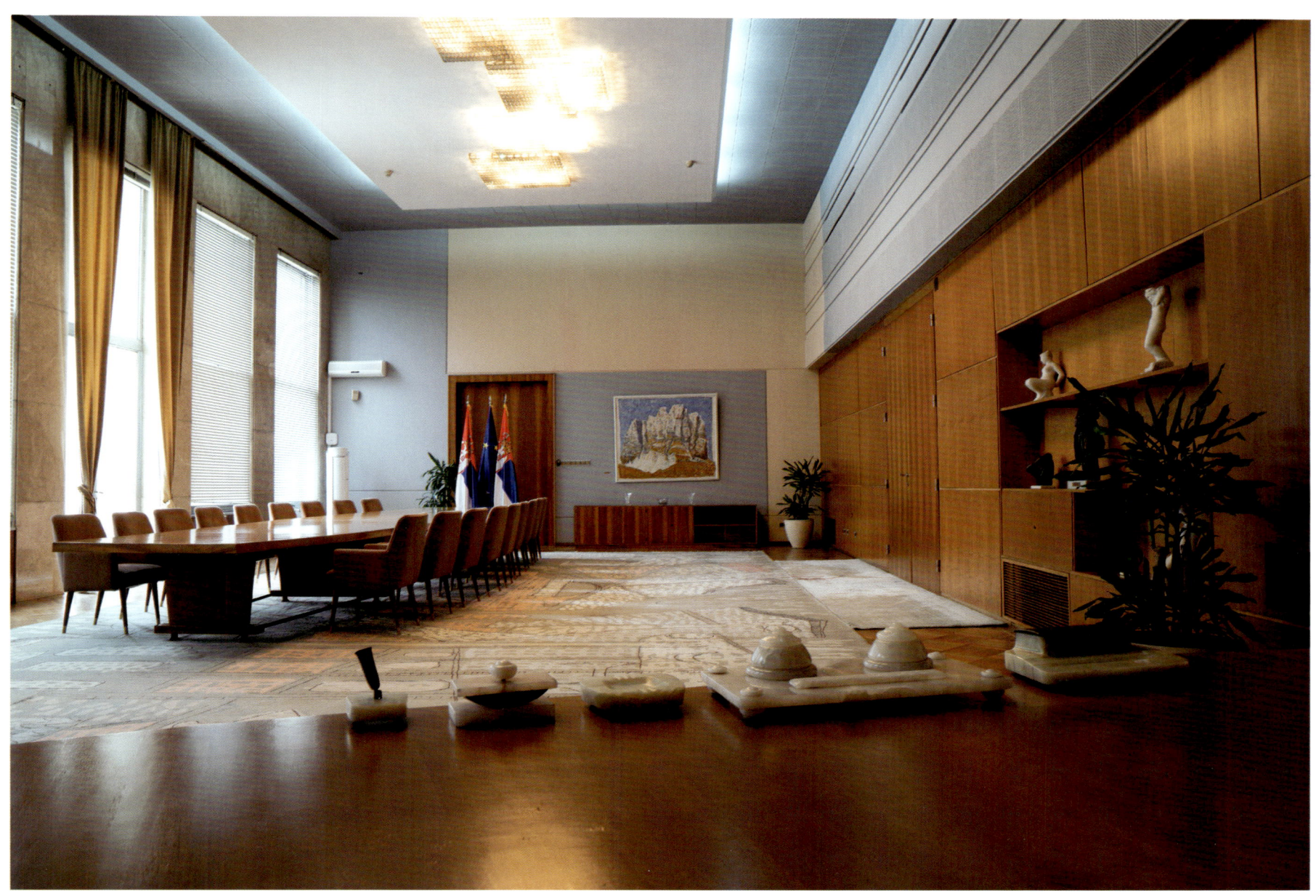

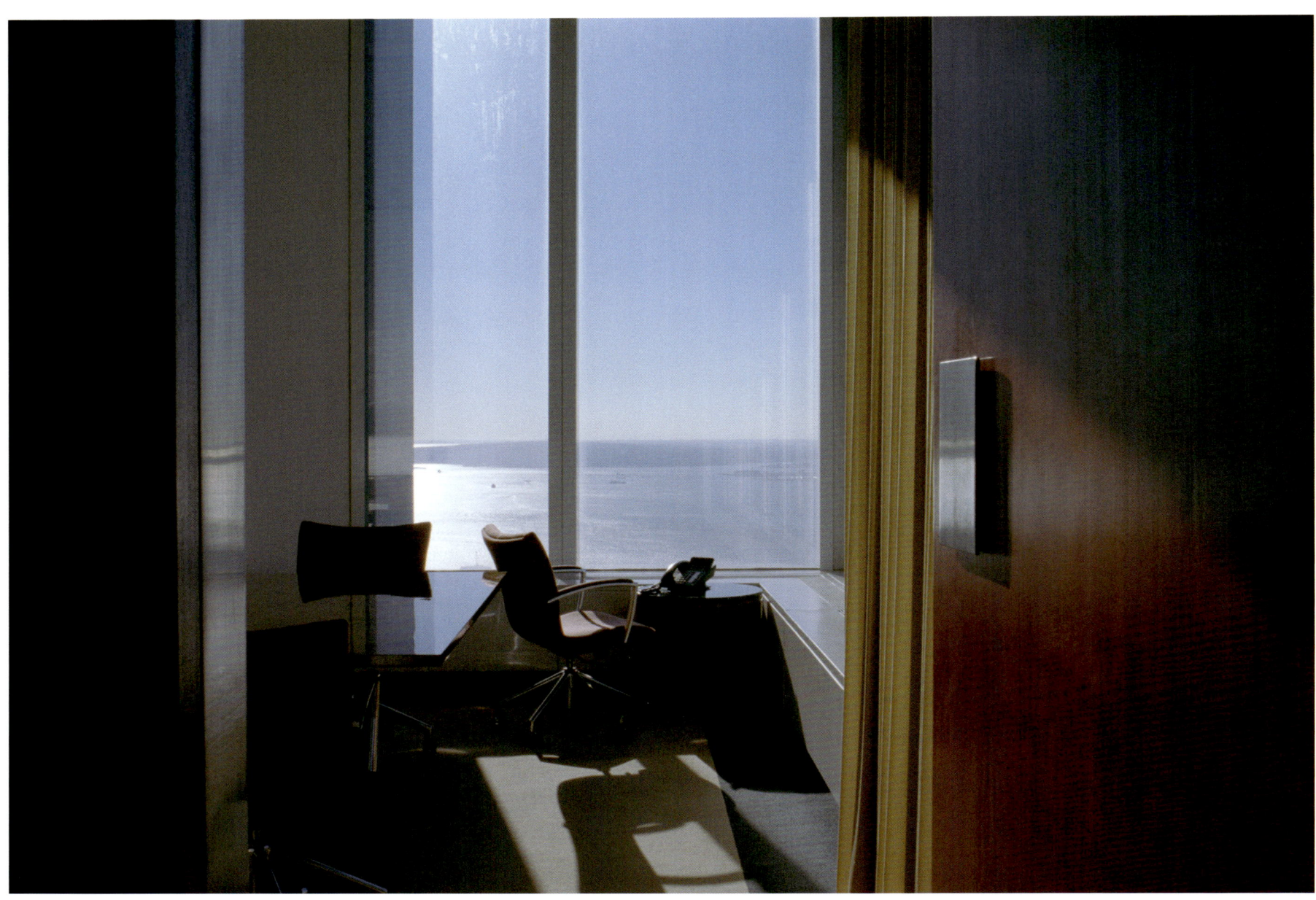

Top Floor Vista. Inside the Chase One Plaza Building, Manhattan, NY

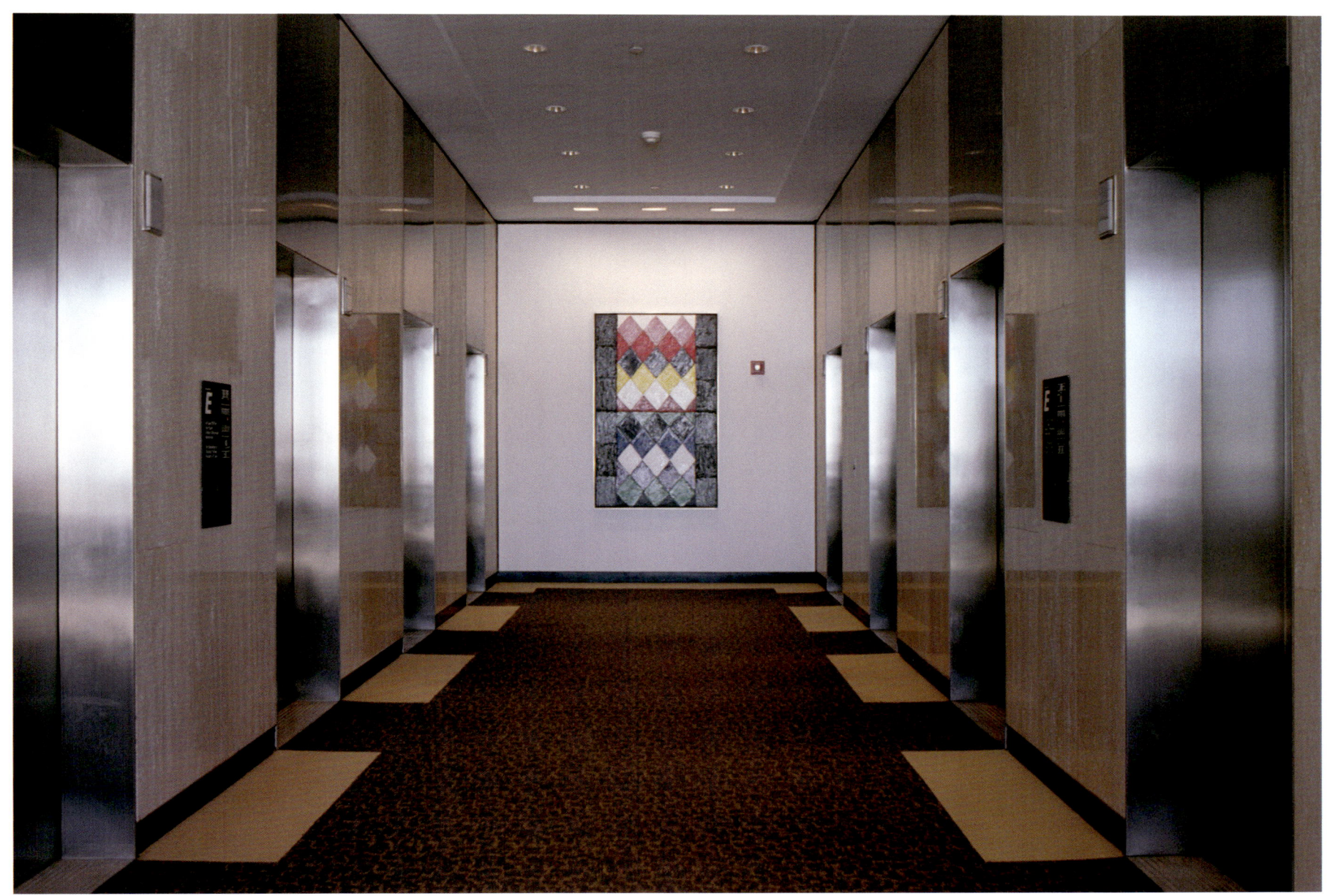

Geometry. Inside the Chase One Plaza Building, Manhattan, NY

Mosaic. Inside the Federal Executive Council Building, Belgrade, Serbia

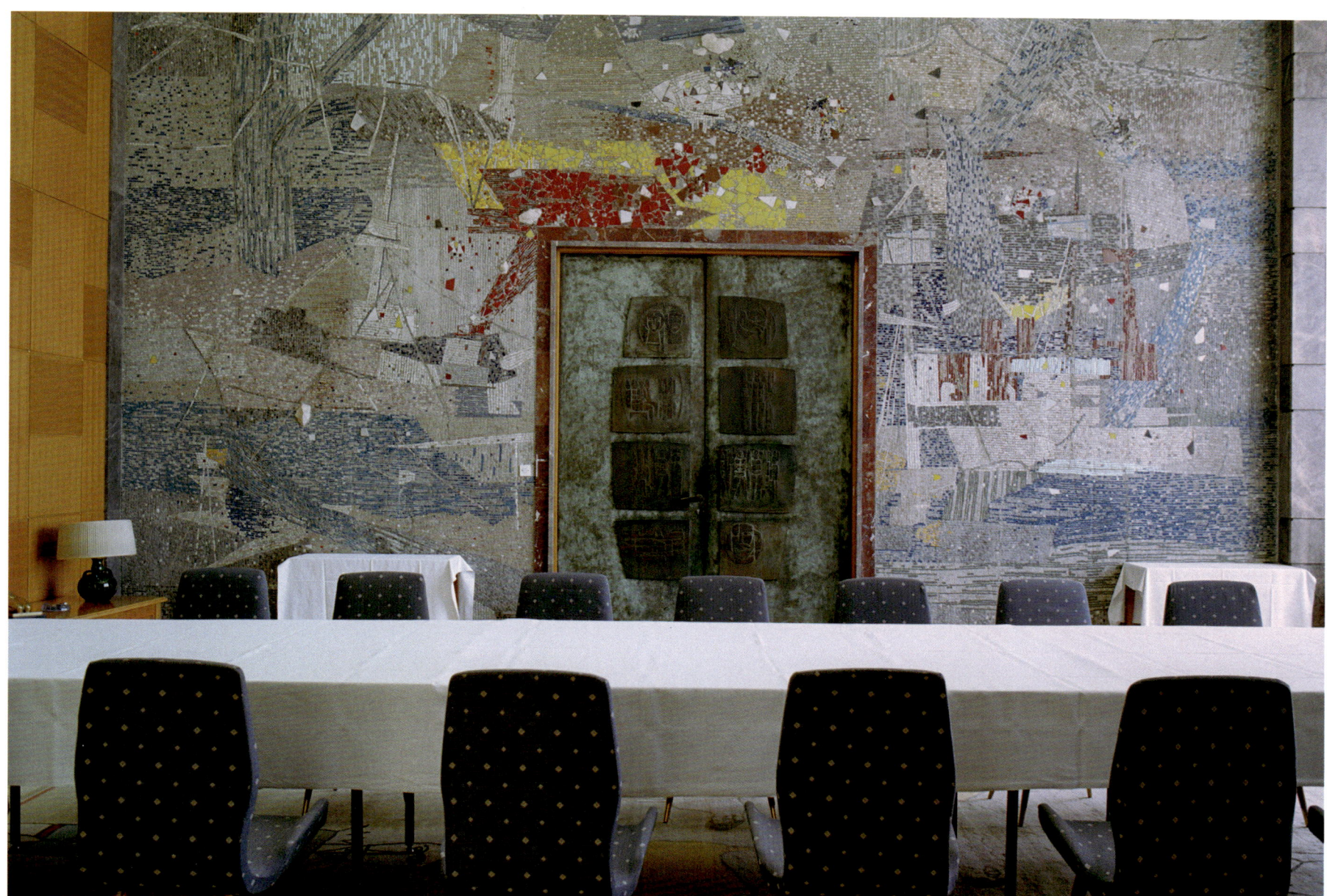

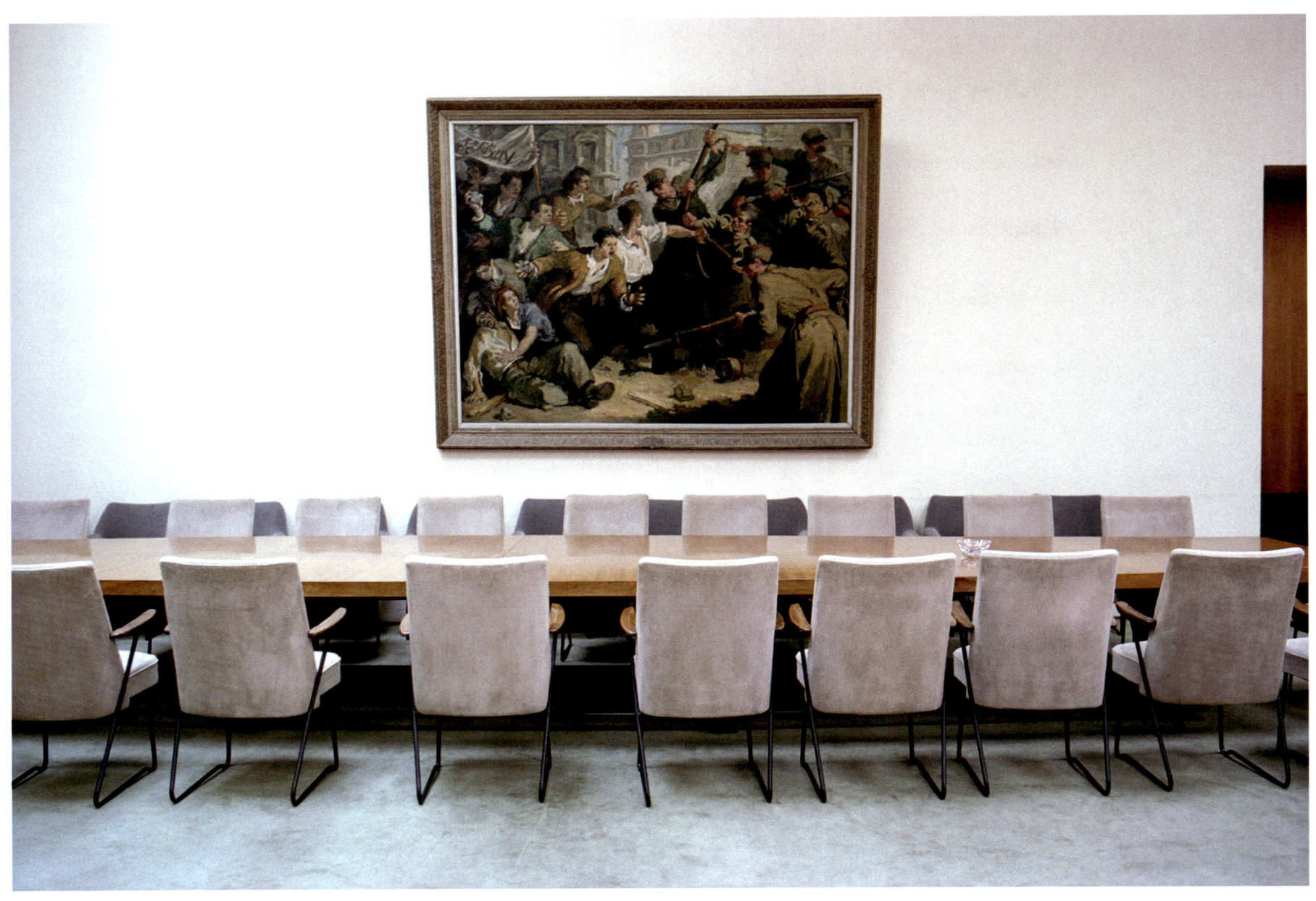

"Mostar" Hall, *14. decembar 1939. - Hleb narodu*, Đorde Andrejević Kun. Inside the Federal Executive Council Building, Belgrade, Serbia

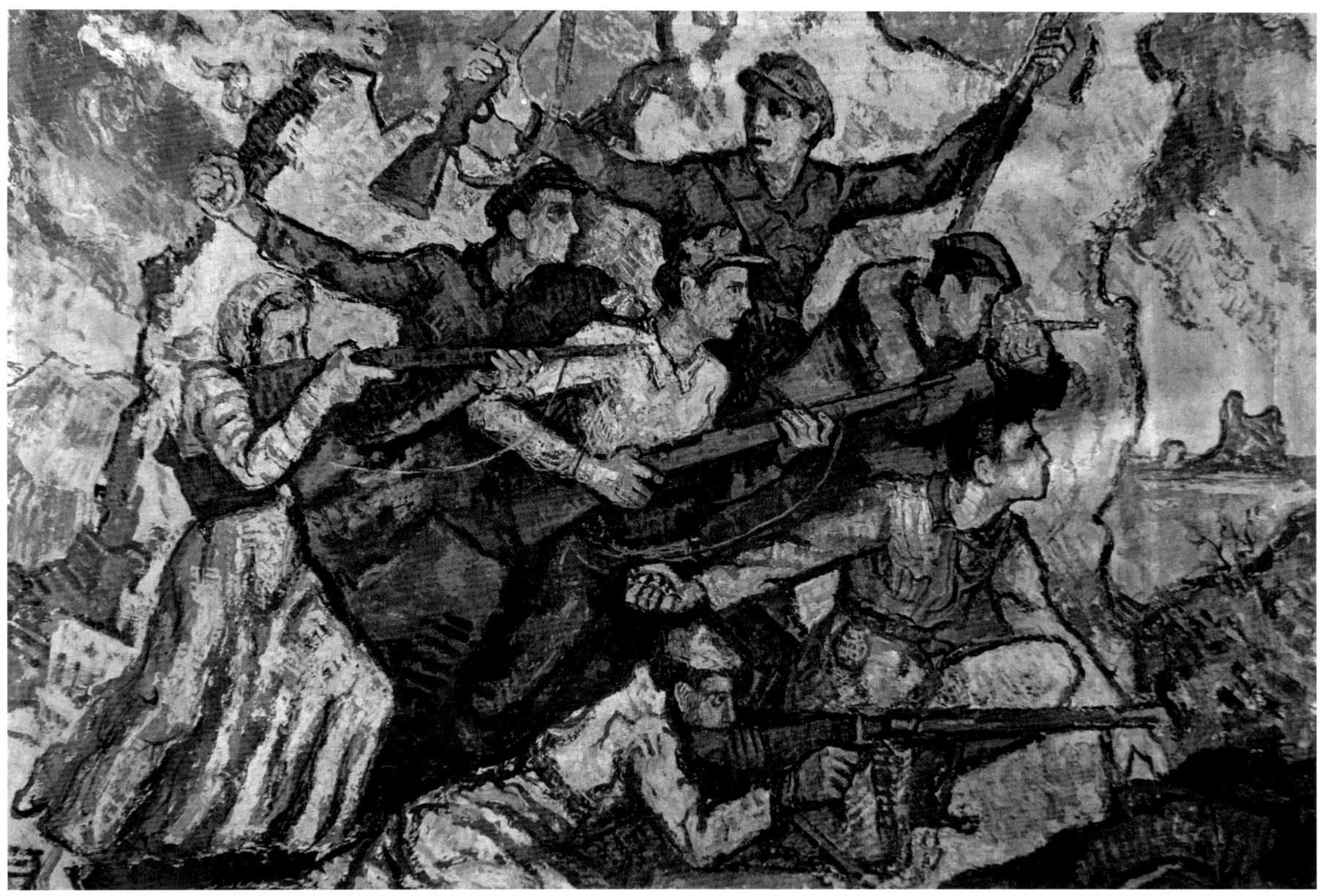

The Salon of the Socialist Republic of Montenegro. Inside the Federal Executive Council Building, Belgrade, Serbia

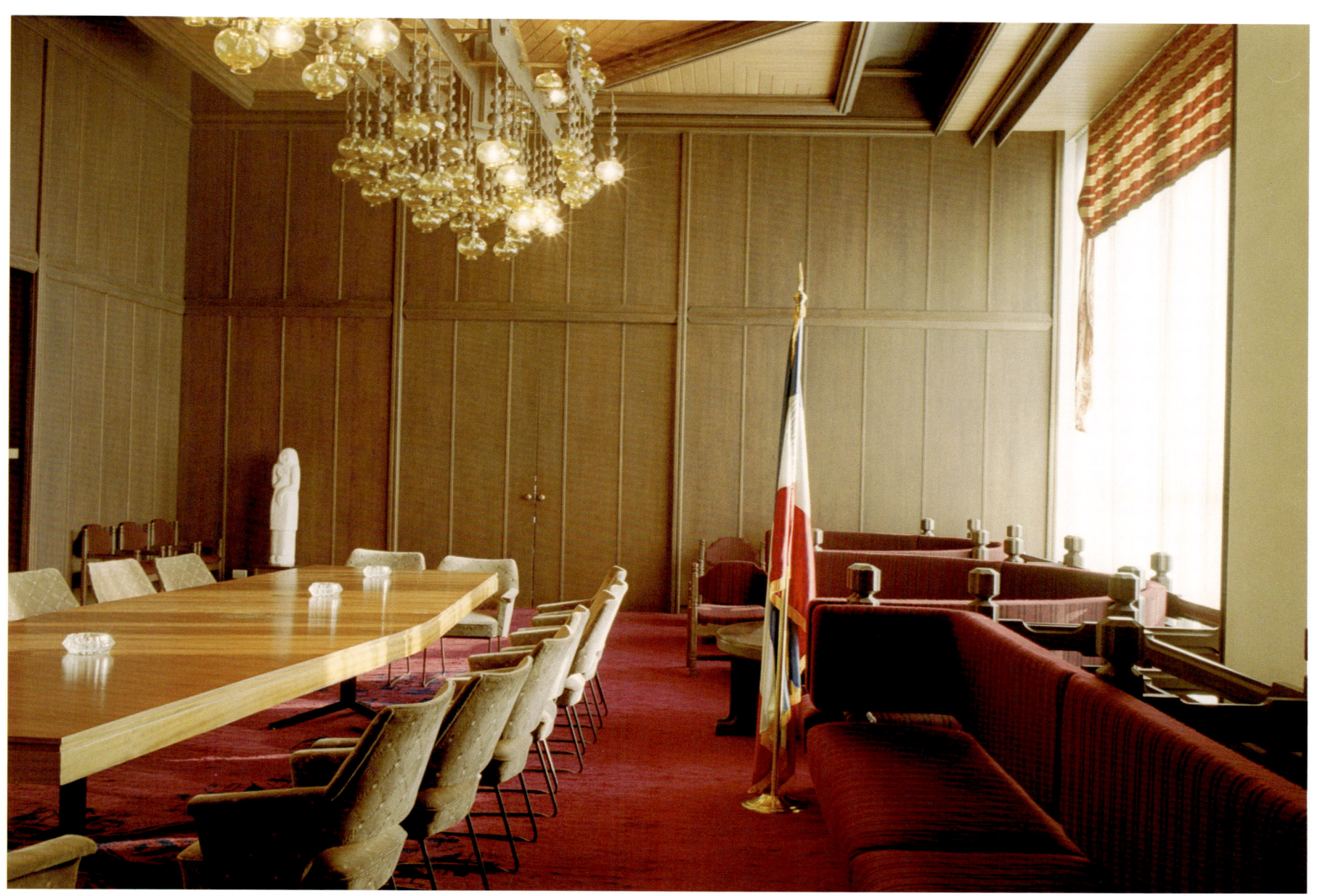

The Salon of the Socialist Republic of Slovenia. Inside the Federal Executive Council Building, Belgrade, Serbia

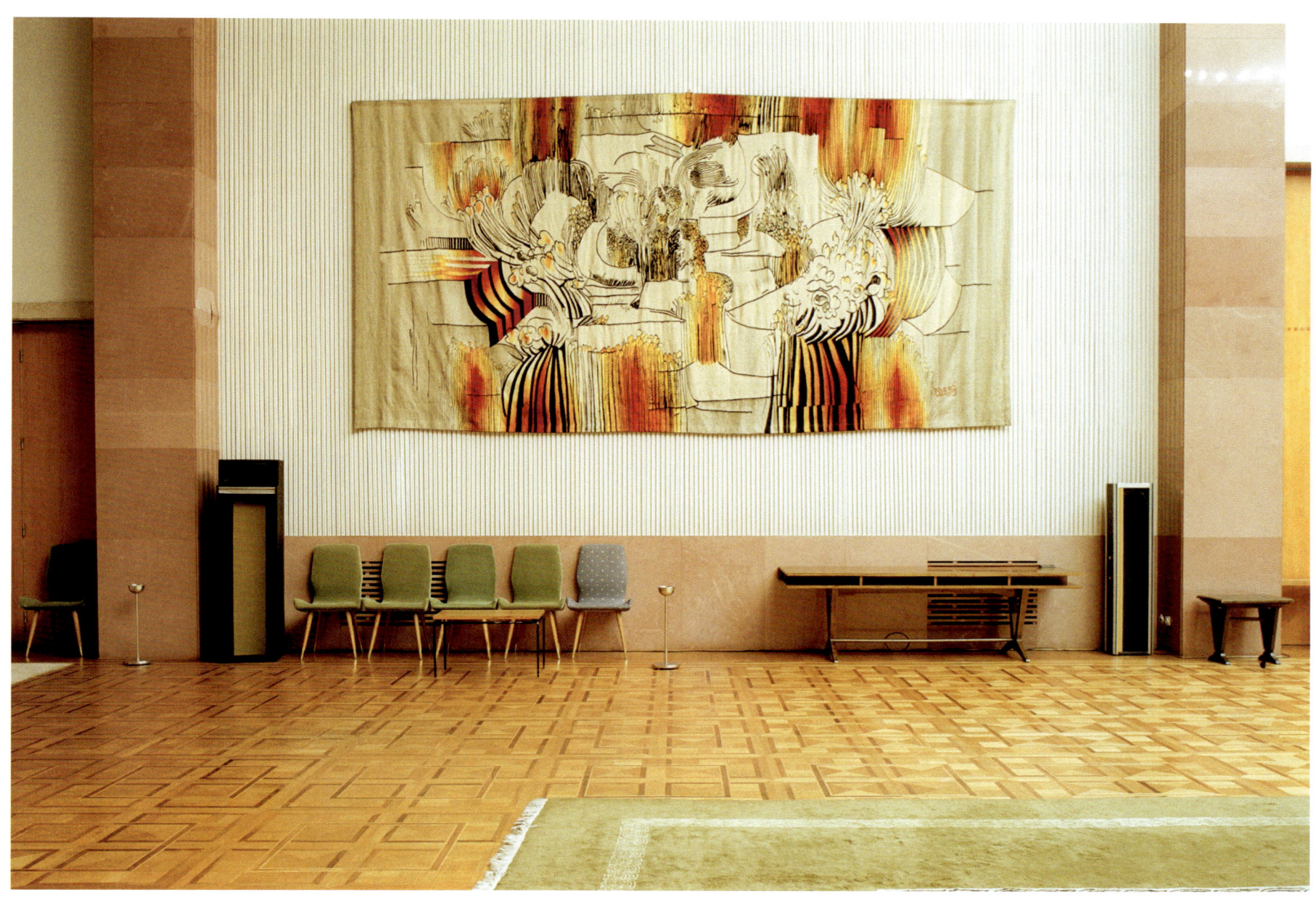

Plant Life II. Inside the Chase One Plaza Building, Manhattan, NY

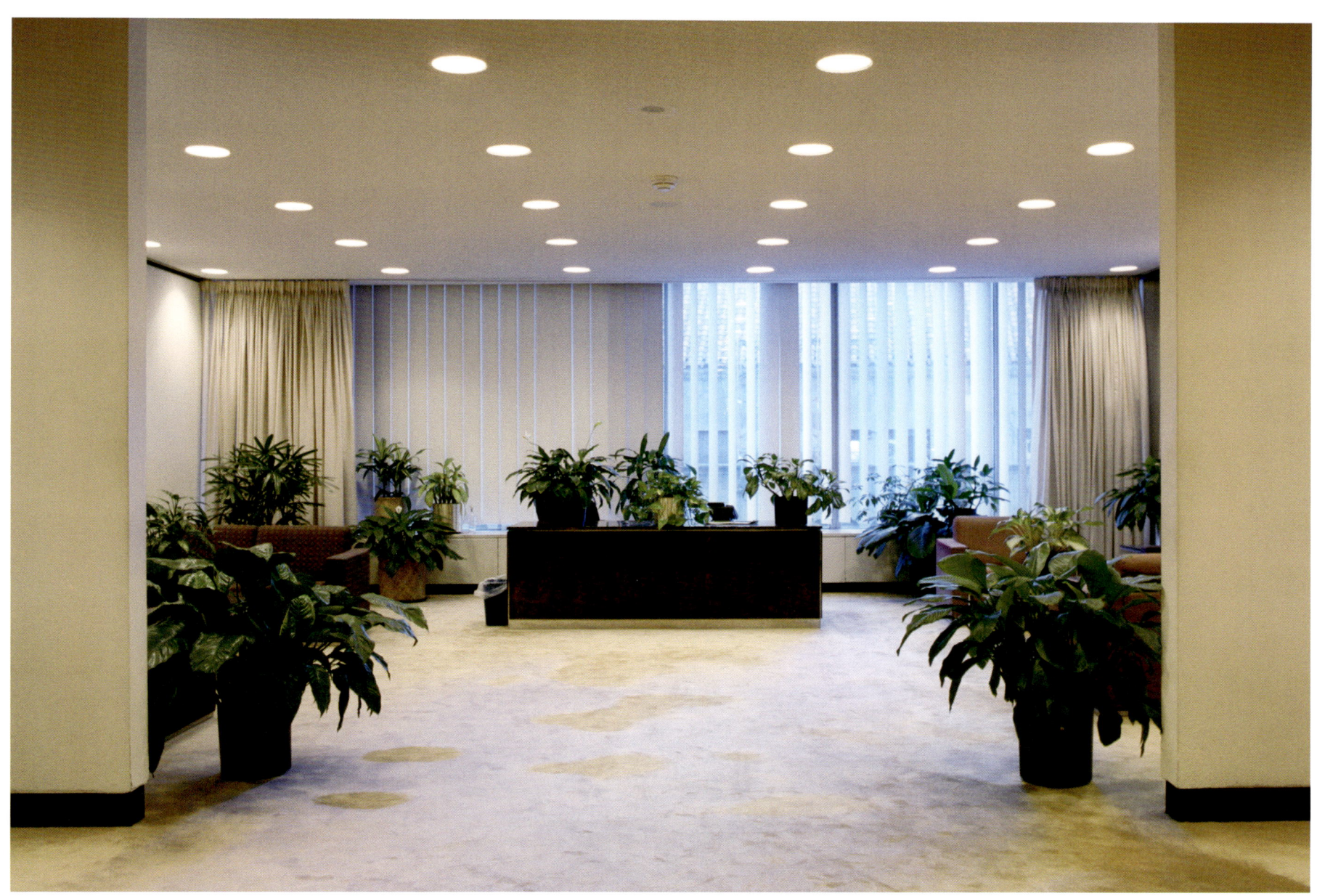

Plant Life I. Inside the Chase One Plaza Building, Manhattan, NY

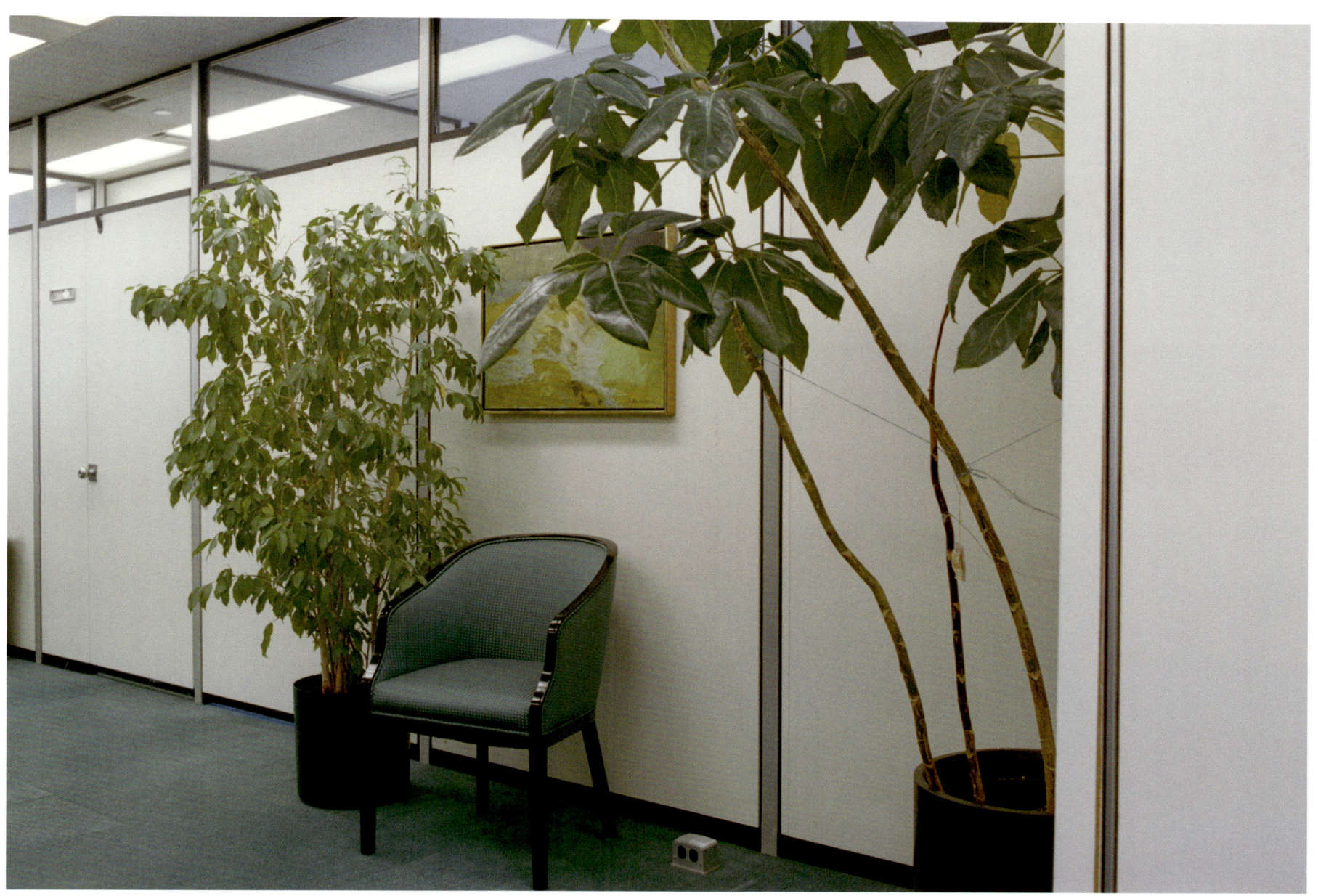

Yugoslavia Hall, *Kompozicija 75 – Vrt*, Mateja Rodići. Inside the Federal Executive Council Building, Belgrade, Serbia

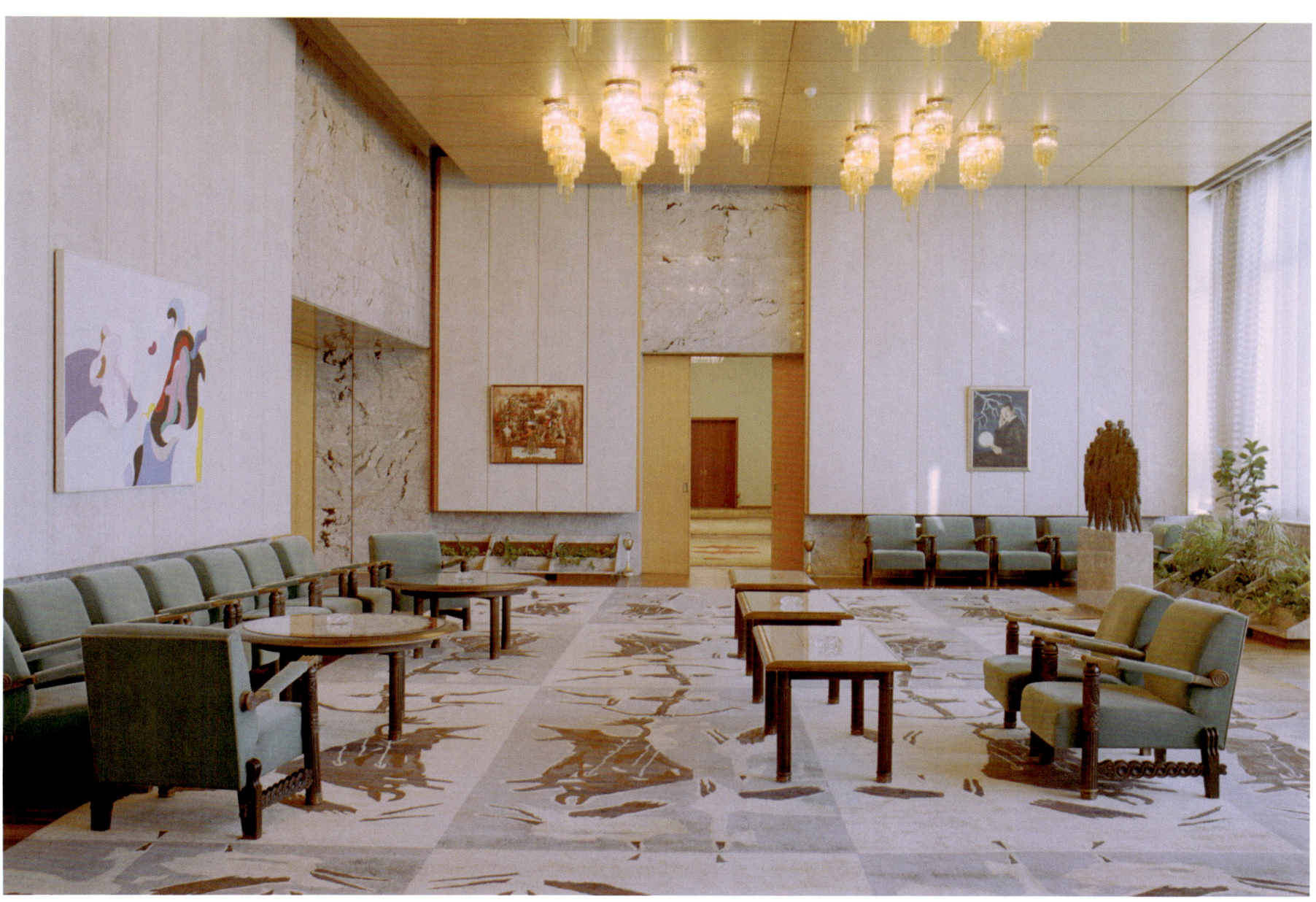

Christmas Sun. Inside the Chase One Plaza Building, Manhattan, NY

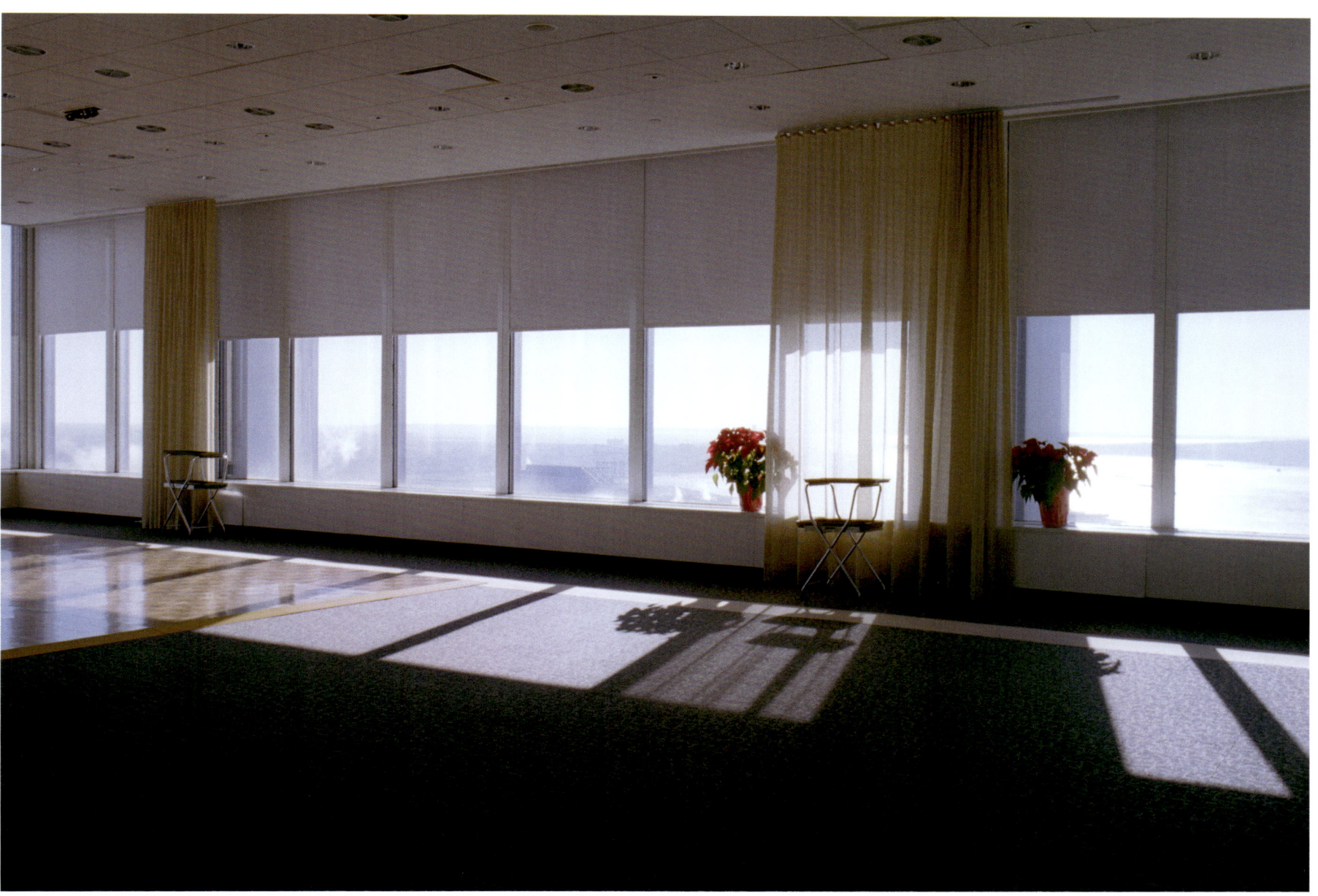

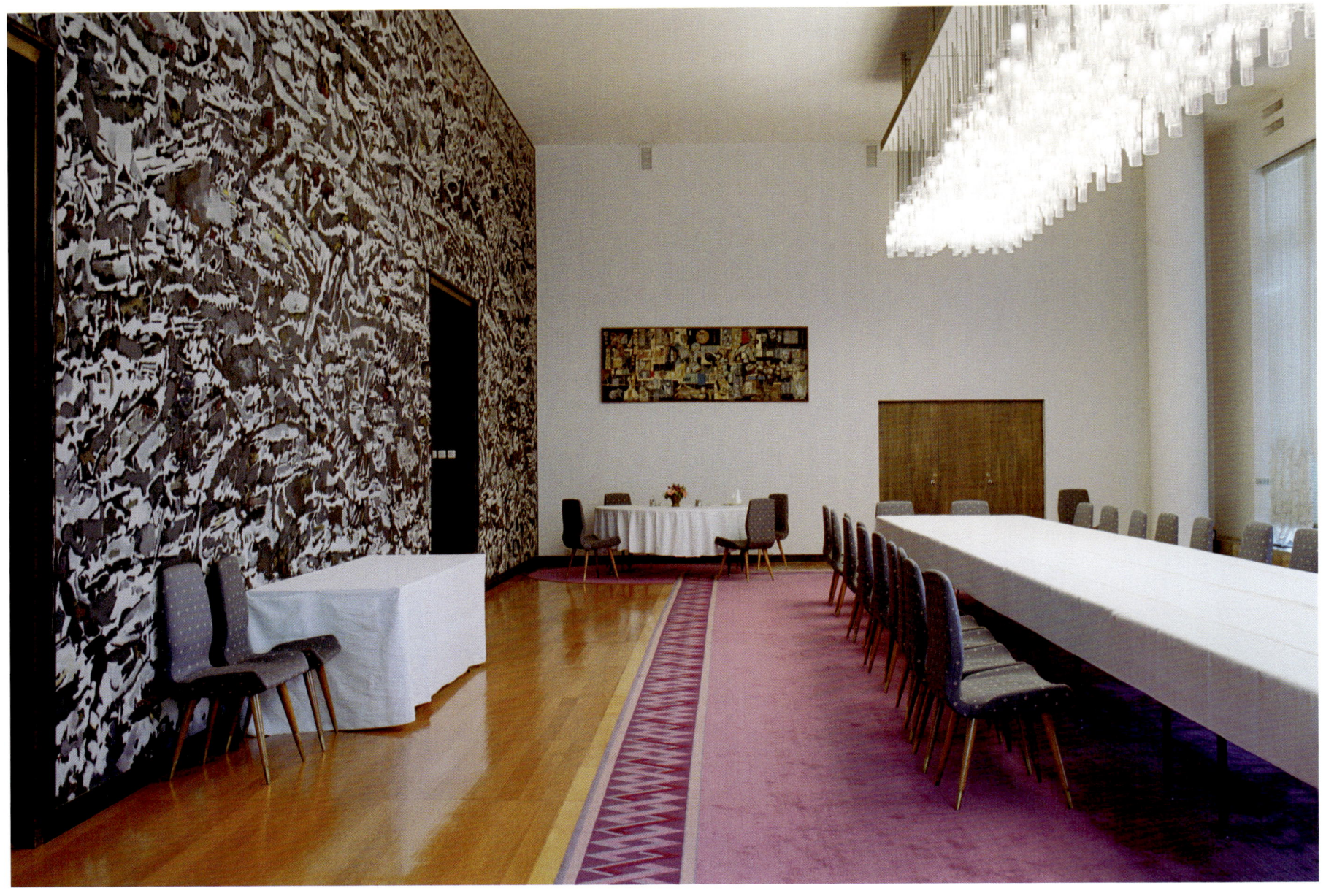

The Salon of the Socialist Republic of Croatia. Inside the Federal Executive Council Building, Belgrade, Serbia

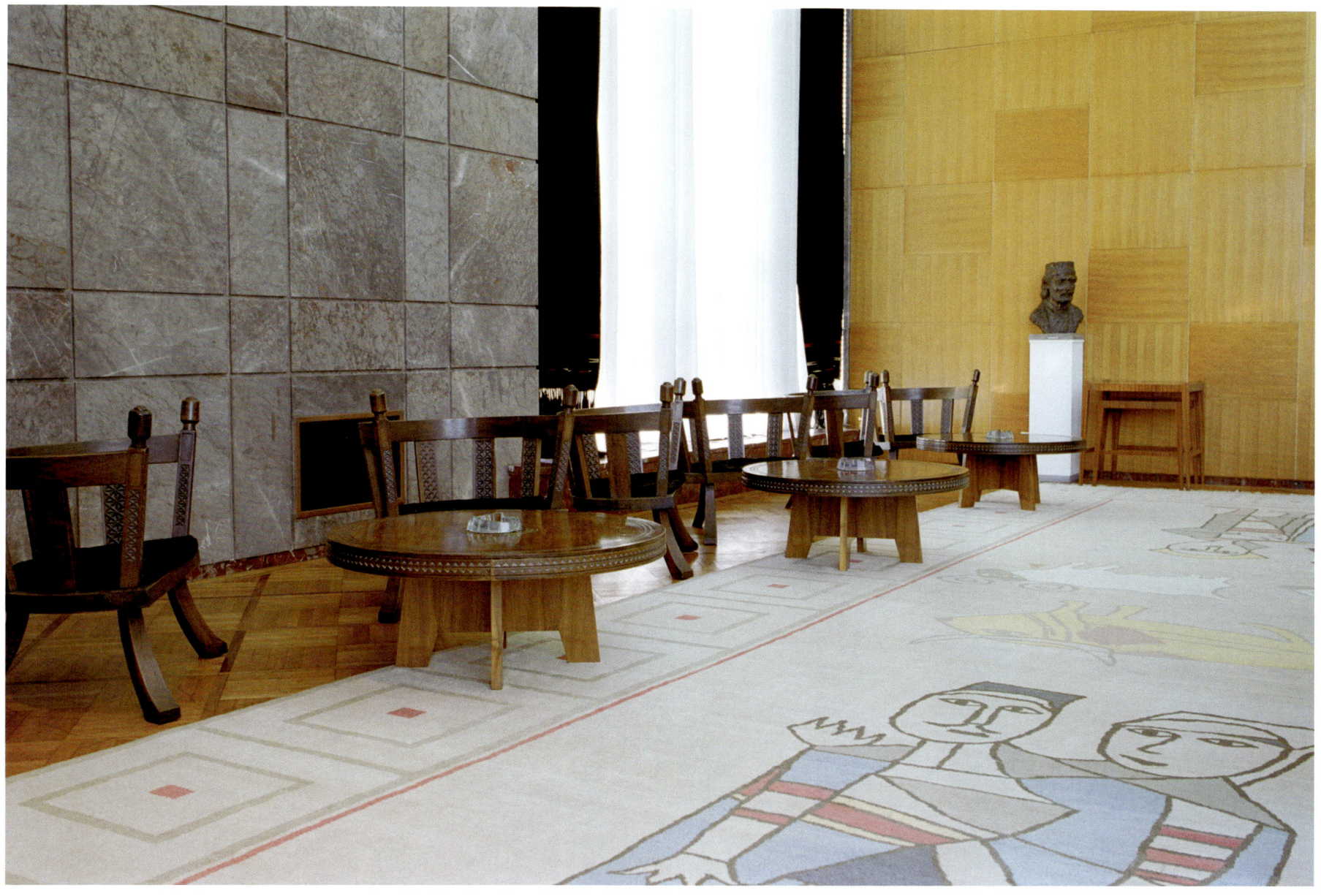

The Salon of the Socialist Republic of Montenegro. Inside the Federal Executive Council Building, Belgrade, Serbia

Waiting Room. Inside the Federal Executive Council Building, Belgrade, Serbia, 2019

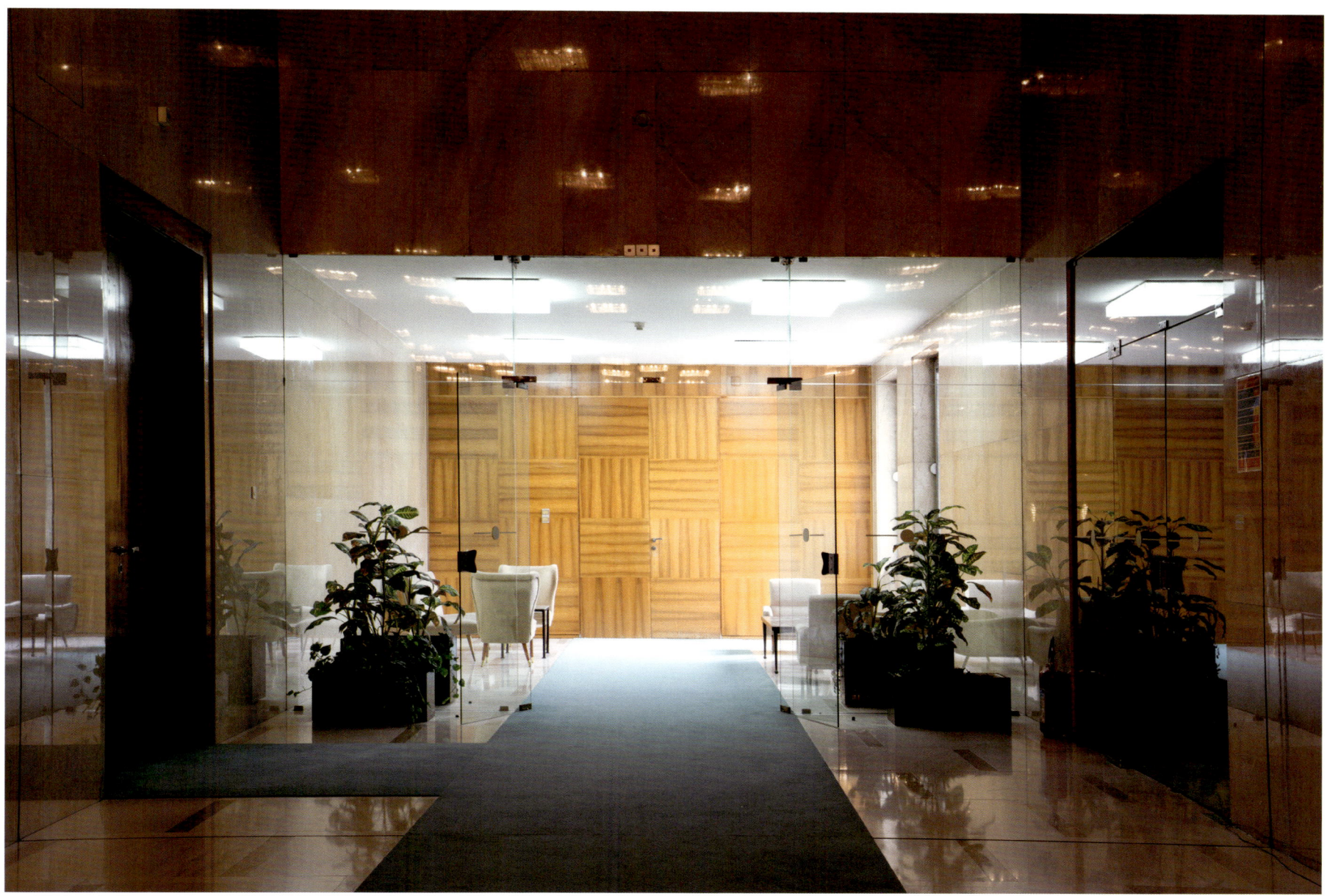

Pattern. Inside the Federal Executive Council Building, Belgrade, Serbia, 2019

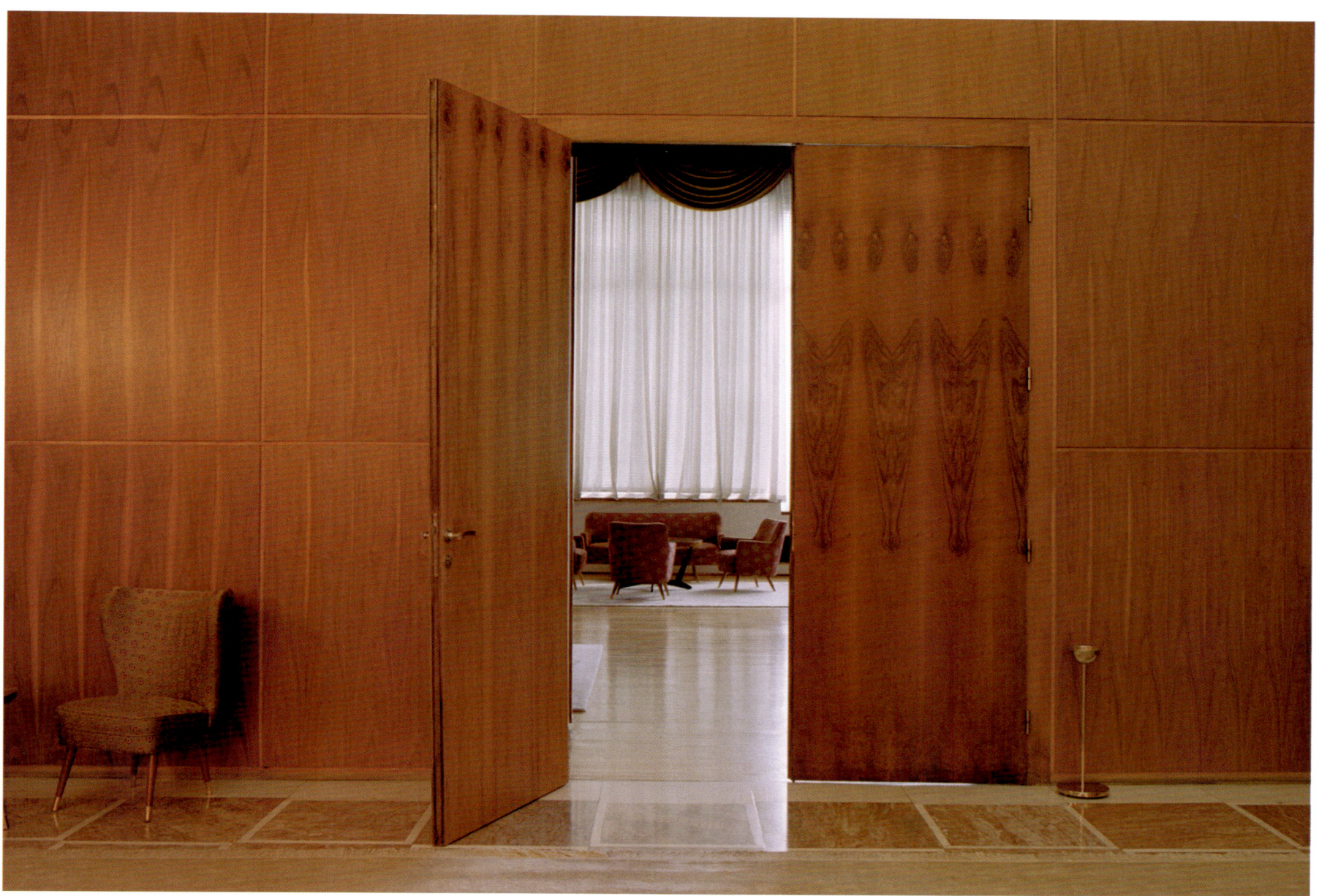

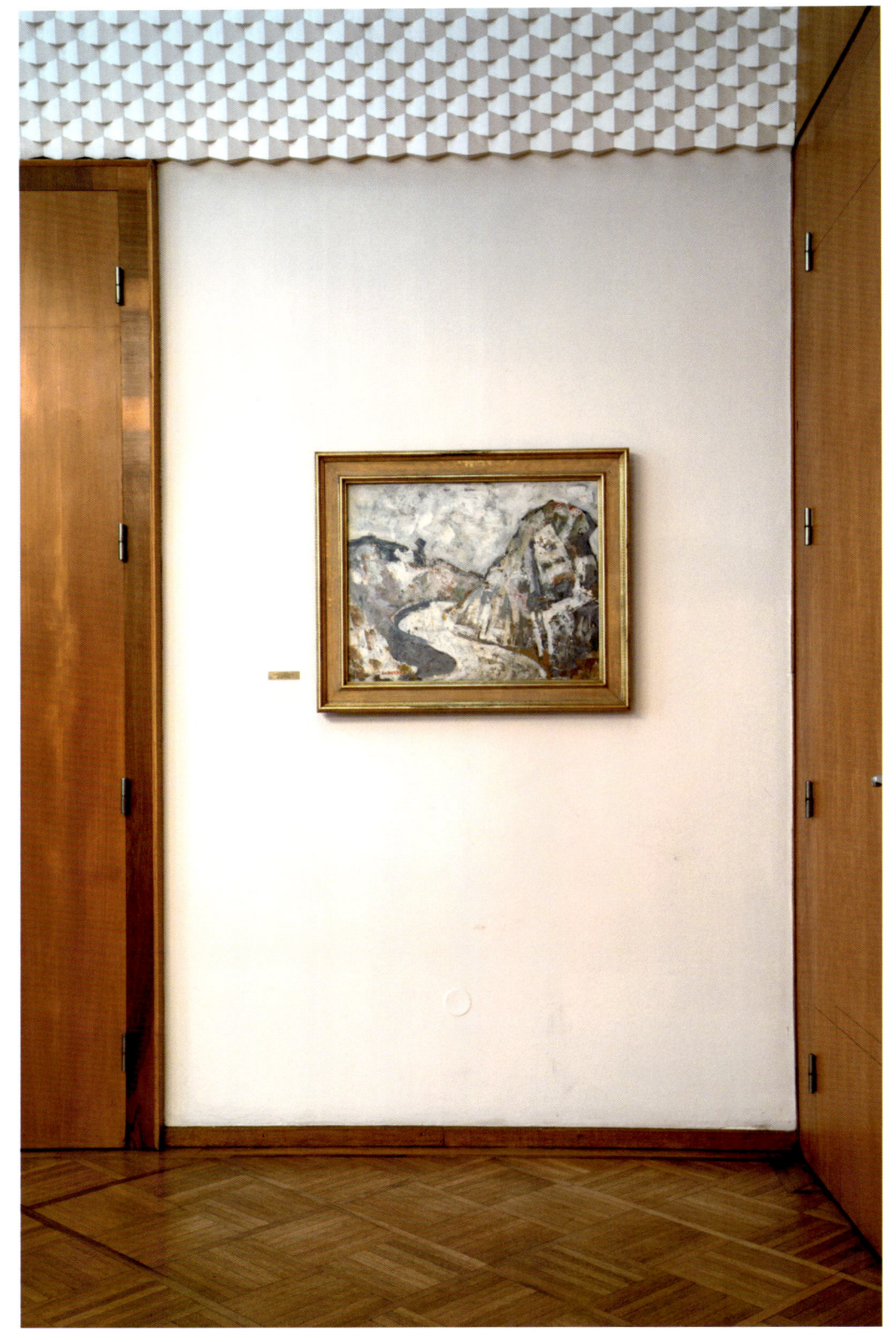

Lubarda. Inside the Federal Executive Council Building,
Belgrade, Serbia, 2019

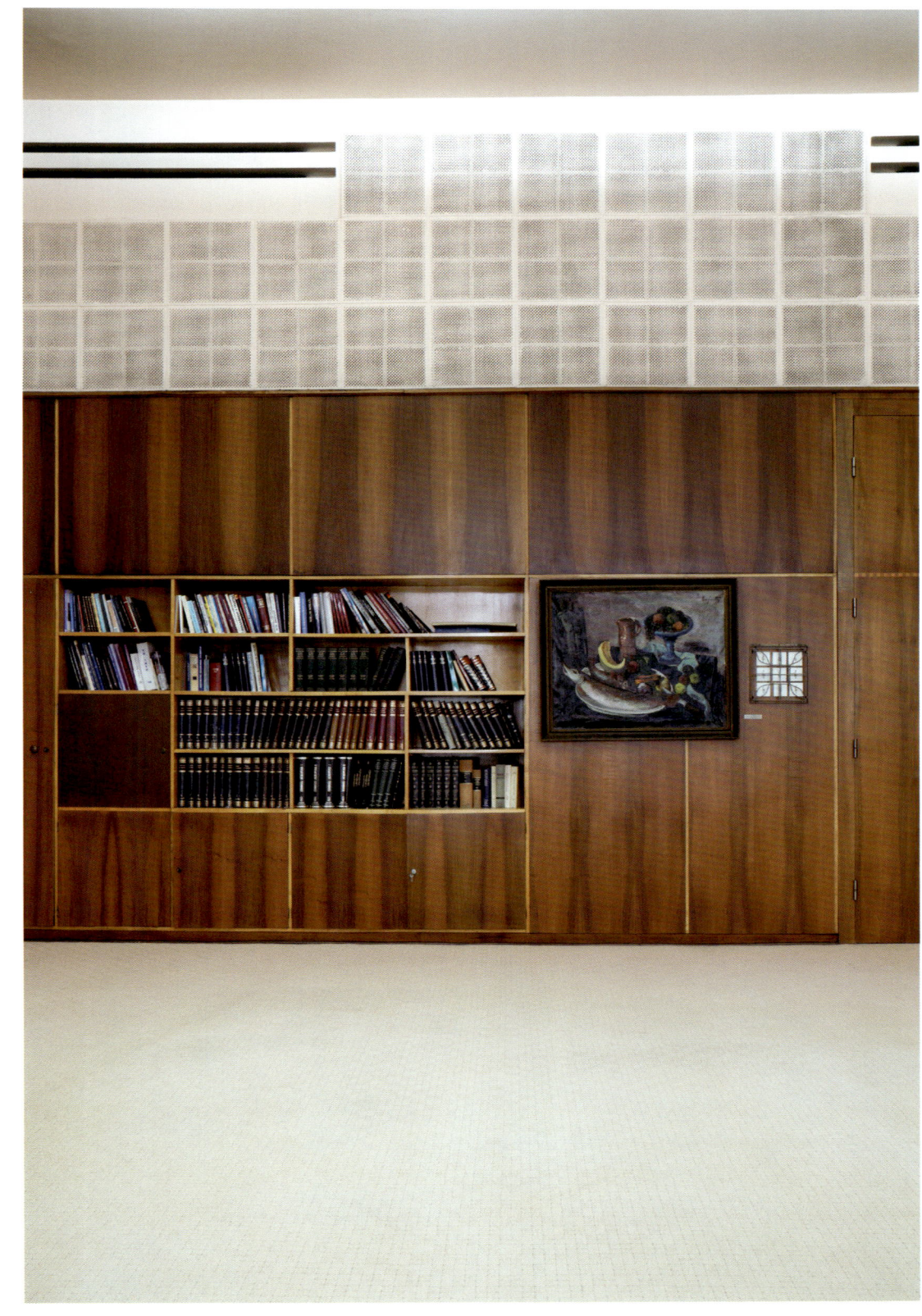

Library. Inside the Federal Executive Council Building,
Belgrade, Serbia, 2019

In-between Cabinet. Inside the Federal Executive Council Building, Belgrade, Serbia, 2019

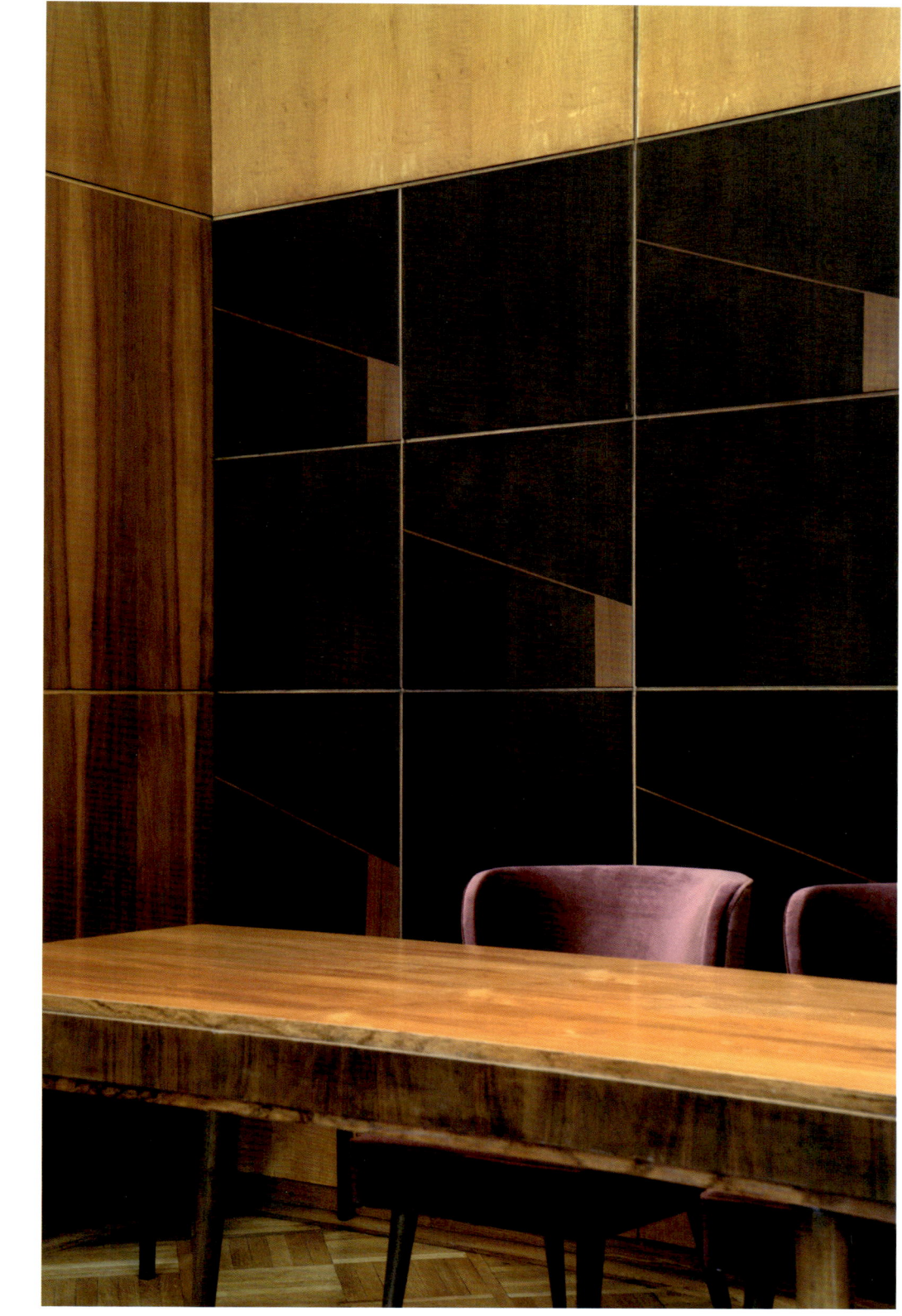

Color Temperature Blue (CTB), 2019

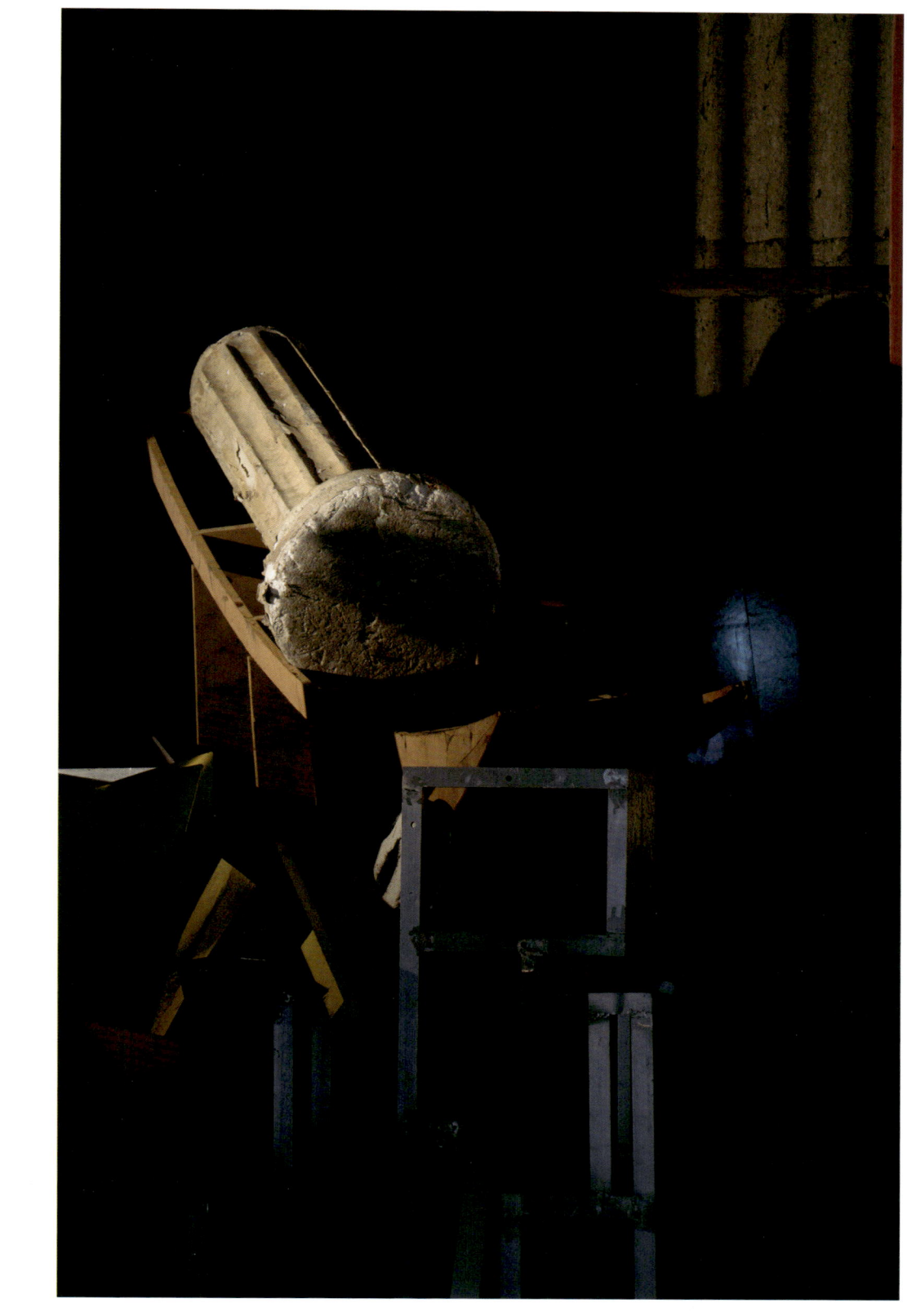

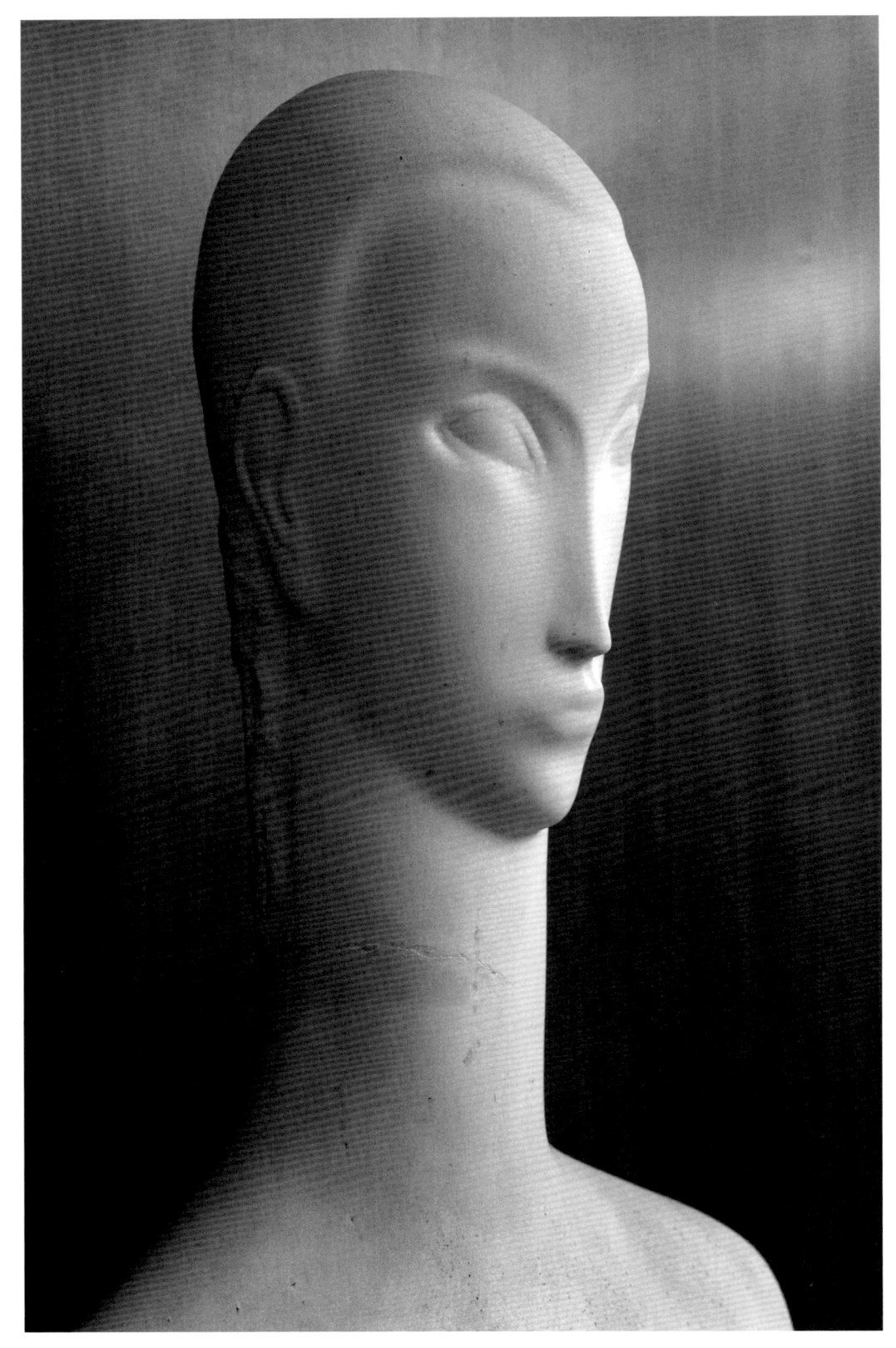

Figure 1. Inside the Federal Executive Council Building, Belgrade, Serbia, 2019

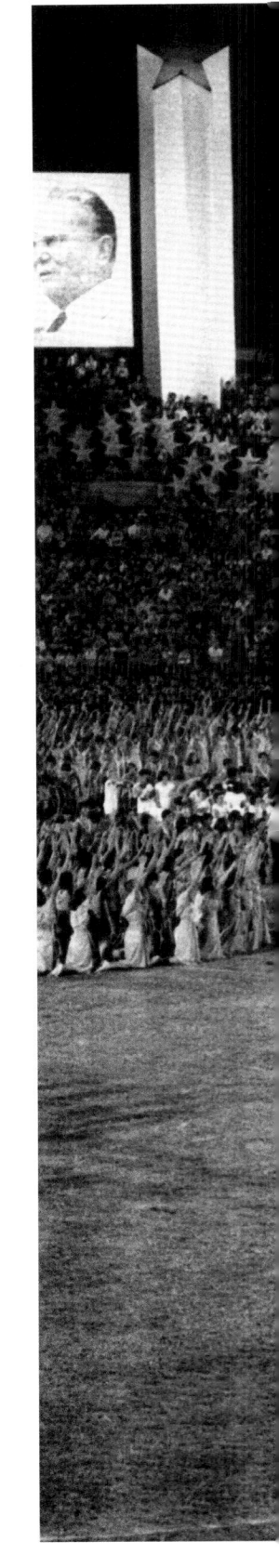

Youth Day Celebration, Yugoslav National Army Stadium, May 25, 1979, 2014

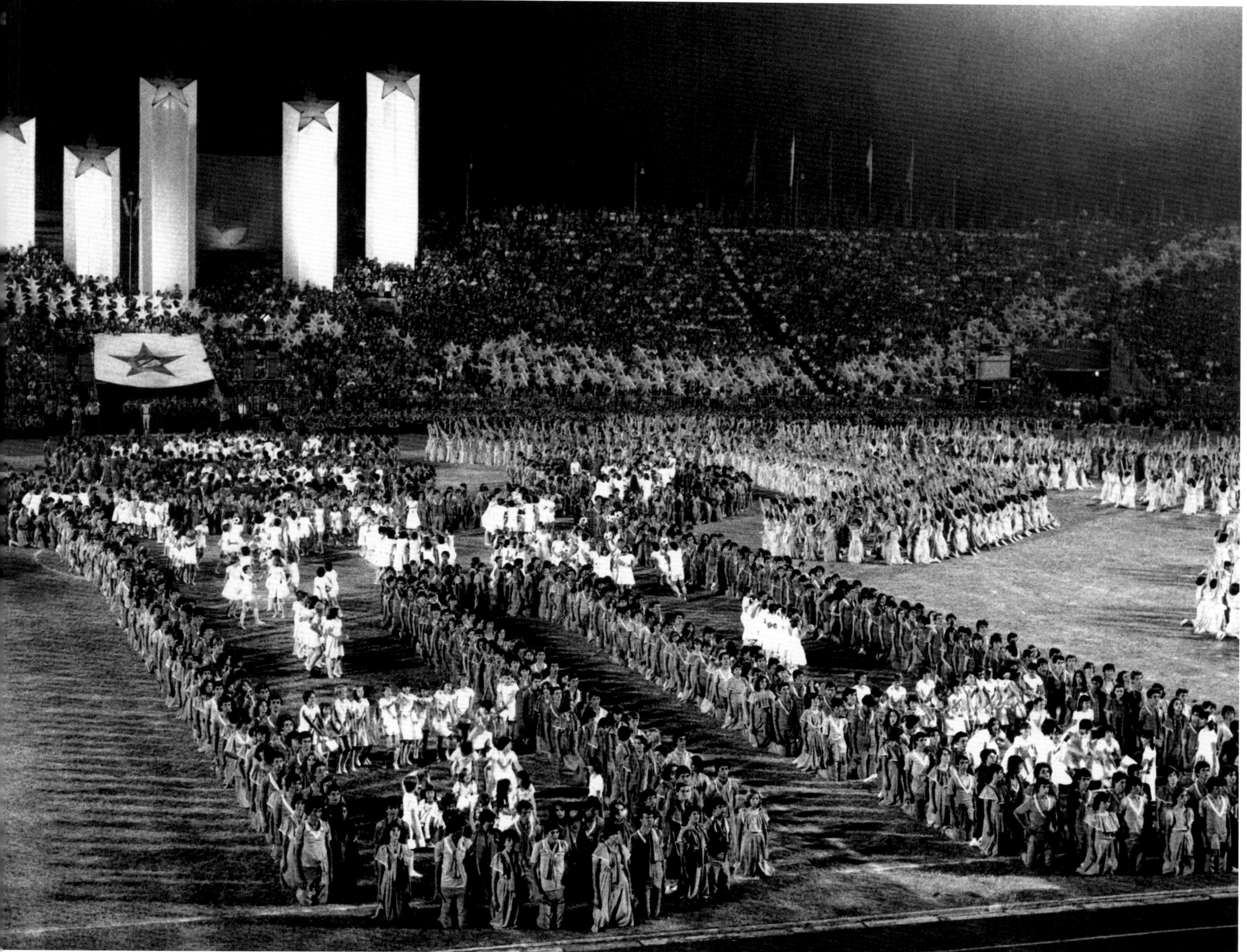

Ceiling Systems, 2019

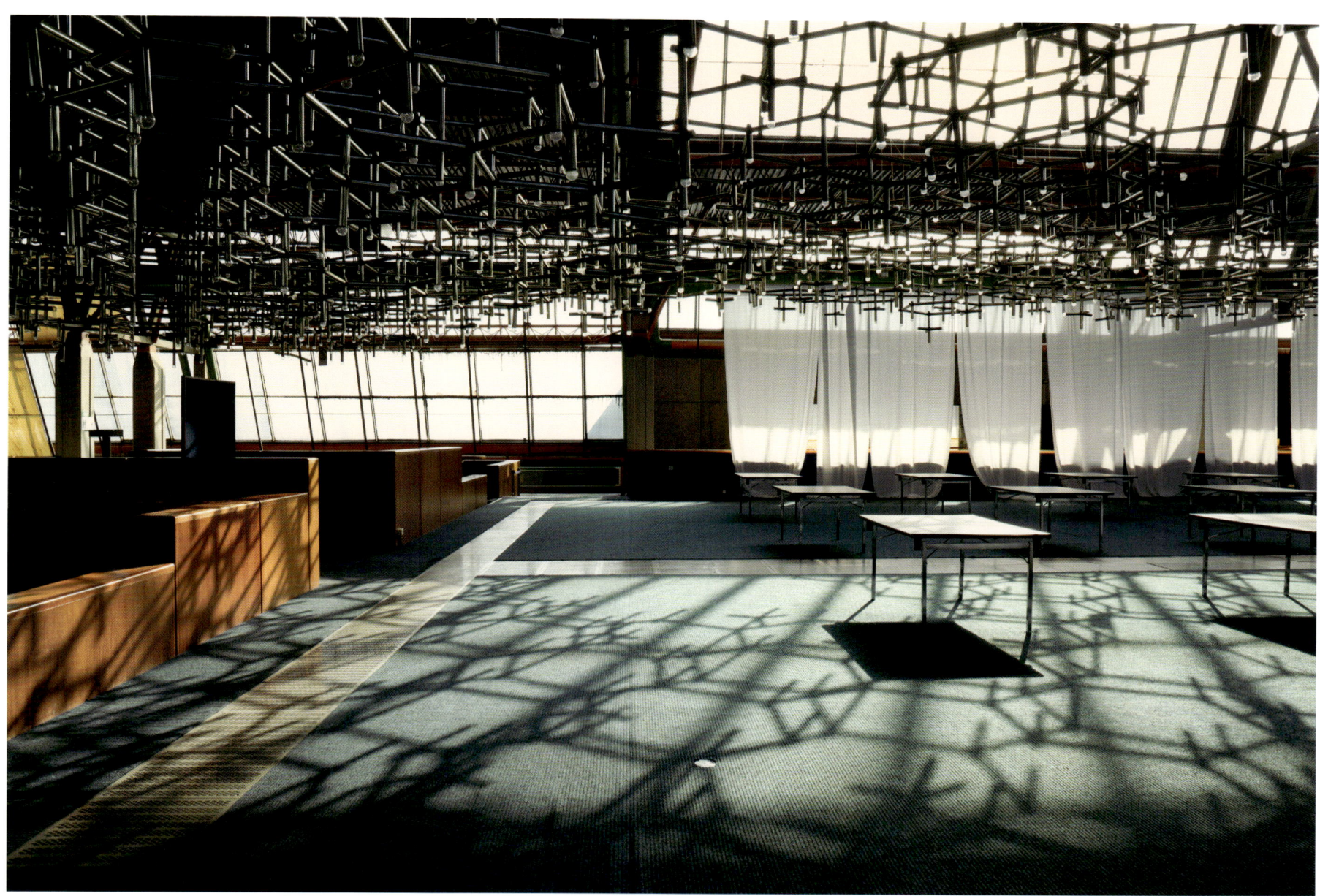

Protocol, 2019

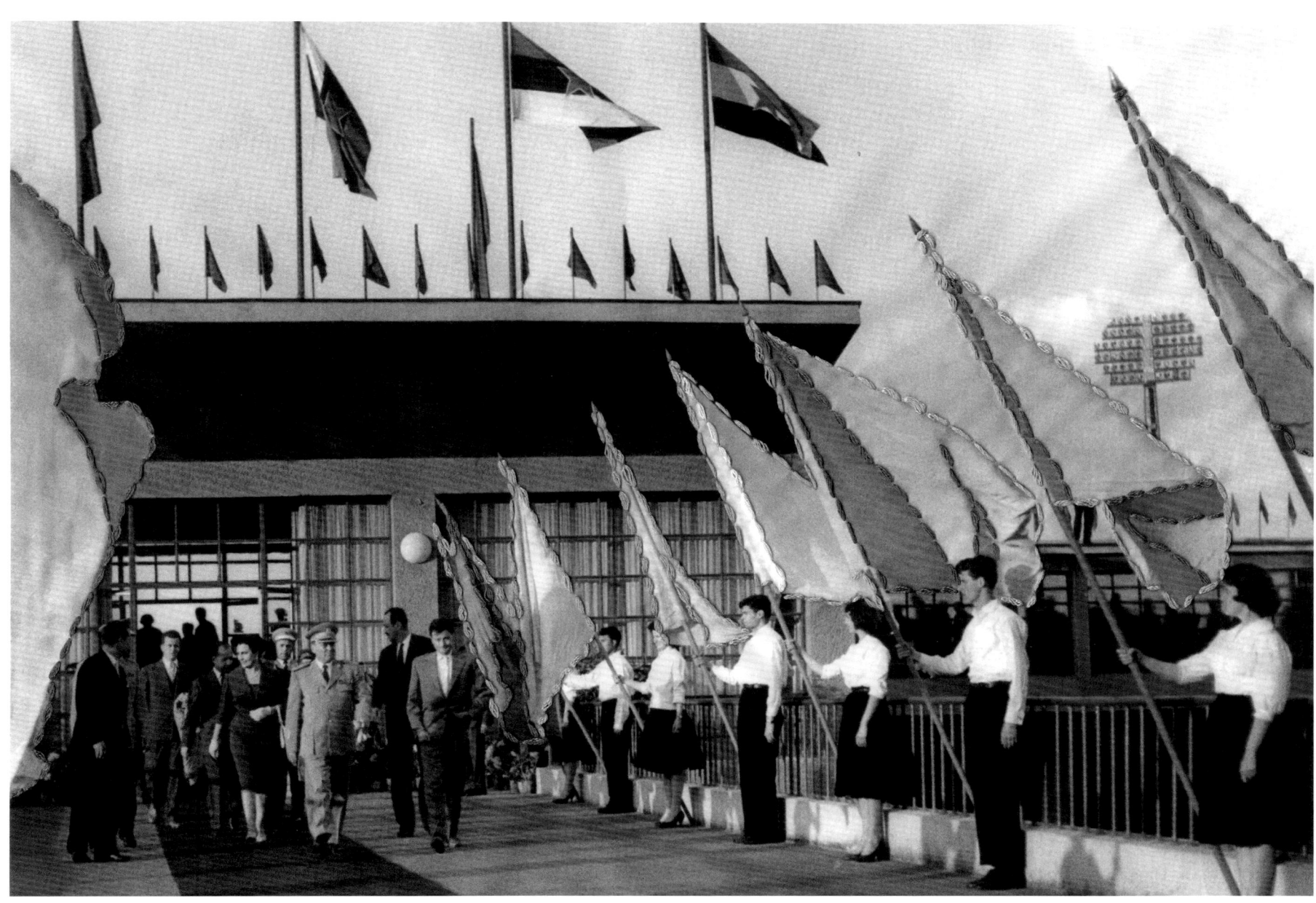

Stadium, 2019

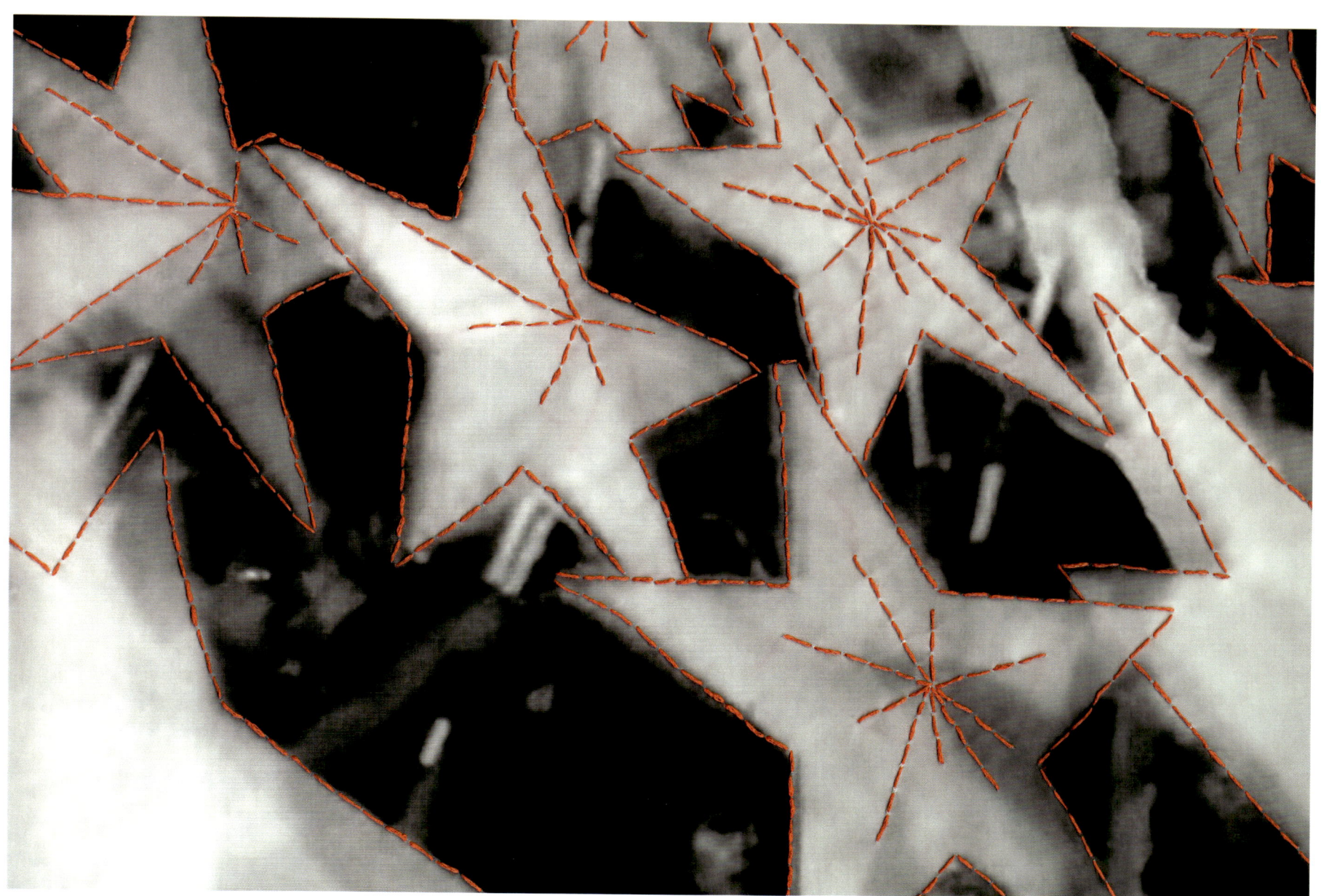

Fireworks, 2019

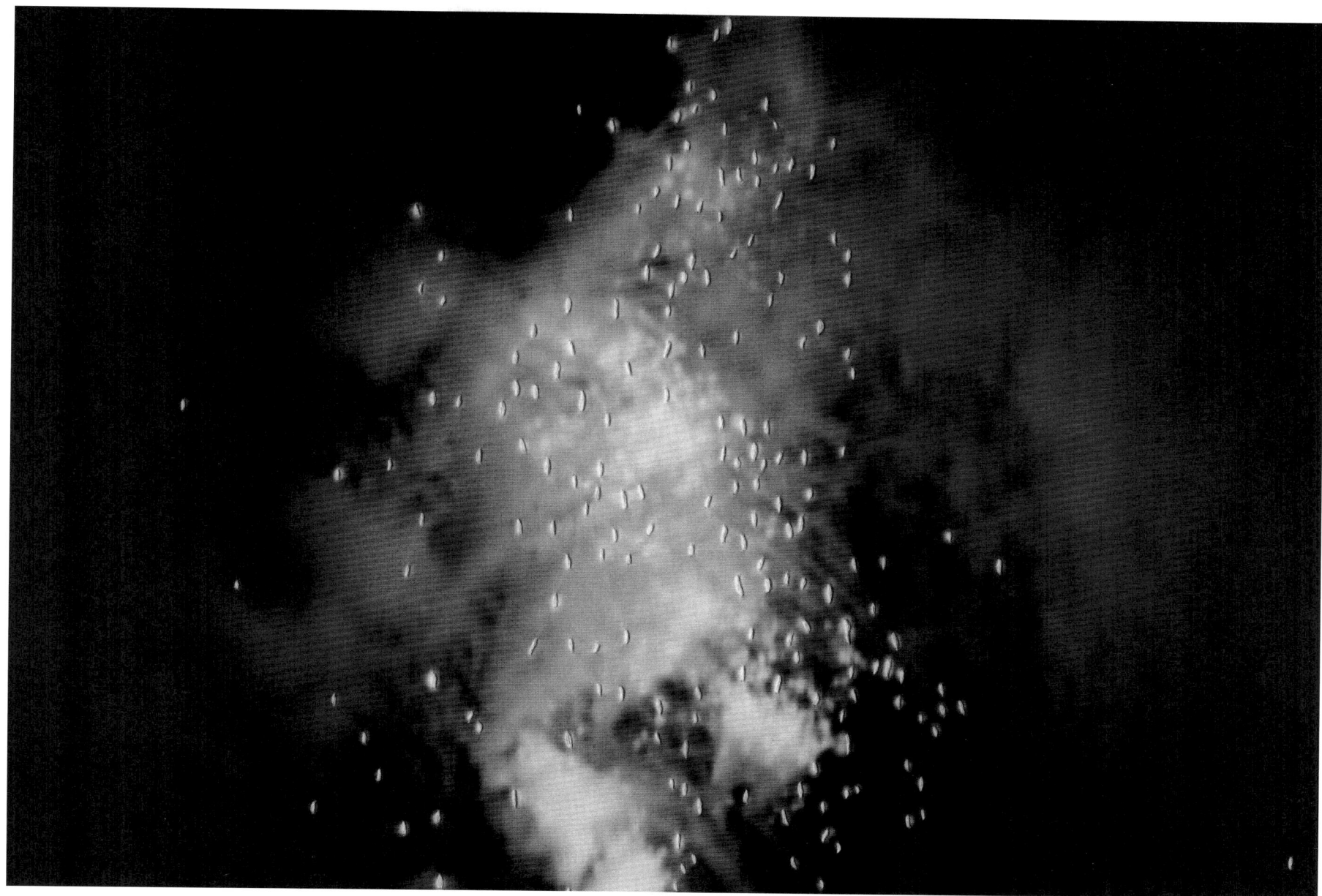

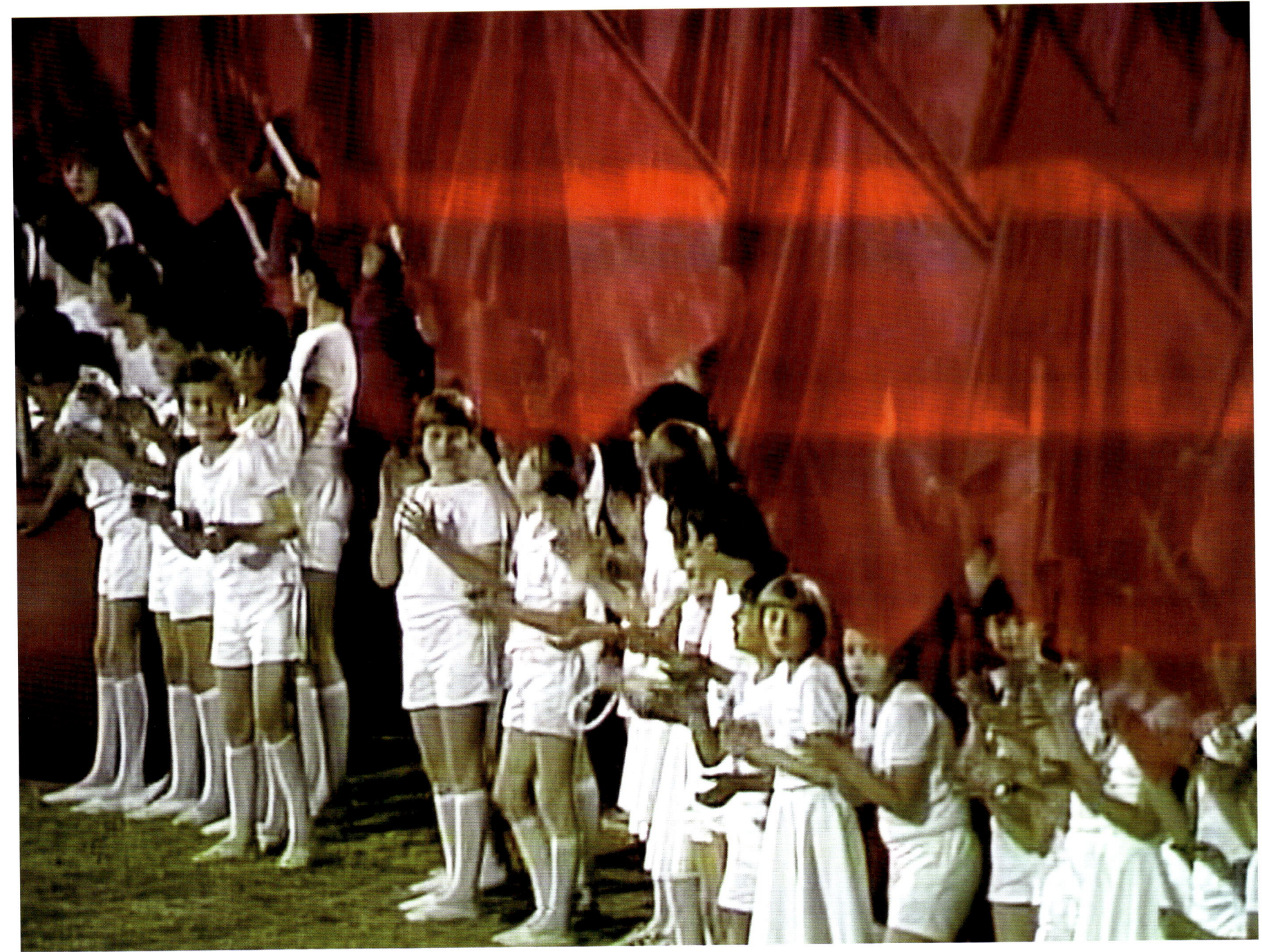

Video Still, May 25, 1979, Television Belgrade, 2015

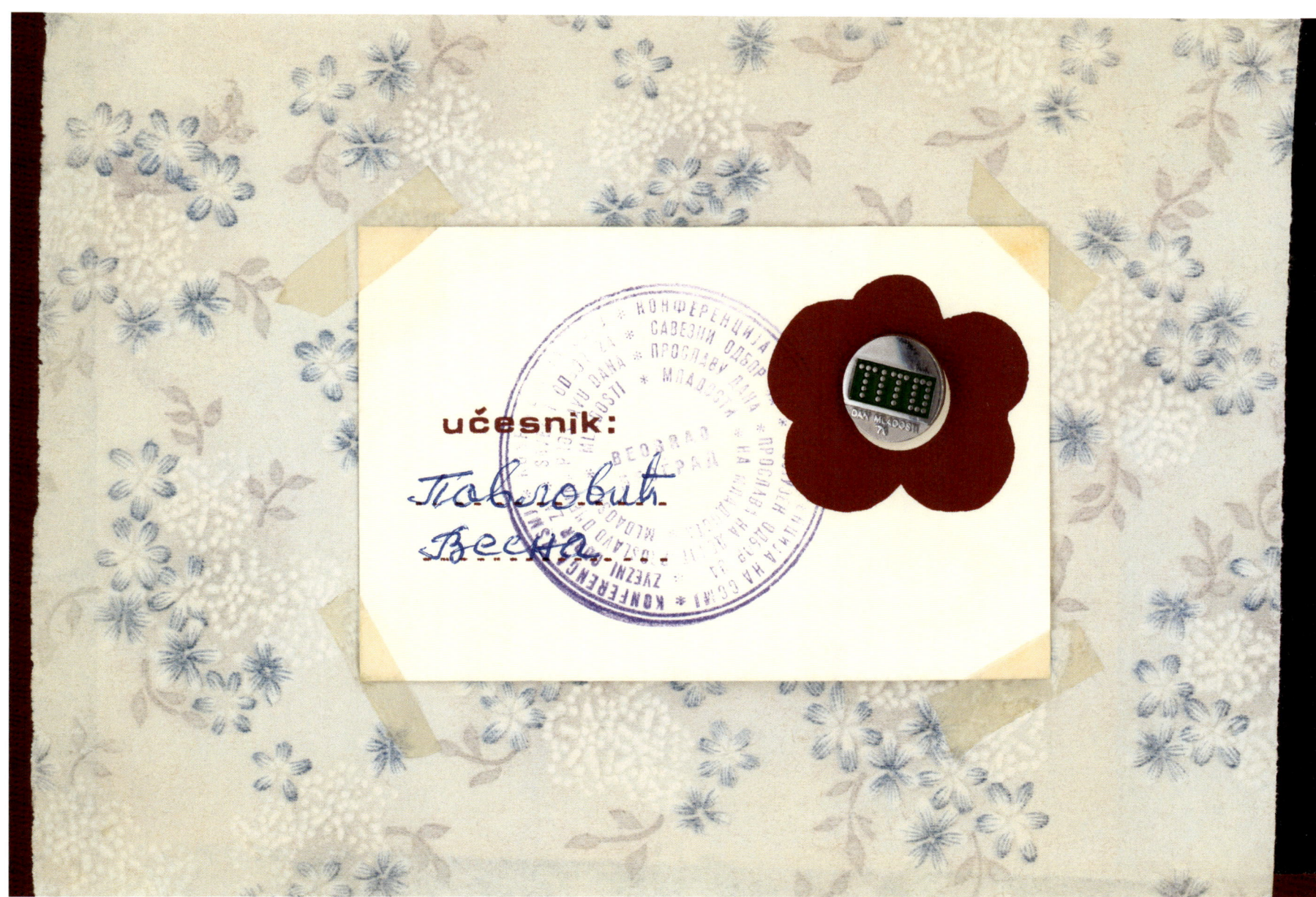

Participant, 2014

Test Card, May 25, 1979, Television Belgrade, 2015

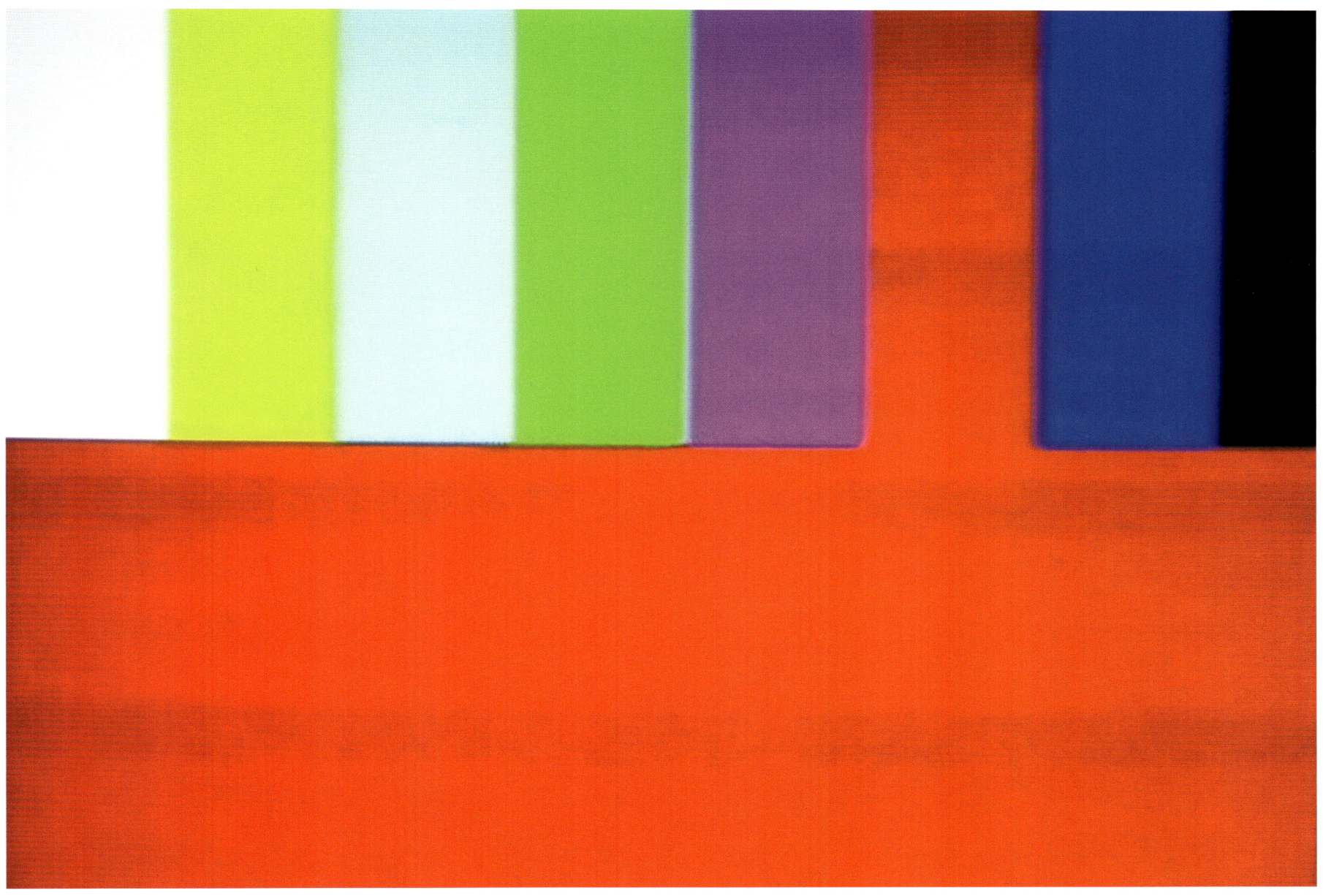

Fototeka (Projection Still III), 2015

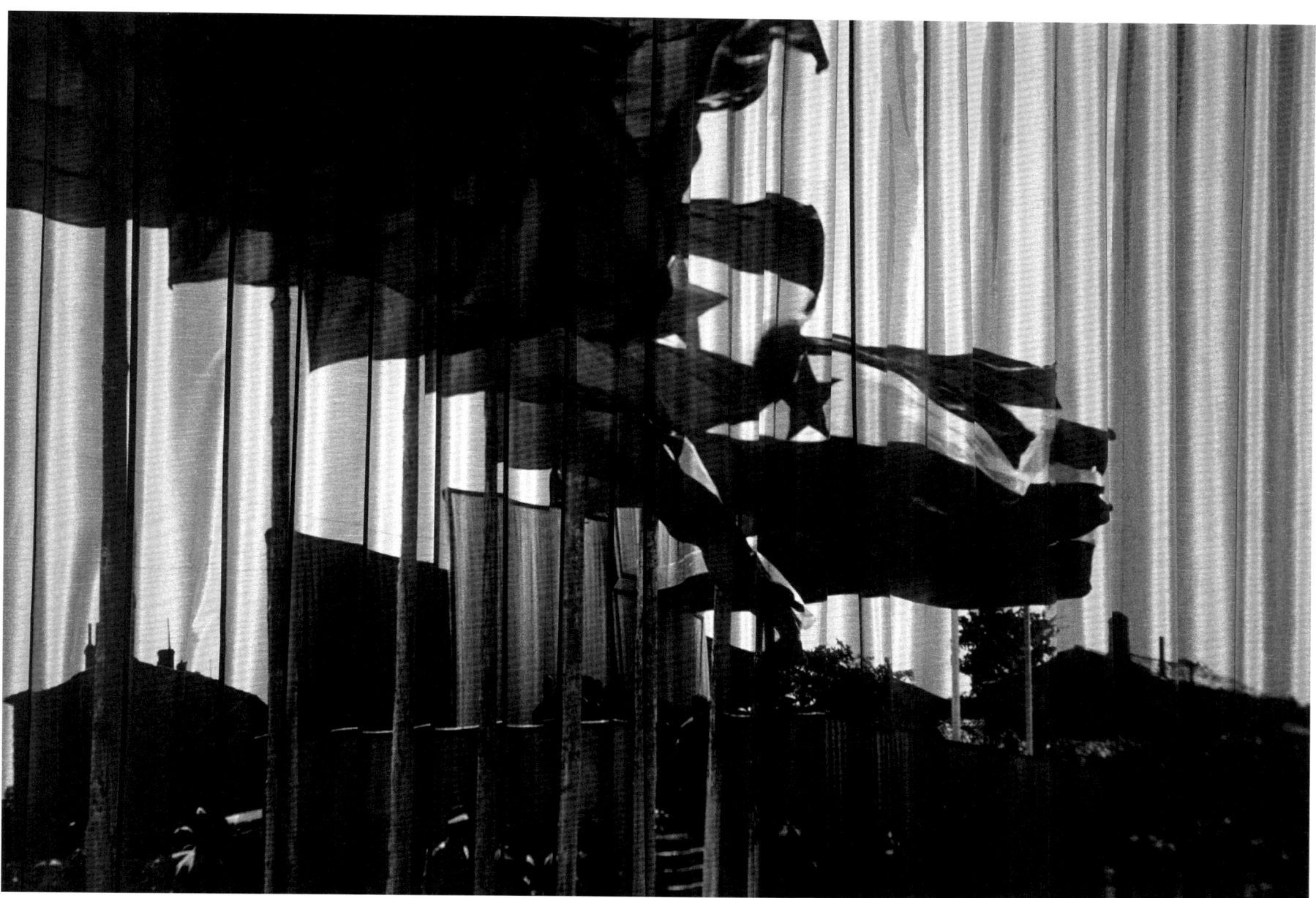

Fototeka (Projection Still VI), 2015

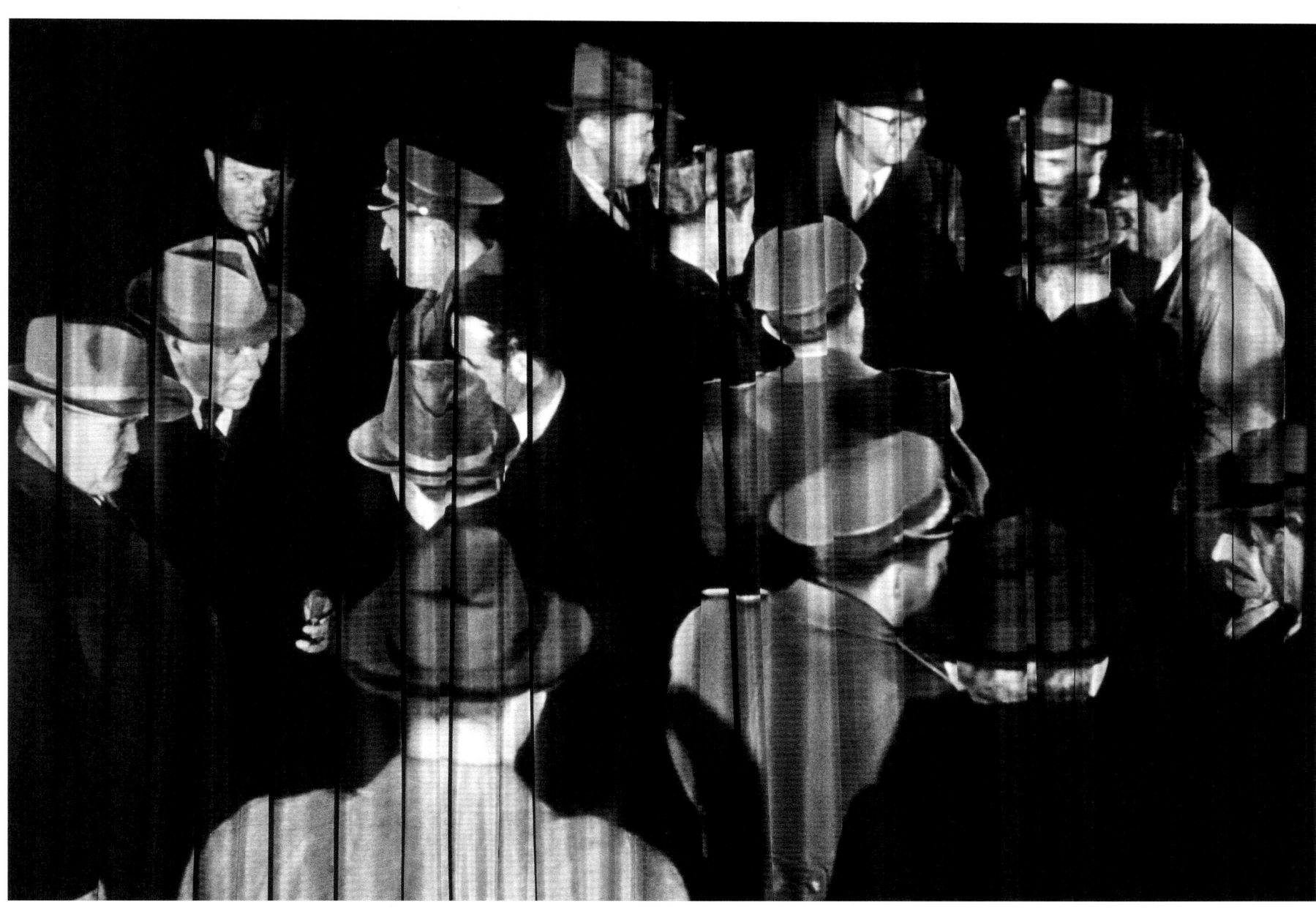

Fototeka (Projection Still IV), 2015

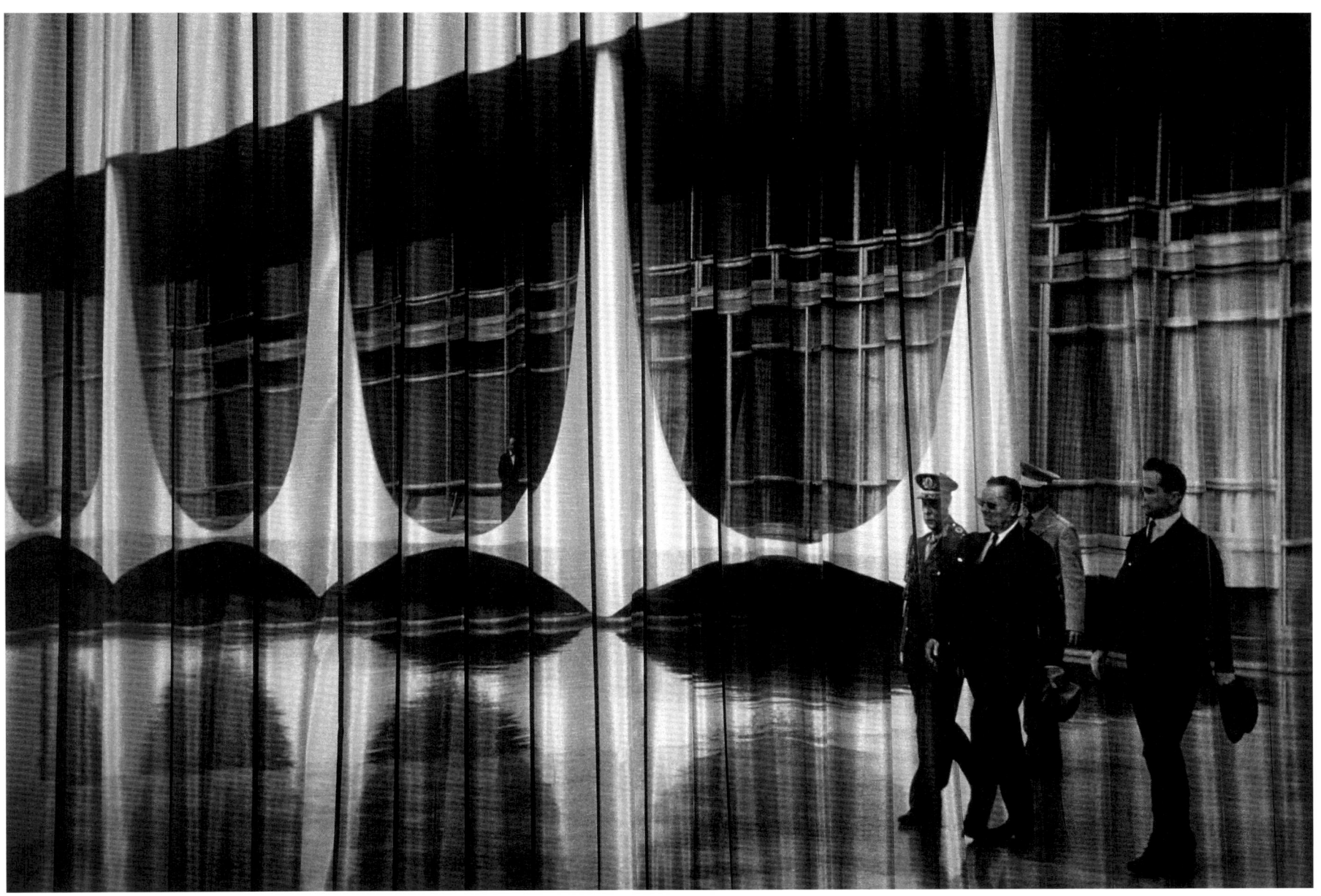

Fototeka (Projection Still I), 2015

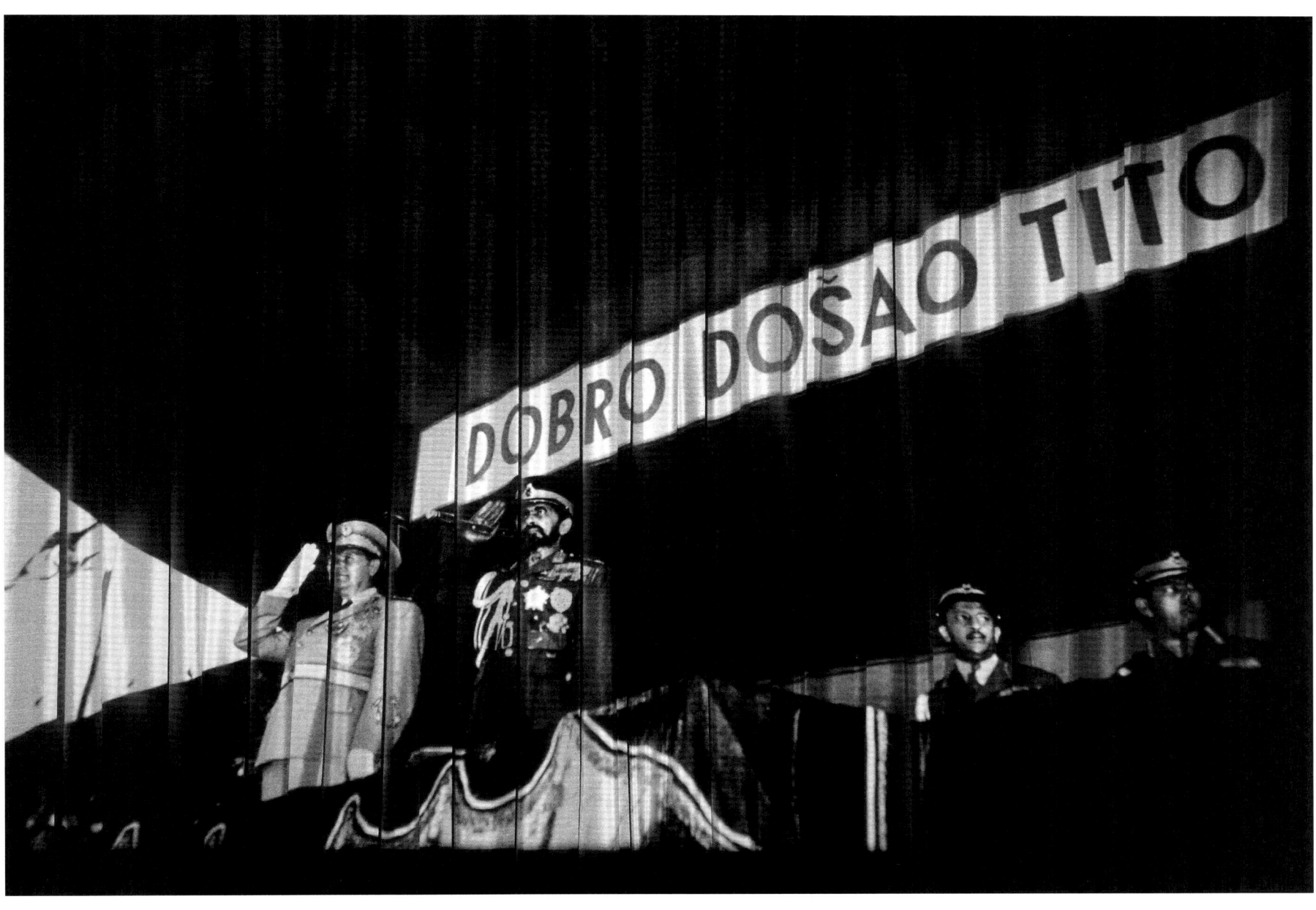

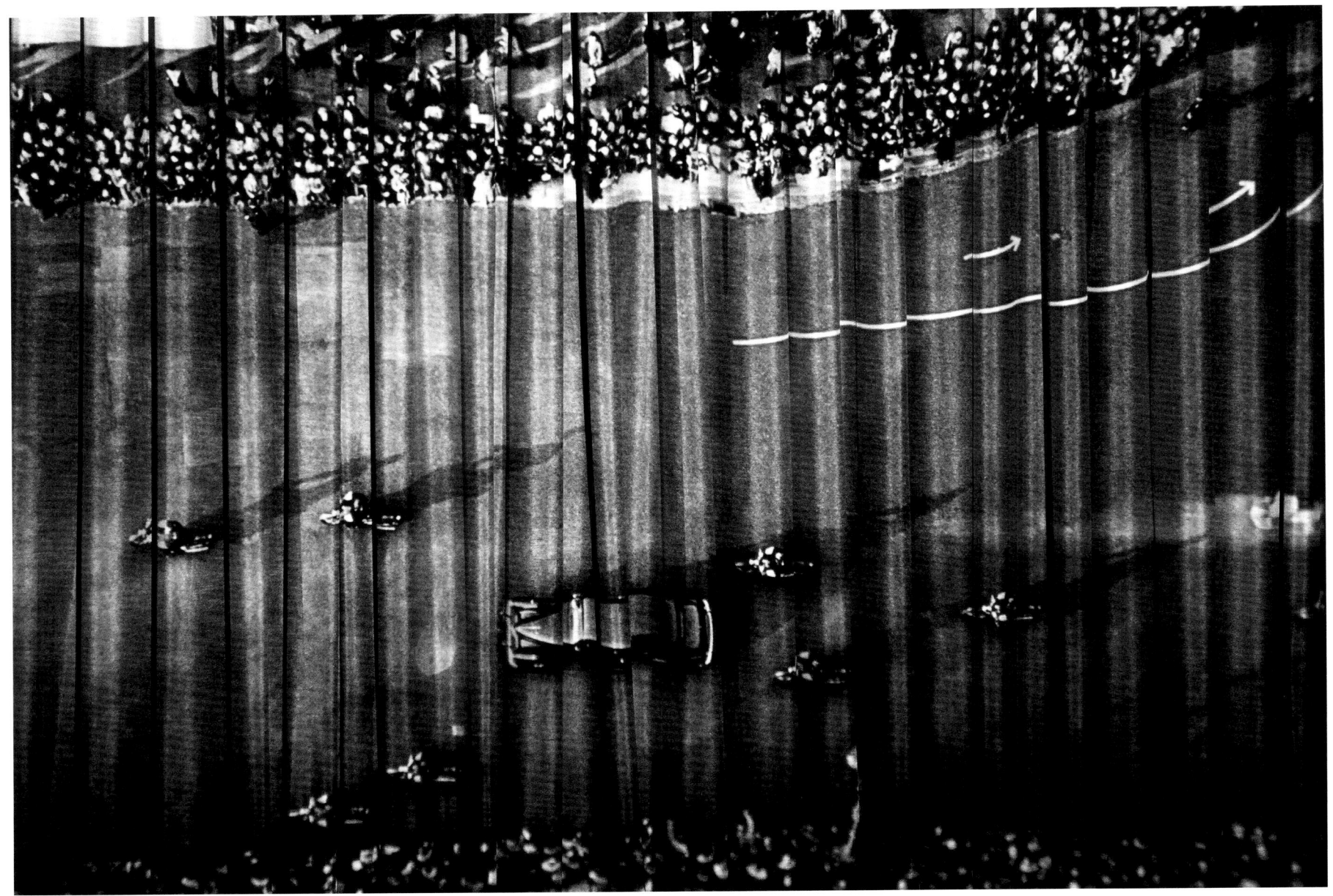

Fototeka (Projection Still V), 2015

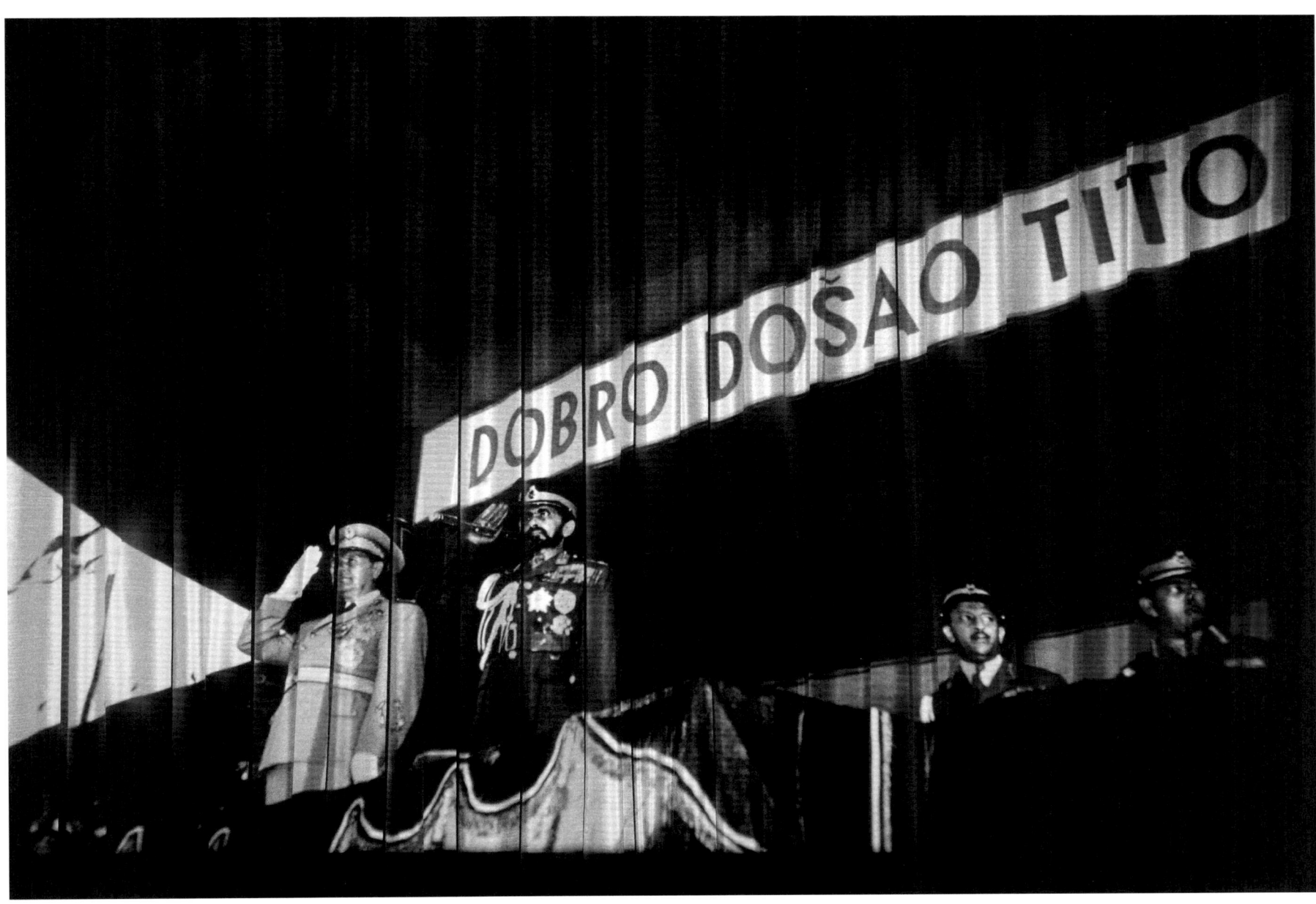

Fototeka (Projection Still VII), 2015

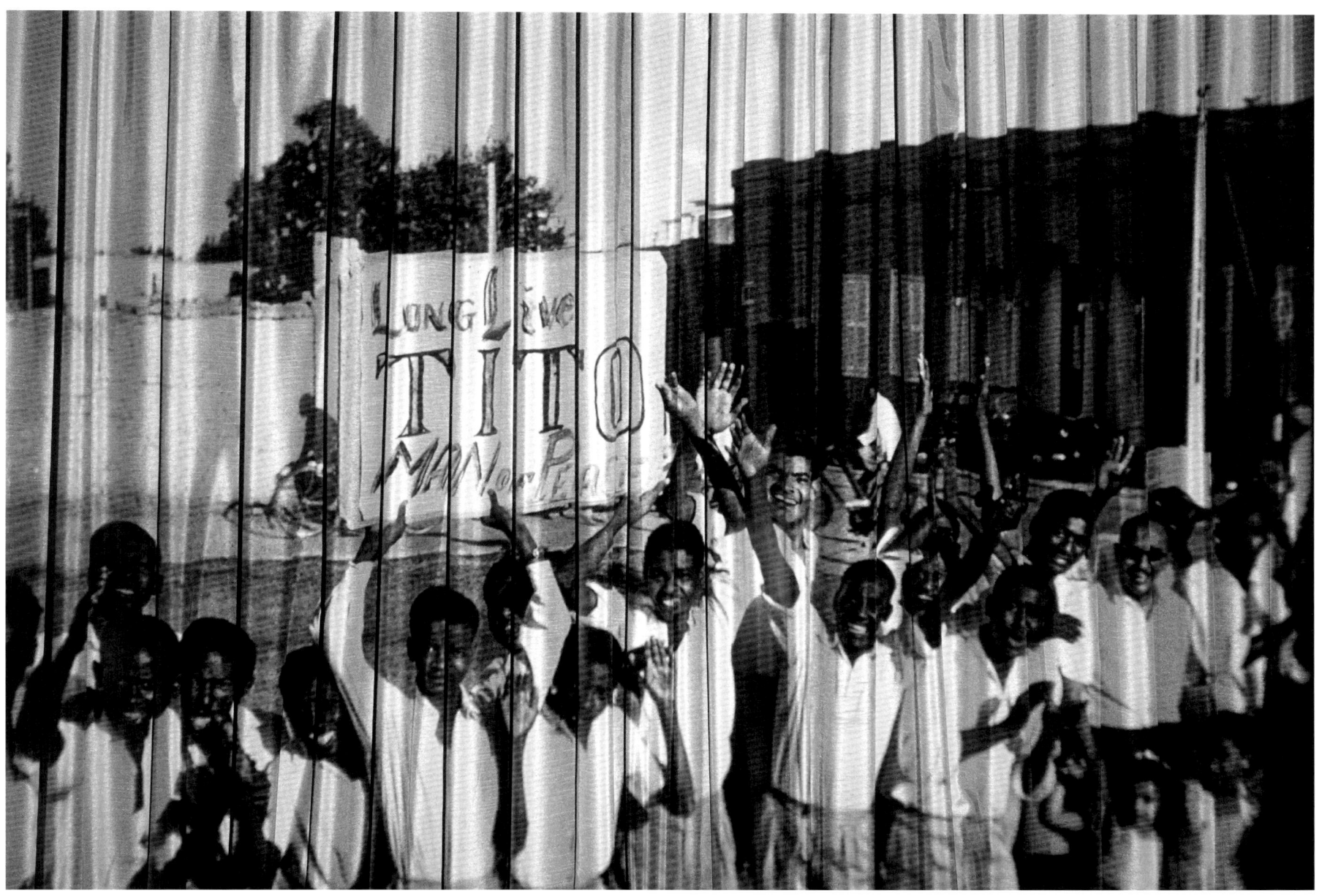

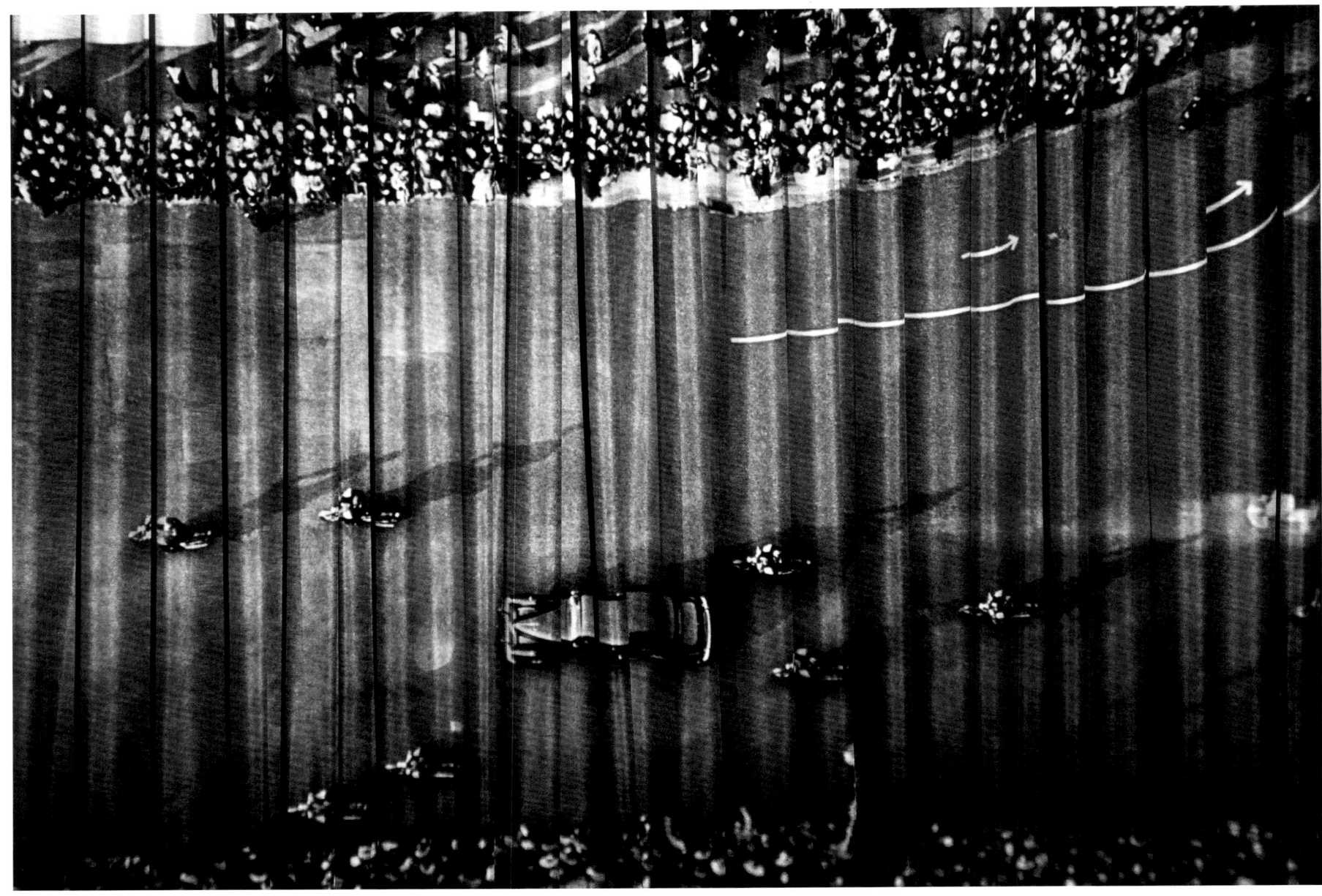

Fototeka (Projection Still V), 2015

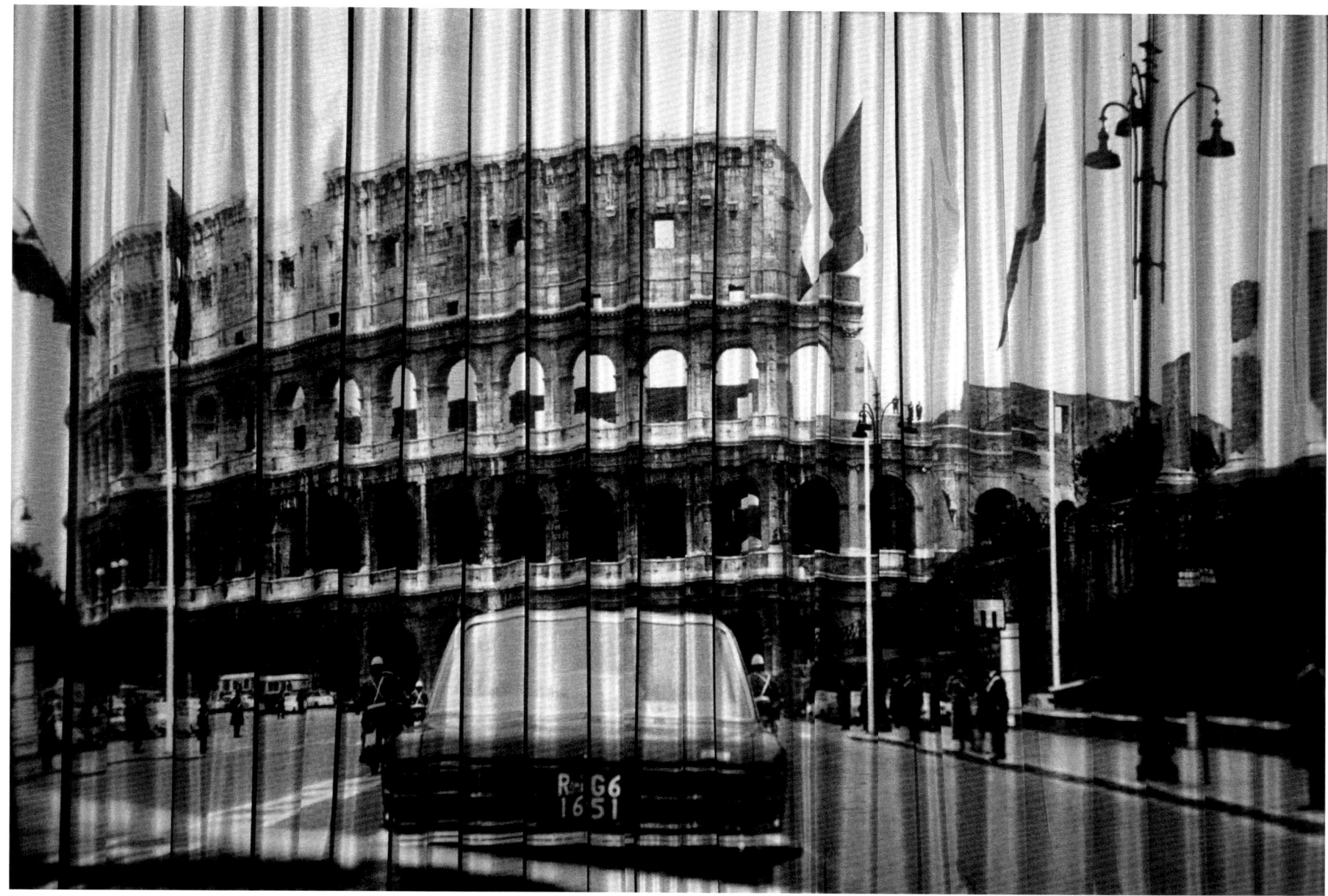

Fototeka (Projection Still II), 2015

Fototeka (Projection Still VIII), 2015

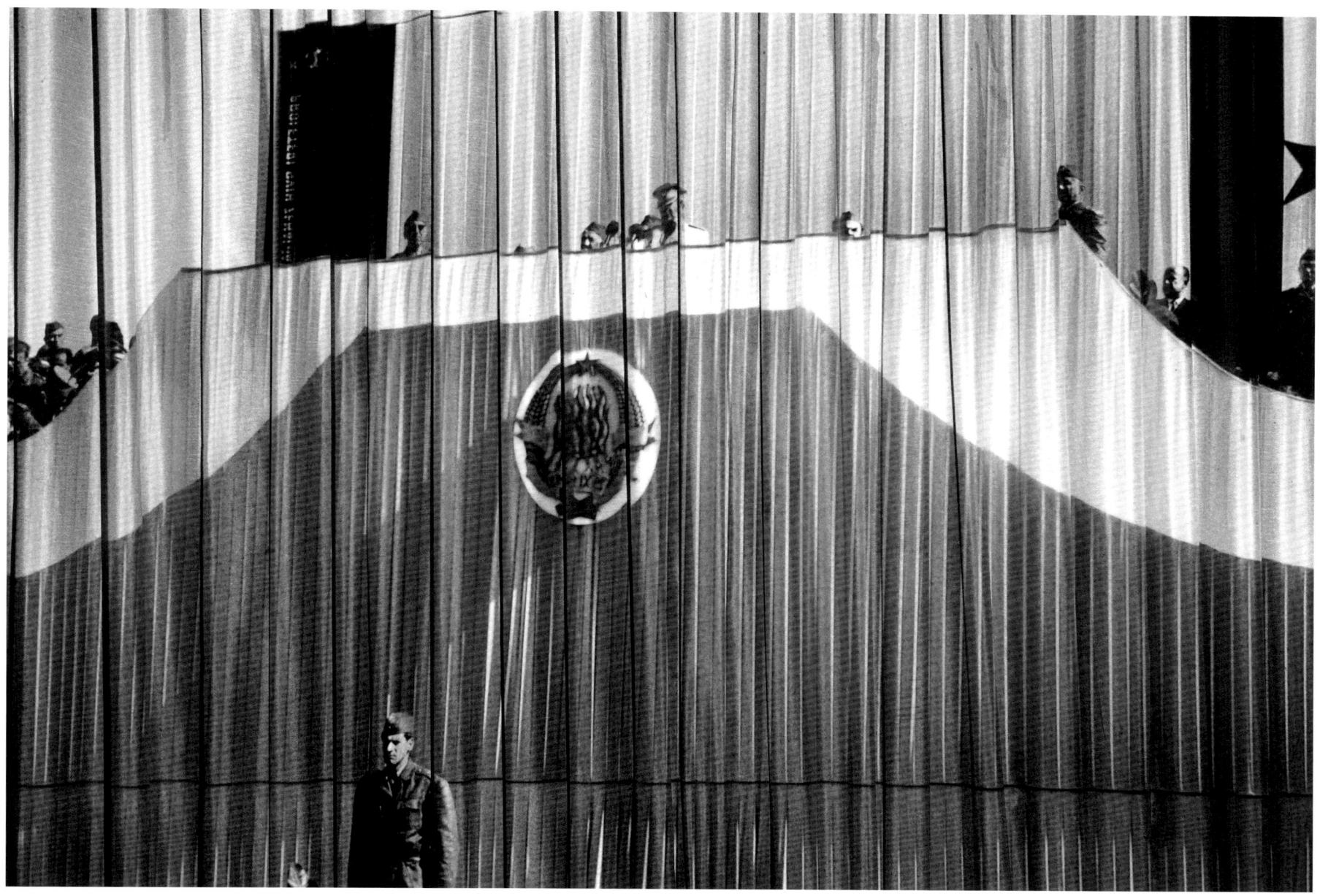

Fototeka (Projection Still IX), 2015

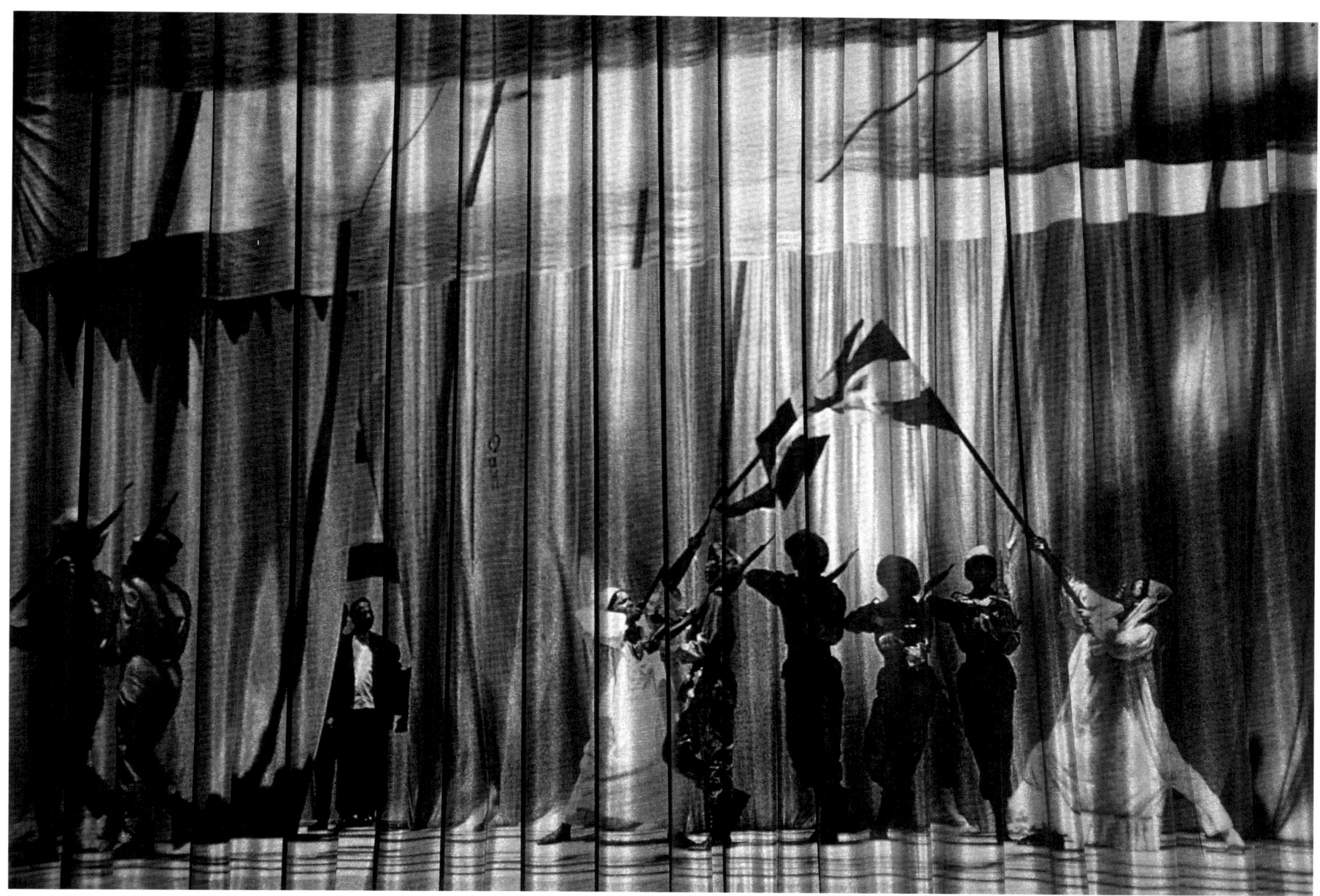

The Archive, 2013

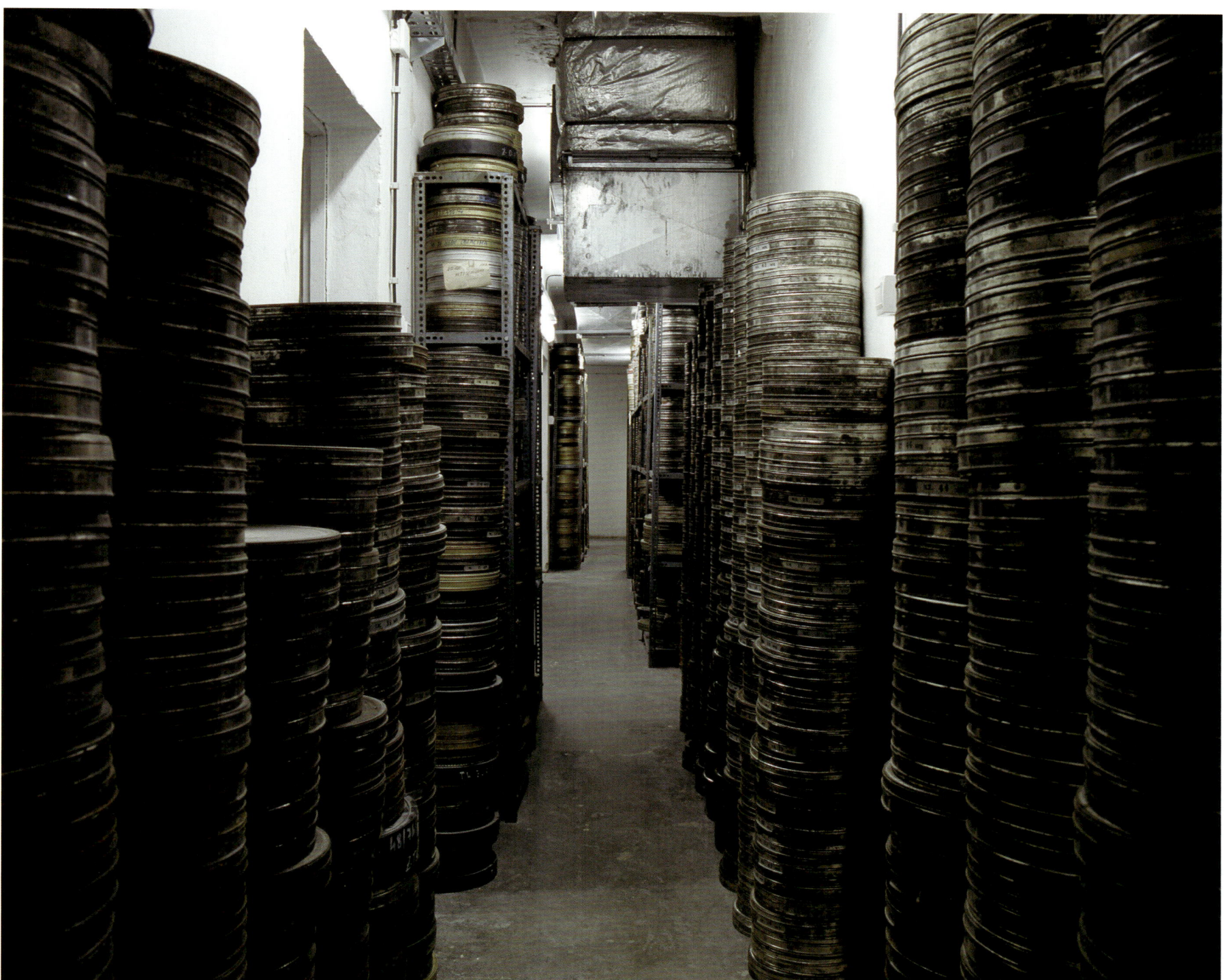

Years of War, Decades of Peace, 2013

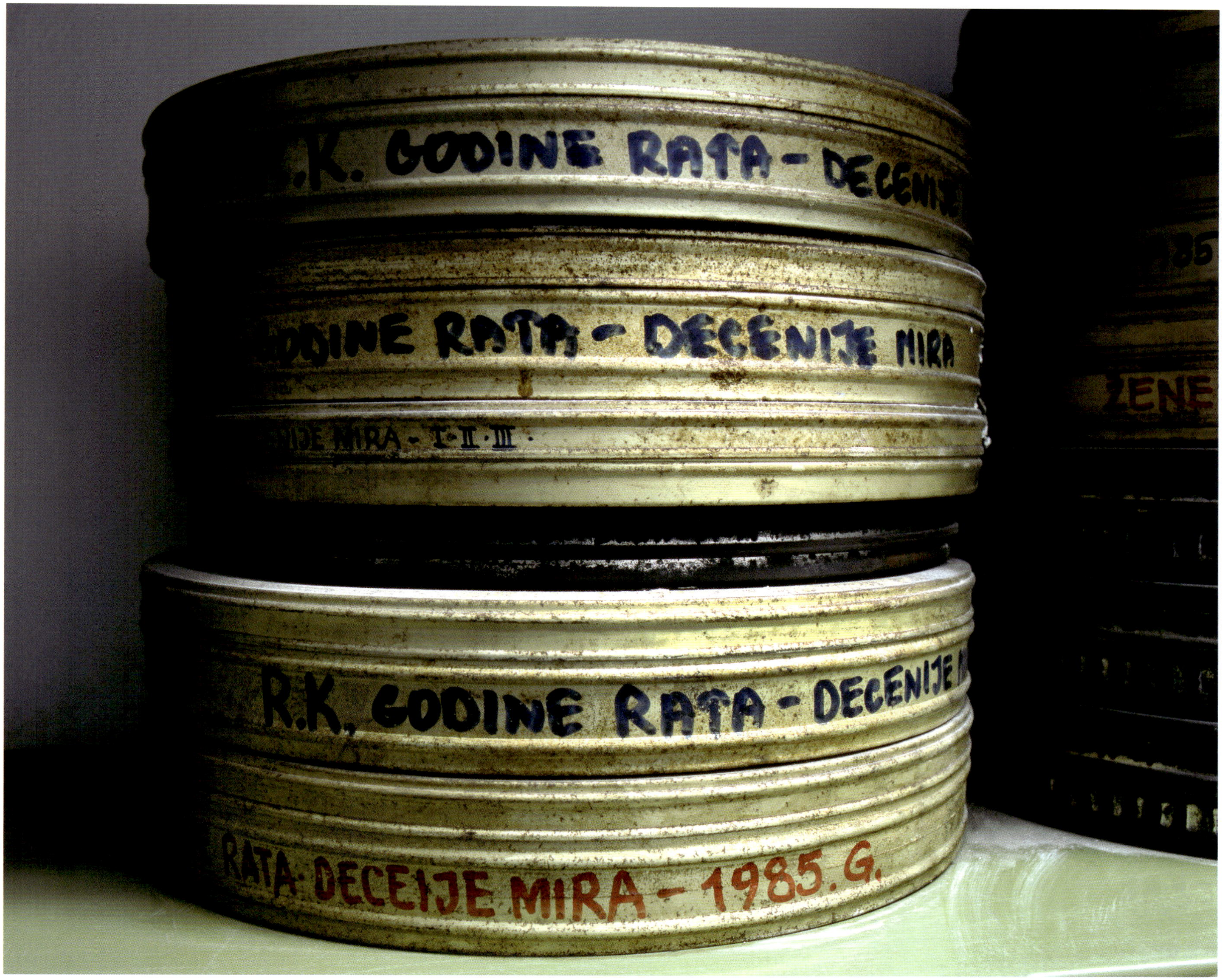
GODINE RATA -
GODINE RATA - DECENIJE MIRA
MIRA - I·II·III
R.K. GODINE RATA - DECENIJE
RATA· DECEIJE MIRA - 1985. G.
ZENE

The 12th Congress League of Communists of Yugoslavia, 2013

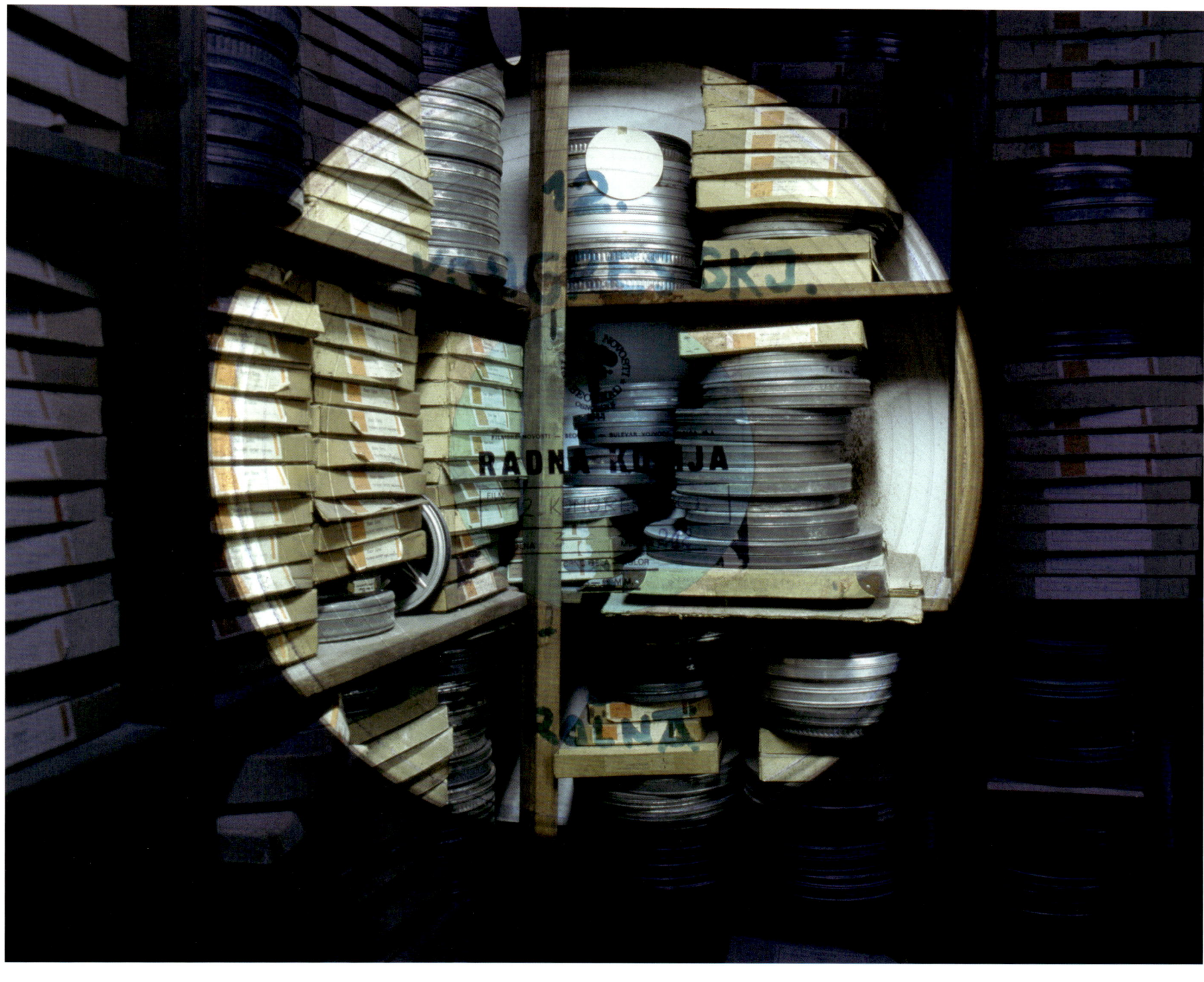

The Belgrade Conference I, 2013

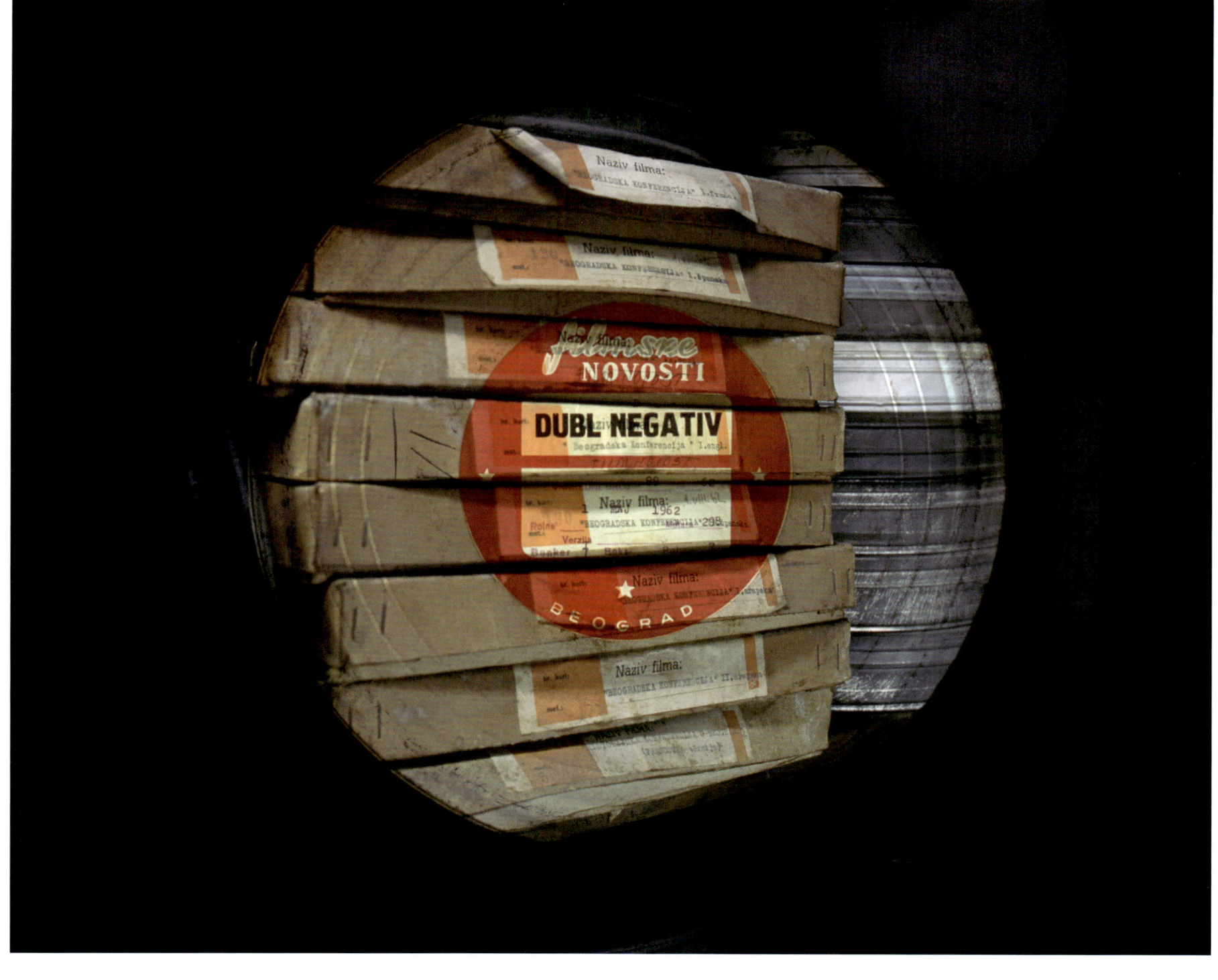

Screening Room, Zastava Film, 2019

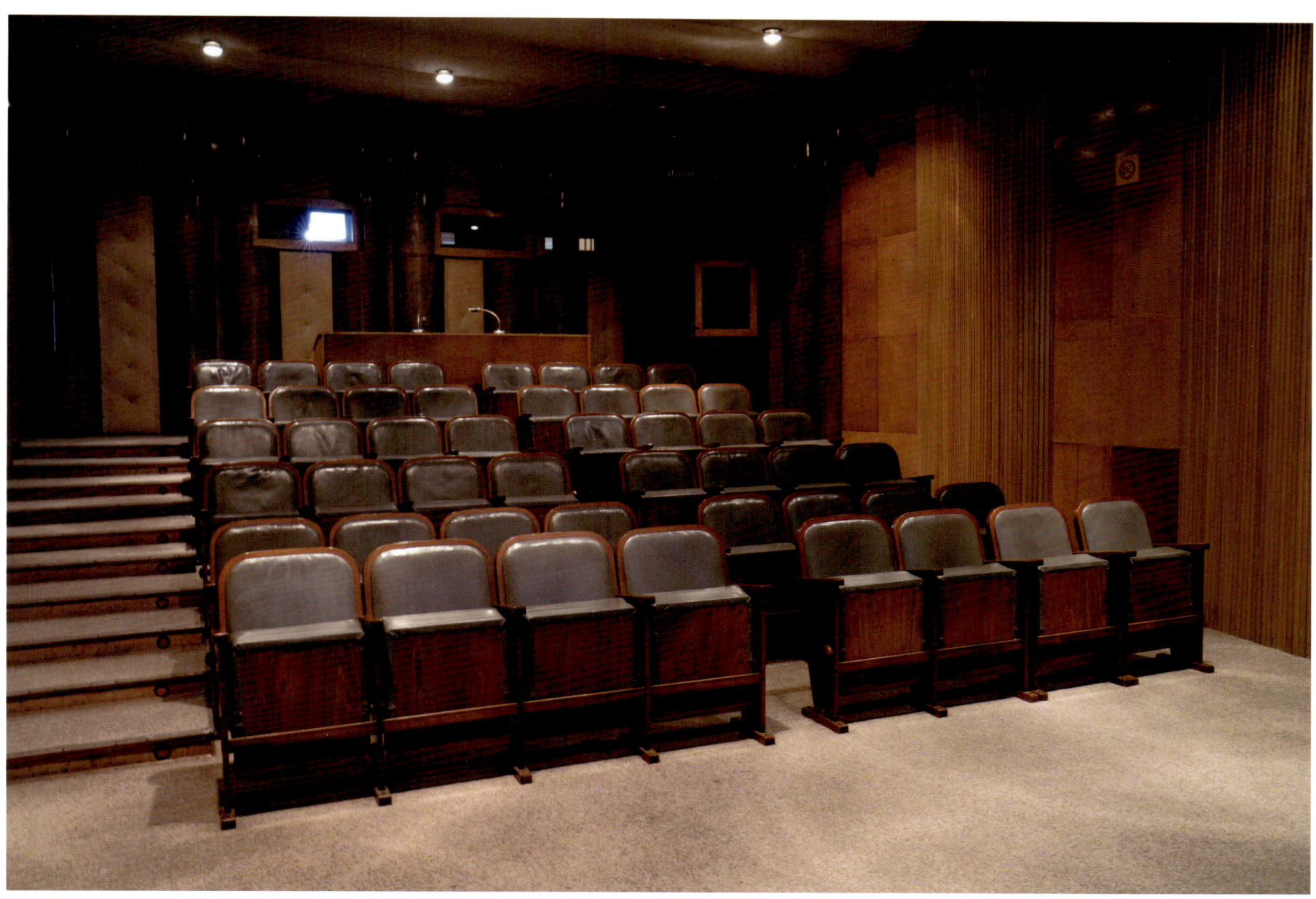

Dubl Pozitiv, 2013

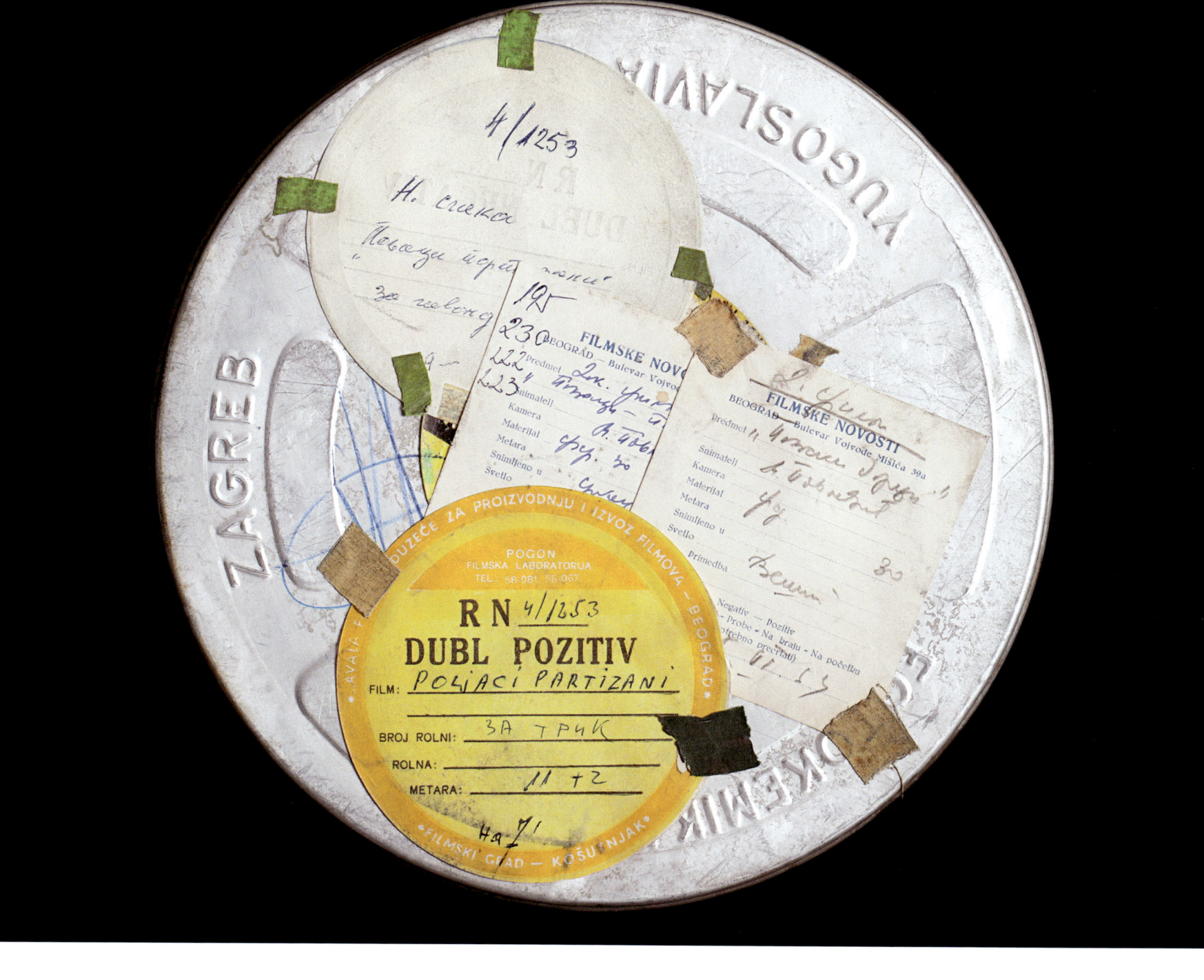

Fluorescent Light, Radio Belgrade, 2019

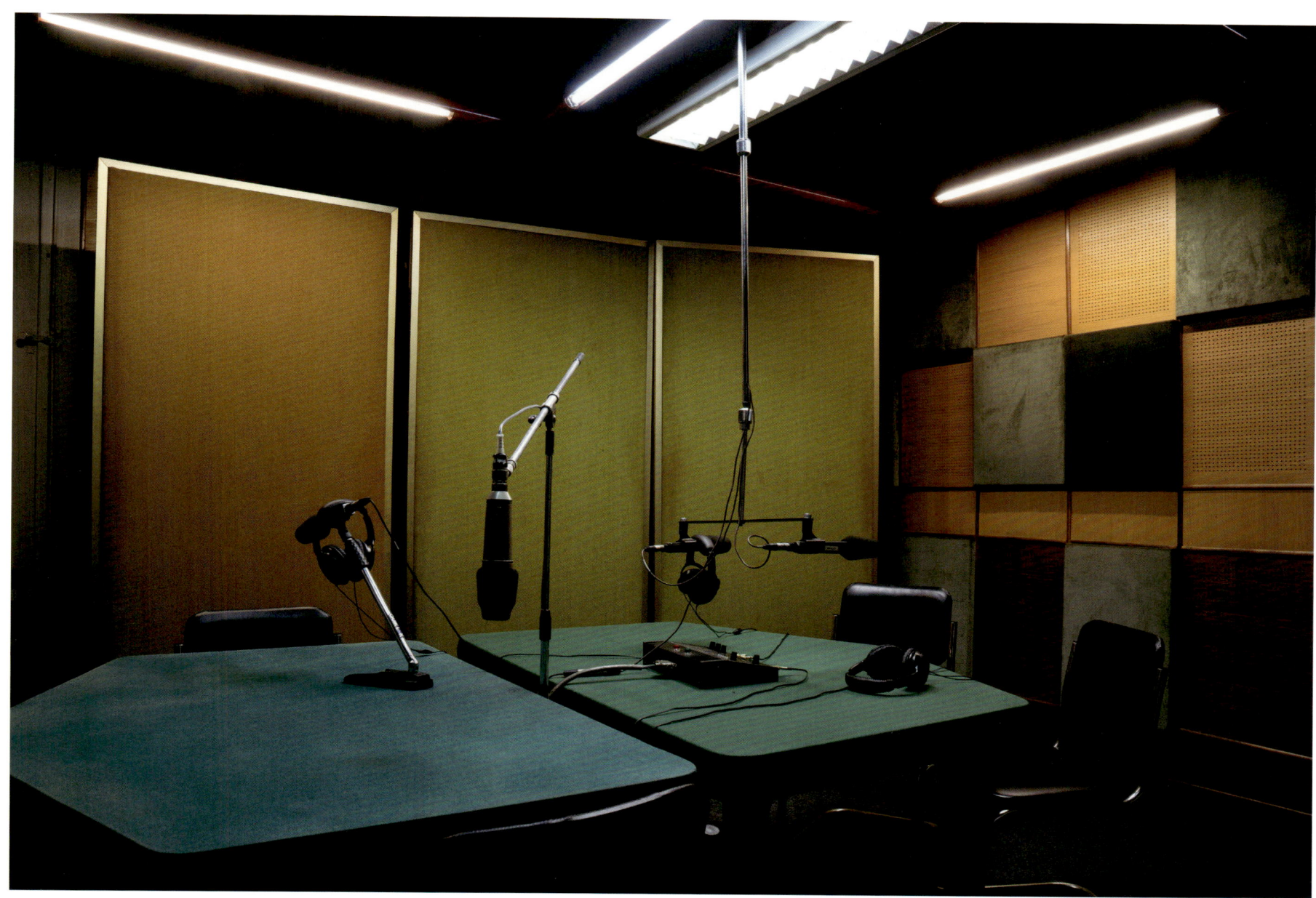

Sava Center Congress Hall, 2019

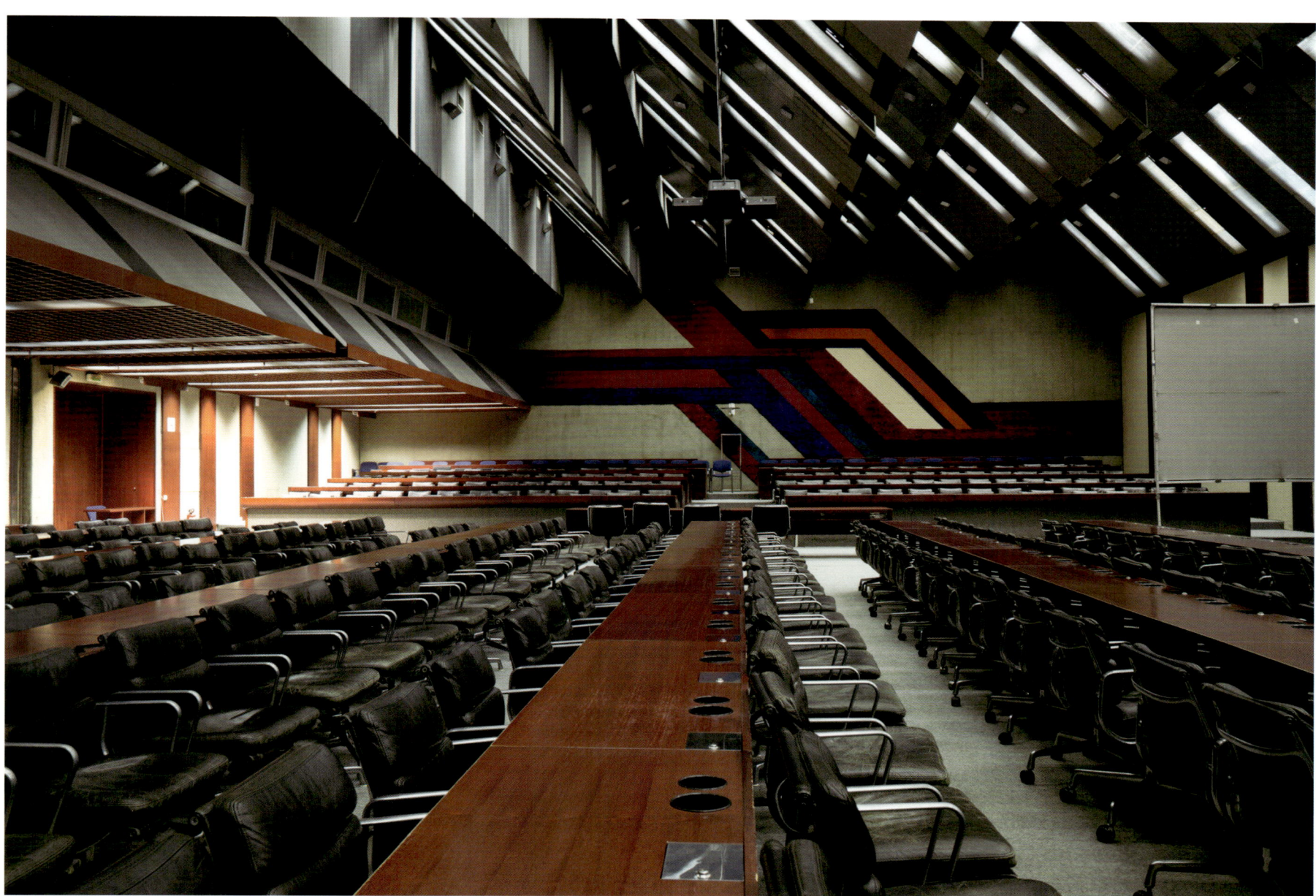

Key Light, 2019

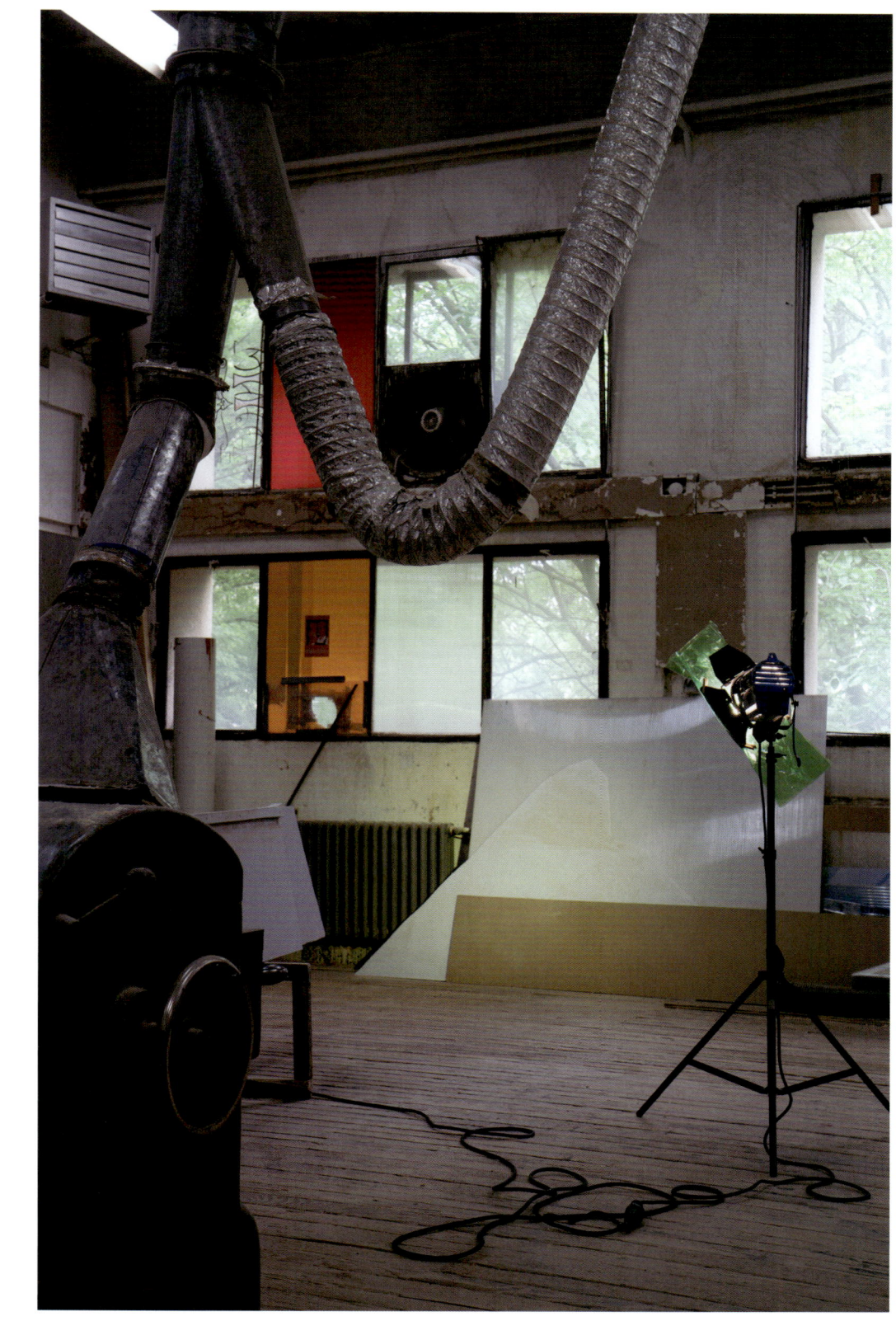

Jugoslavija, 2019

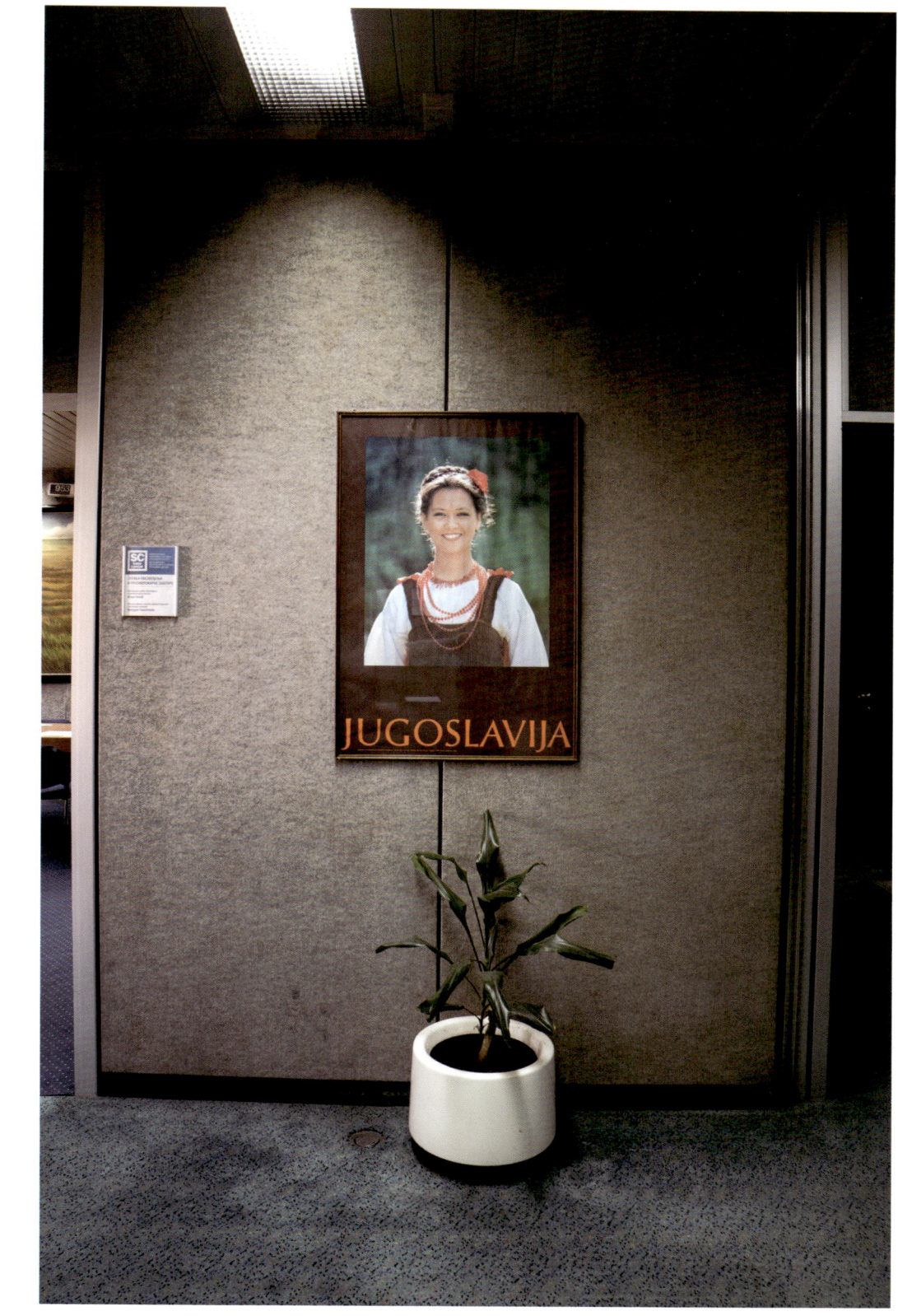

Diffused Reflections, 2019

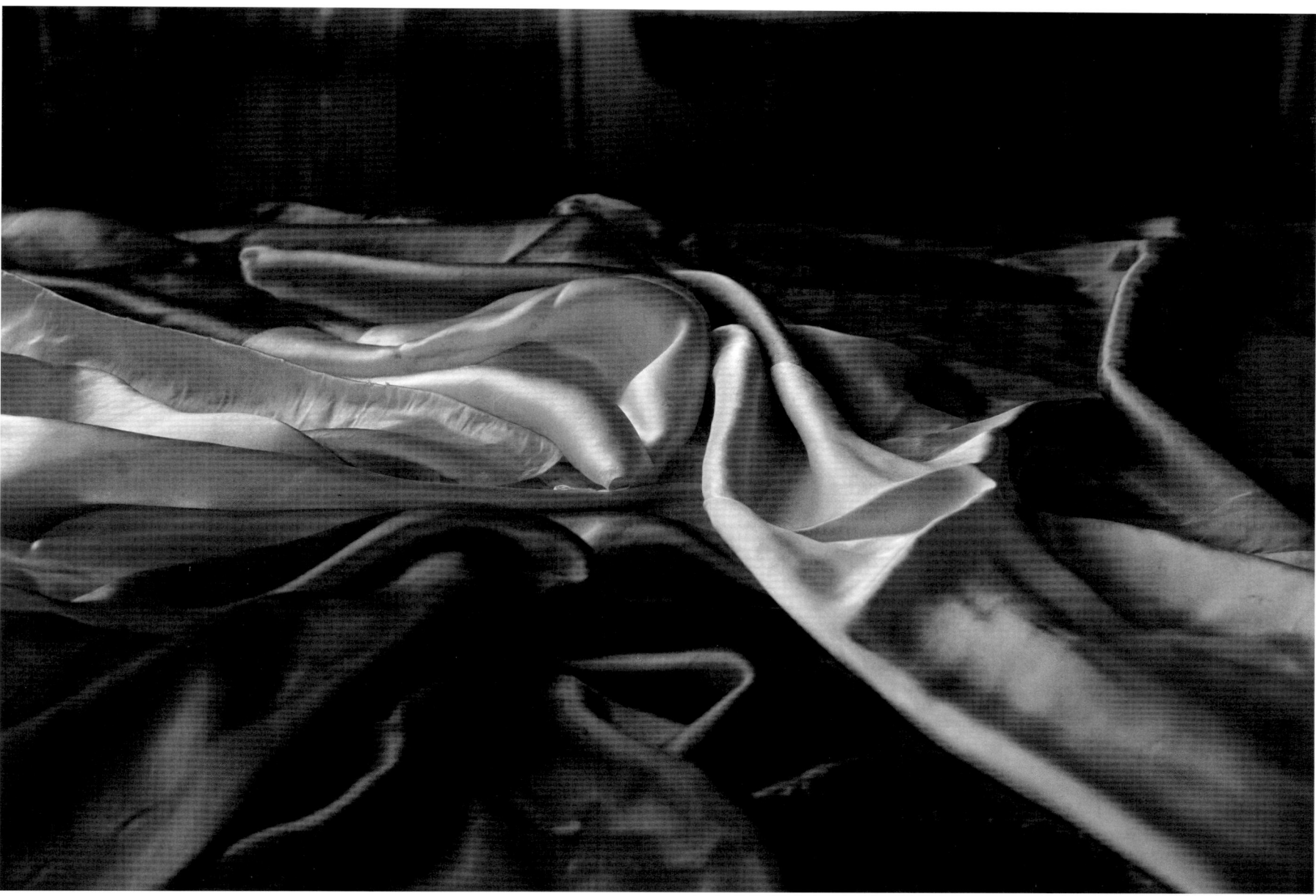

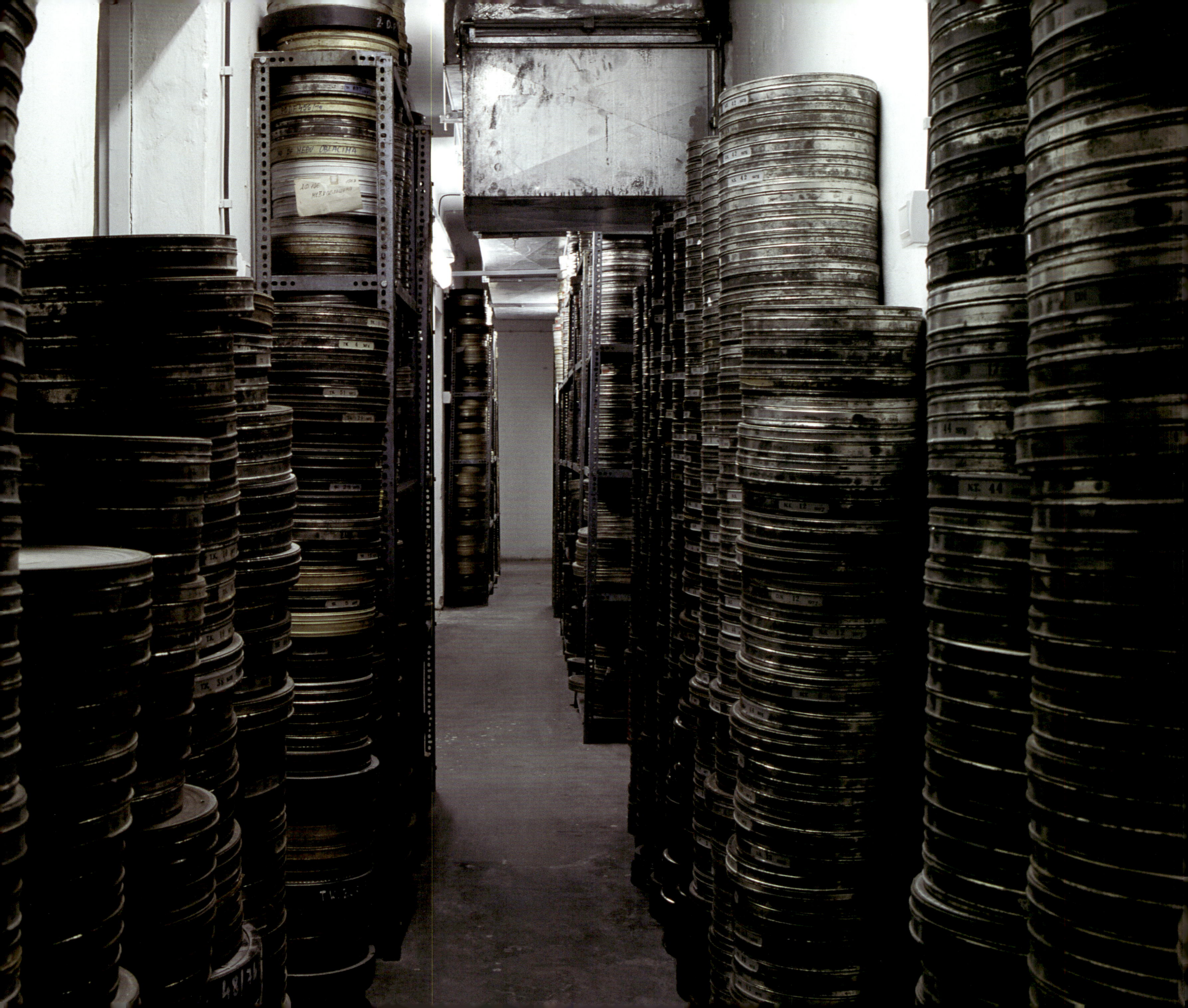

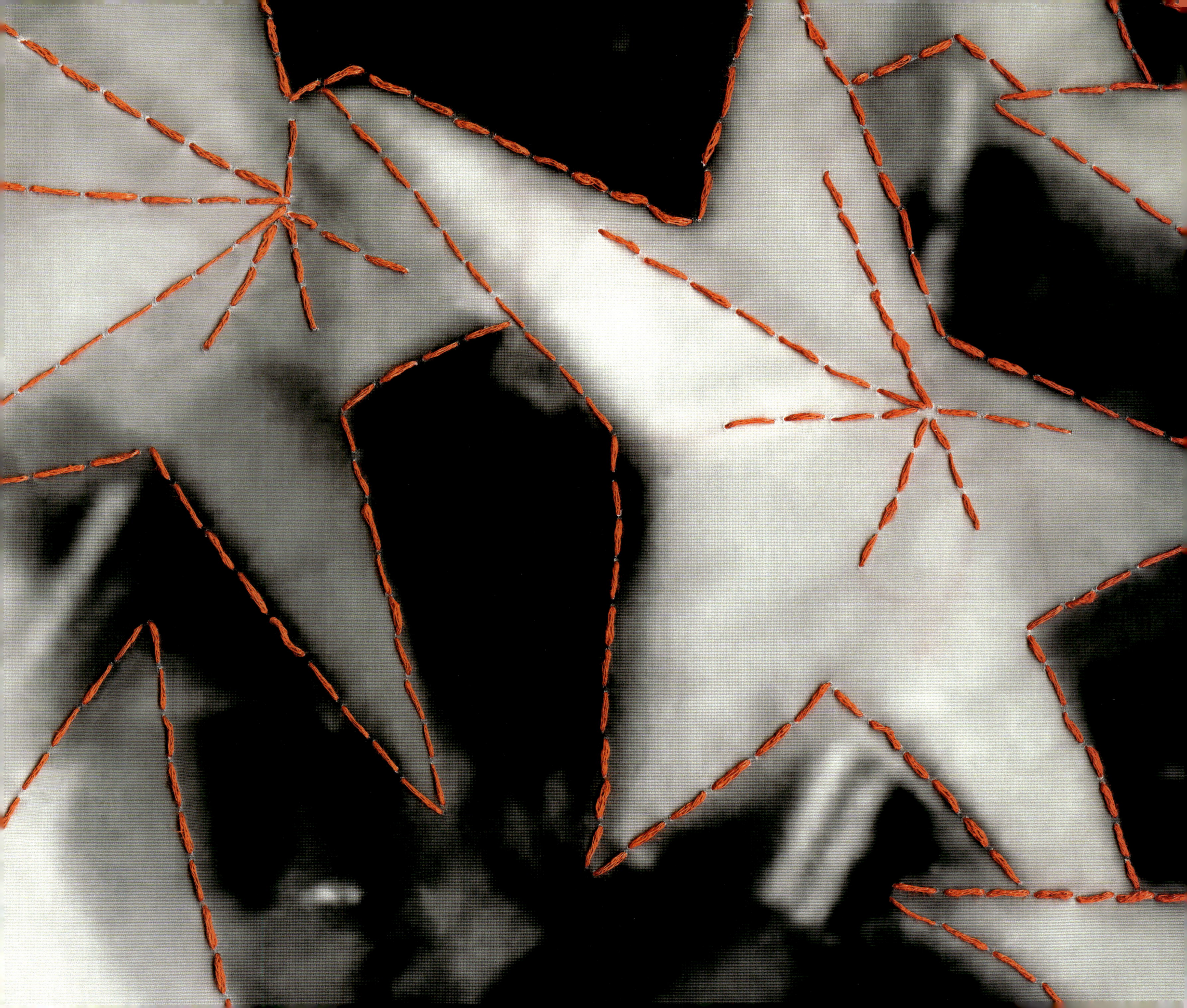

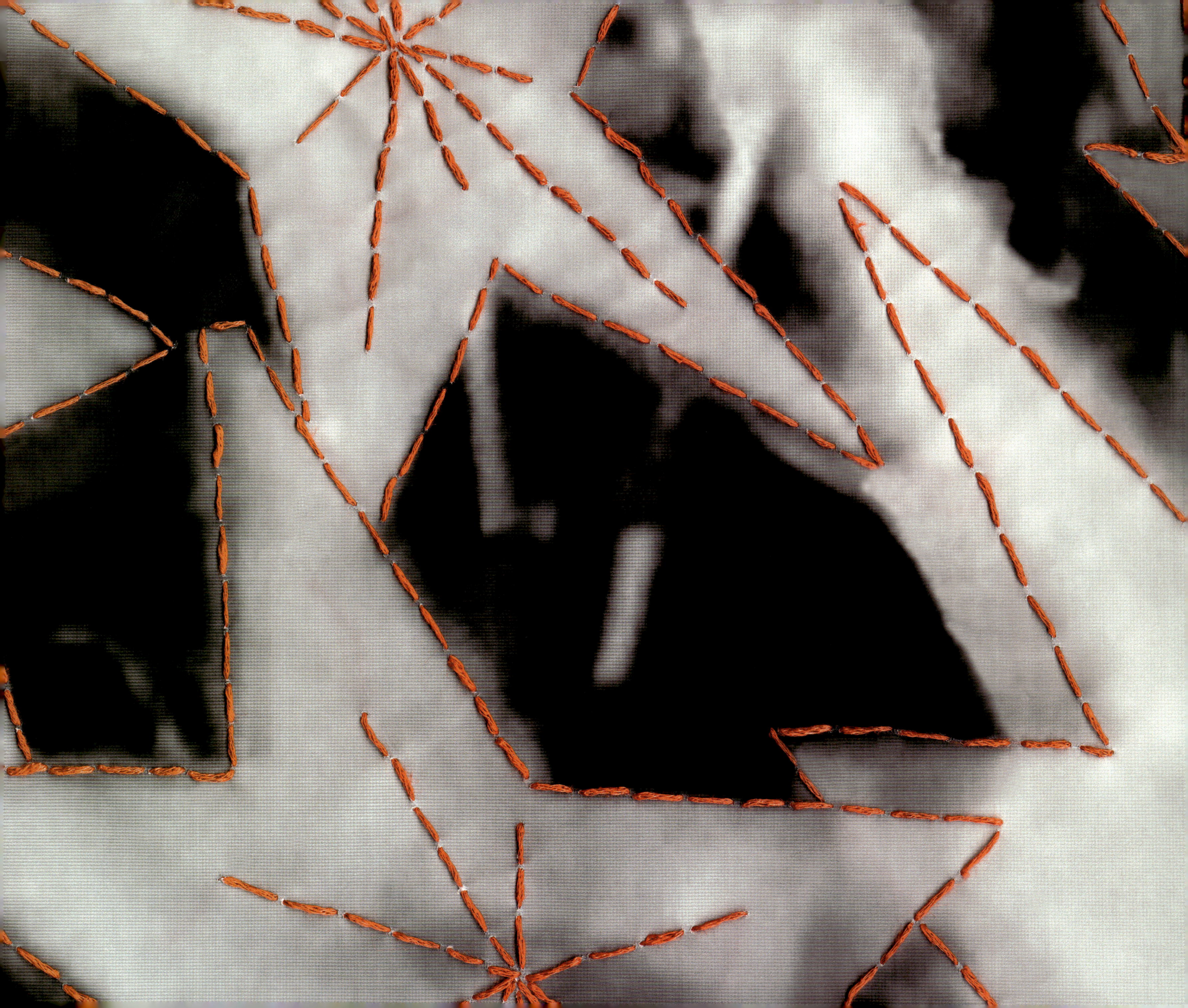

VESNA PAVLOVIĆ obtained her MFA degree in visual arts from Columbia University in New York in 2007. She is an associate professor of art at Vanderbilt University where she teaches photography and digital media. Her projects examine the evolving relationship between memory in contemporary culture and the technologies of photographic image production. Expanding the photographic image beyond its frame, traditional format, and the narrative is central to her artistic strategies. She examines photographic representation of specific political and cultural histories, which include photographic archives and related artifacts.

Pavlović has exhibited widely, including solo shows at the Phillips Collection in Washington, DC, the Frist Art Museum in Nashville, the Museum of History of Yugoslavia in Belgrade, and the Crocker Art Museum in Sacramento. She has participated in a number of group shows, including at the Untitled, 12th Istanbul Biennial, 2011, in Turkey; the Museum of Modern Art in Ljubljana, Slovenia; the 13th Havana Biennial, Rios Intermitentes in Matanzas, Cuba; the MAC—Metropolitan Arts Center in Belfast, Northern Ireland; the 5th Biennial of Contemporary Art in Konjic, Bosnia and Herzegovina; the Württembergischen Kunstverein in Düsseldorf, Germany; the KUMU Art Museum in Tallinn, Estonia; Zachęta, the National Gallery of Art in Warsaw, Poland; the City Art Gallery, in Ljubljana, Slovenia; the New Art Gallery Walsall, UK; the Paço das Artes, São Paulo, Brazil; the Bucharest Biennale 5 in Bucharest, Romania; the Museum of Contemporary Photography in Chicago; Le Quartier Center for Contemporary Art in Quimper, France; NGBK in Berlin, Germany; Photographers' Gallery in London and Kettle's Yard in Cambridge, UK; and the FRAC Center for Contemporary Art in Dunkerque, France.

In the 1990s, in Belgrade, Pavlović worked closely with the feminist pacifist group Women in Black. Vesna Pavlović is the 2020 Smithsonian Artist Research Fellow. She was the recipient of the Fulbright Scholar Award in 2018, George A. and Eliza Gardner Howard Foundation fellowship in 2017, and the City of Copenhagen Artist-in-Residence grant in 2011. In 2013, she was a Marian O. Naumburg Fellow at the MacDowell in Peterborough, New Hampshire. She was a Southern Prize Fellow in 2018 and has received the 2012 Art Matters Foundation grant.

Her work is included in major private and public art collections, including the Phillips Collection, the Hirshhorn Museum and Sculpture Garden, the Museum of Women in the Arts, and the Art in Embassies Program in Washington, DC; Princeton

University Art Gallery, Princeton, New Jersey; the Center for Creative Photography at the University of Arizona in Tucson, Arizona; and the Museum of Contemporary Art, Belgrade, Serbia, among others. *Vesna Pavlović's Lost Art: Photography, Display, and the Archive*, edited by Morna O'Neill, was published in 2018 by Hanes Art Gallery at Wake Forest University.

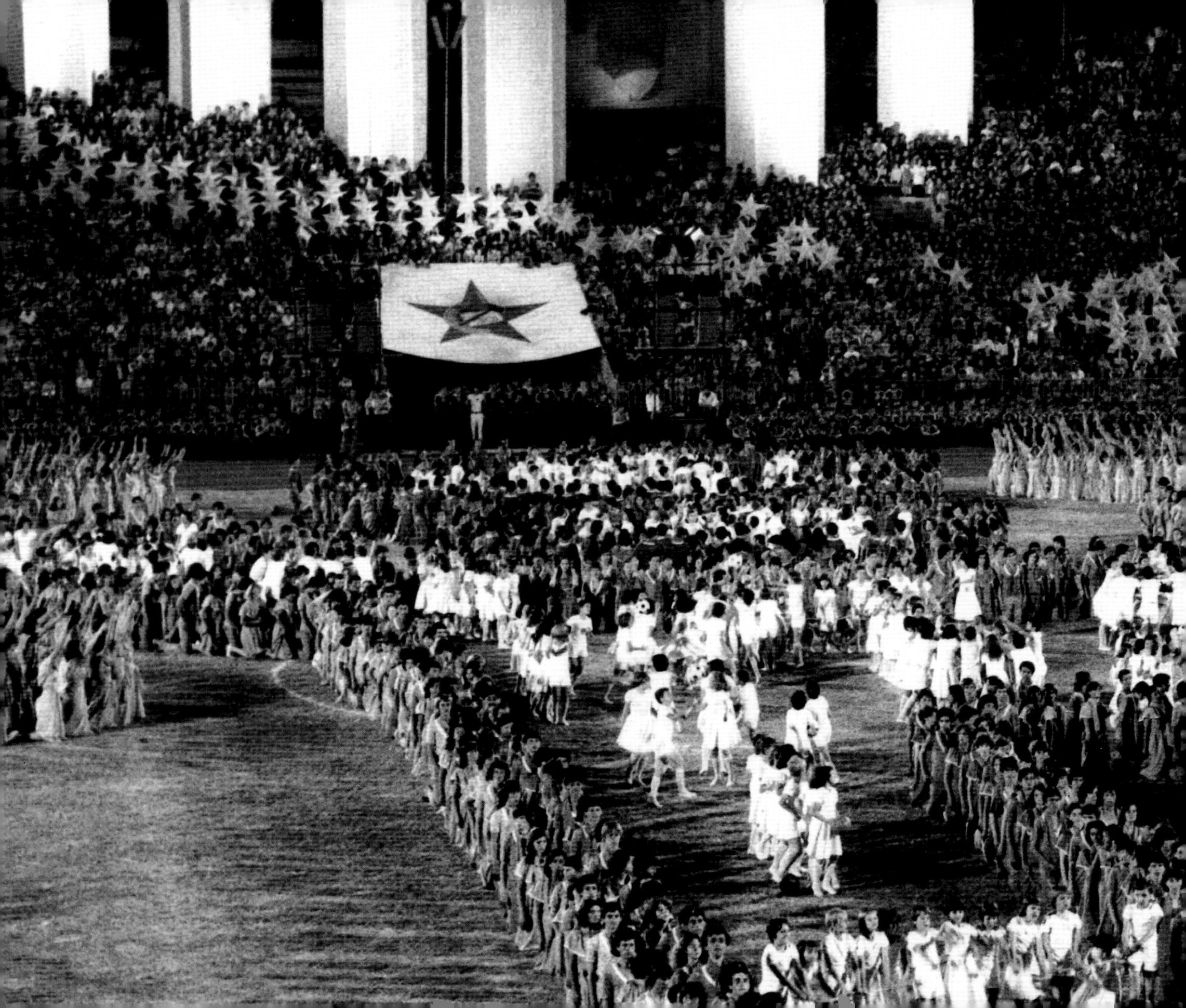

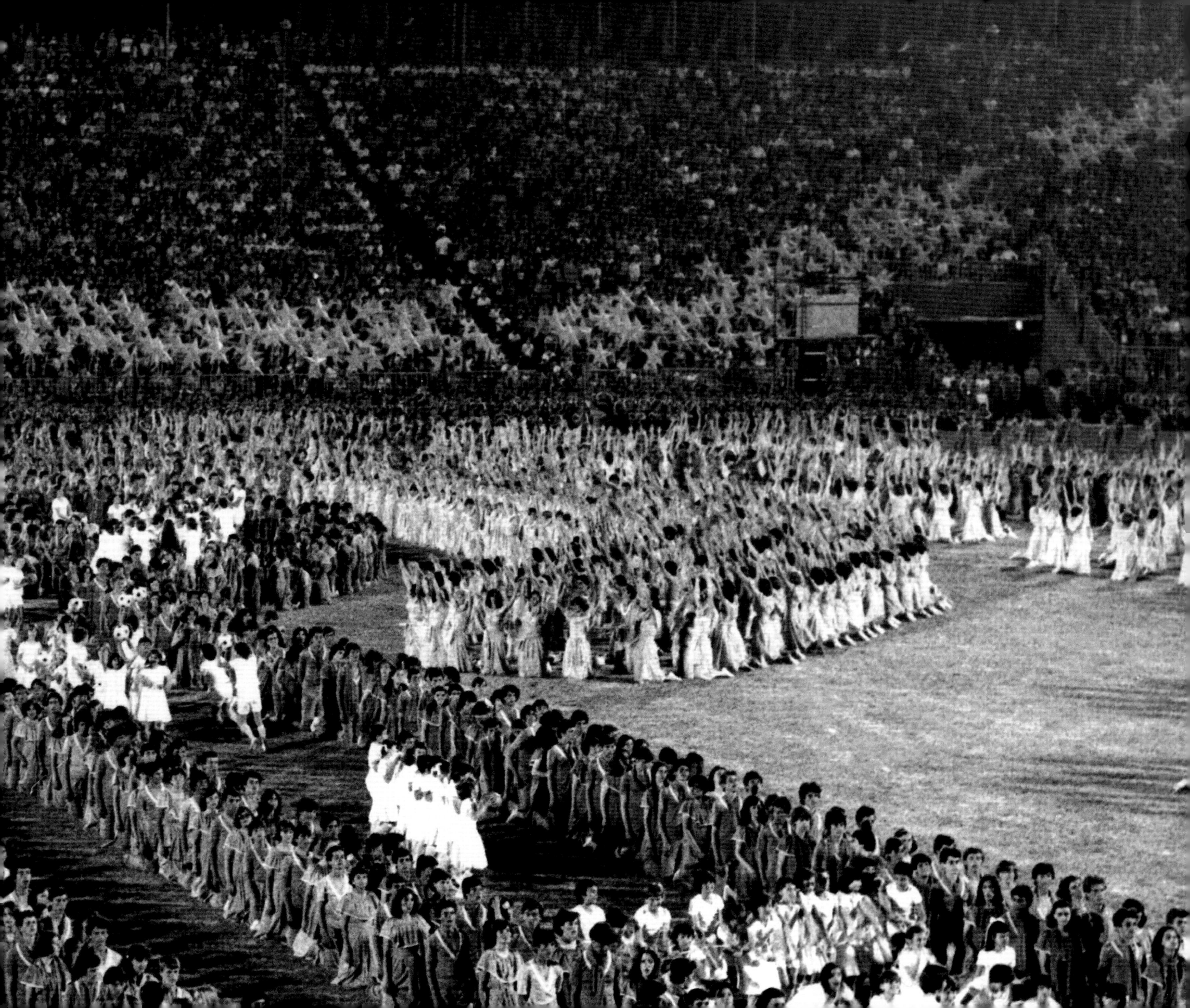

DR. JELENA VESIĆ is an independent curator, writer, editor, and lecturer. She is active in the field of publishing, research, and exhibition practice that intertwines political theory and contemporary art. She is the cofounder of Prelom Collective; coeditor of *Red Thread*—a journal for social theory, contemporary art, and activism; a member of the board of *Art Margins*; and a member of the advisory board of *Mezosfera*. Her most recent exhibitions are *Story on Copy* (Akademie Schloss Solitude, Stuttgart) and *We Are Family* (with Natasa Ilić) presented in Pawilion, Poznan. Vesić also curated *Lecture Performance* (MoCA, Belgrade, and the Kölnischer Kunstverein, with Anja Dorn, Kathrin Jentjens and Radmila Joksimović) as well as the collective exhibition project *Political Practices of (Post-)Yugoslav Art*, which critically examined art historical concepts and narratives on Yugoslav art after the dissolution of Yugoslavia. Her recent book *On Neutrality* (with Vladimir Jerić Vlidi and Rachel O'Reilly) is part of the Non-Aligned Modernisms series from the Museum of Contemporary Art, Belgrade.

DR. JOHN J. CURLEY is an associate professor of art history in the Department of Art at Wake Forest University, where he teaches classes on modern and contemporary art history as well as photographic history. He has published widely on American and European postwar art and photography, with essays in journals and catalogues for major museum exhibitions. He is the author of *A Conspiracy of Images: Andy Warhol, Gerhard Richter, and the Art of the Cold War* (Yale University Press, 2013). His second book, *Global Art and the Cold War*, appeared in January 2019 (Laurence King). His new book project, *Dead White Men: Scenes from the End of American Modernism, 1955–1975*, reconsiders the nefarious sides of American high modernism, including chapters on Willem de Kooning, Morris Louis, and Donald Judd. His research has been supported by the Getty Research Institute, the Yale Center for British Art, the Deutscher Akademischer Austauschdienst (DAAD), and the Henry Moore Foundation, among others.

DR. JORDAN AMIRKHANI is a professorial lecturer in modern and contemporary art history at American University in Washington, DC. Amirkhani has published scholarship on the Franco-Cuban painter and polemicist Francis Picabia, the British conceptual art collective Art & Language, the Belgrade-based art collective Grupa Spomenik/Monument Group, and the photographic work of Crow artist Wendy Red Star. Recent curatorial projects include *Identity Measures*, an exhibition of twenty-three New Orleans–based artists for the Contemporary Art Center of New Orleans' 2019 Open Call exhibition, and *DIALOGUES*, an inaugural exhibition of thirty-two artists for STABLE—a subsidized studio, gallery, and educational space in northeast Washington, DC. In addition to her academic scholarship, Amirkhani also writes art criticism for a number of contemporary art publications including *Artforum*, *Art Practical*, *Baltimore Arts*, and *Burnaway*. Her emphasis on contextualizing contemporary art and artists working in the American Southeast garnered her a prestigious Creative Capital/Andy Warhol Foundation "Short-Form" Writing Grant in 2017 and three nominations for the Rabkin Prize in Arts Journalism in 2017, 2018, and 2019.

DR. BRANISLAV DIMITRIJEVIĆ is professor of history and theory of art at the College of Art and Design in Belgrade. He teaches and writes internationally on art and culture of socialist Yugoslavia, and also on avant-garde, contemporary art, and exhibition histories. His books include *Consumed Socialism: Culture, Consumerism and Social Imagination in Yugoslavia, 1950–1974* (2016), *Dušan Makavejev's Sweet Movie* (2017), *On Normality: Art in Serbia 1989–2001* (2005, with B. Anđelković and D. Sretenović), and most recently *Yugoslavia: How and Why?* (2019, with I. Erdei and T. Toroman). His curatorial projects include *Good Life* (2012, with M. Hannula) and *No Network* (2011), and the first edition of the Time Machine Biennial in the nuclear bunker in Konjic, Bosnia and Herzegovina. For selected texts see independent.academia.edu/BranislavDimitrijevic.